SIMP-LEE THE BEST

SIMP-LEE THE BEST

MY AUTOBIOGRAPHY

LEE McCULLOCH

WITH MARK GUIDI

BLACK & WHITE PUBLISHING

First published 2013
by Black & White Publishing Ltd
29 Ocean Drive, Edinburgh EH6 6JL

1 3 5 7 9 10 8 6 4 2   13 14 15 16

ISBN: 978 1 84502 606 6

A CIP catalogue record for this book is available from the British Library.

Typeset by Creative Link, North Berwick
Printed and bound by CPI Group (UK) Ltd, Croydon, CR0 4YY

To Amanda, Callum and Jack; to my parents and brothers.
The best I could ever wish for. Love you all.

ACKNOWLEDGEMENTS

Lee McCulloch

I would like to thank my family for your help and support and encouragement over the years. You have all given invaluable guidance and support when I've been writing this book.

The idea of writing this book was something I gave careful consideration to and was initially hesitant to get involved in. But my main motivation was to thank the people who have helped mould me as a person, a partner, a father, a son, a brother and a footballer. It also appealed for my two young sons, Callum and Jack, to have this book to look back on and learn what my career was all about.

Mum and Dad always put their three sons first, never thinking of themselves. They have wonderful family values and the upbringing they gave me has made me the man I am today. I'll never forget the things both of you taught me. I am eternally grateful.

To my brothers, Gregor and Wullie. Gregor, thanks for your support, smooth style and wit. Wullie, for sharing a bedroom with me and sharing all you had in your life. And for never once letting me win at football when you used to play with me.

To all of my previous managers in football – from Boys Club through to the professional game – thanks for your patience and support, especially Tom Forsyth and Jim Griffin at Motherwell for giving me the confidence to kick on. To all of the staff at Motherwell, Wigan, Rangers and Scotland for being part of your club and sharing some brilliant memories.

My two closest mates, Christopher Reid and John Paul Curran, for the childhood times we had, the fun, the laughter and for sticking with me through the rough times and always being there. Your loyalty and honesty has been priceless. Great memories. Thanks for your input.

To the Motherwell fans that backed me all the way and the incredible Wigan fans that helped take us to the Premiership. To the hundreds of thousands of Glasgow Rangers fans for your amazing support and dedication for helping to keep our club alive and with your energy and commitment we WILL get back to where we belong.

My thanks also to all the staff at Glasgow Rangers FC.

To Campbell Brown and his staff at Black & White Publishing. Thanks for your professionalism and for believing in this book.

Stuart Gilmour at the Bothwell Brasserie, thanks for the endless coffees and great meals. You provided us with a great base to write this book.

Dylan and Mathew, my wee nephews and pals. It's been a joy to watch you both grow up. You both have been like little brothers to me. My big cousin, Derek Anson, who passed away when I was younger. I loved it when you used to take me out to play football and the time you gave me to help me become streetwise.

To my friend and mentor, Davie Weir, thanks for doing me the honour of your foreword.

Thanks to Mark Guidi, who has helped bring my book together. Your humour helped me get through some long days. Your calmness was invaluable when I got stressed. You're a genuine, honest and hardworking guy and for that I thank you.

Special thanks to your lovely family – Anne, Eva, Sophia and Claudia – for allowing me your time.

And, of course, to my wife-to-be, Amanda. Your love and support has never dwindled. It's been great to share so many high times and special moments together, from the English Second Division to the Champions League. Your calmness and sense of perspective helped me cope with the lows.

And our two sons, Callum and Jack. You both give me so much love and bring me more happiness than you could ever imagine. Keep up your energy to help keep me young. Nothing gives me more pleasure than being a dad to you both.

Mark Guidi

My thanks to Lee for choosing me to work with him on his book. From start to finish, it was a pleasure and a privilege. Thoroughly enjoyed your company.

To Amanda, Callum and Jack, thanks for making me welcome in your home.

To Iris and John. Your recollections of Lee were of great help. Really appreciated it all.

Brian McSweeney and Gavin Berry were brilliant for me in their assistance and research.

To Campbell Brown, Alison McBride, Janne Moller, Kristen Susienka and all staff at Black & White Publishing. Thanks for publishing this book and your invaluable guidance throughout the whole process.

CONTENTS

FOREWORD
BY DAVID WEIR

IT WAS the summer of 2007 and my mobile phone was red hot. Nothing to do with the decent weather we had during that period. No, it was because of Lee McCulloch. My Scotland colleague wanted kept up-to-date if we were going to become team-mates at club level.

I was at Glasgow Rangers, having decided to stay on under Walter Smith after I had initially signed on a six-month loan deal from Everton. It was always an ambition of mine to play for Rangers, the team I supported as a lad.

Lee was exactly the same. He was at Wigan Athletic, doing very well in the English Premiership for them, but he knew Rangers wanted him and he was desperate for the move to go through. So was I.

I played against Lee when I was with Hearts and he was just kicking off his career in the Motherwell first team. Our paths also crossed in the English Premiership when I was with Everton. It was when he started to get involved with the Scotland set-up that we got to know each other. We struck up an affinity right away because he is a likeable guy and we had lots in common. So, when Rangers and Wigan haggled over a transfer fee, Lee used me as his 'inside man' at Ibrox to keep him in the loop, to notify him of any developments at our end, just in case Wigan kept things from him.

I wanted Lee to get his move. I knew how much it meant to him. And I believed he would be a great signing, a true asset on and off the park.

And so the phone calls continued. It was incessant – three or four times a day, for the best part of two months. He wanted updates, to find out if Walter had mentioned anything to me, if progress had been made. I tried to give him encouraging news but it was difficult. I doubt Walter would have listened to me or told me anything confidential. So, I just urged Lee to be patient.

He got his wish in mid-July 2007 when he signed for Rangers. I was delighted for him. And for me. No more blisters on my ears!

Rangers were Lee's boyhood team. A lot of people pay lip service to that but it was genuine from him. His mum and dad made sure he was steeped in the tradition of the club. That helped the bond we had because I felt proud and privileged to be a part of Rangers.

But it wasn't always full of the joys for him. He had to go through tough times at the club during his first eighteen months. Lee wasn't happy with his form for periods and felt he wasn't contributing as much as he should have been. It's not easy to play for Rangers, it really isn't, especially when you have been brought up as a supporter and live in the West of Scotland. If things don't go well on a match day then some people look upon you as a failure. It's hard. I was fortunate I could head back down the road to Manchester and escape. For Lee, though, there was no hideaway, whether it was dropping kids off at school, going to the supermarket, or whatever. It can take over your life.

He was desperate to do well, but I felt he tried too hard to succeed. I told him to relax, that his talent would shine through eventually. But he wanted it all in an instant. He wanted to play every week and to score goals every week. He tried to force it, but he was doing it all for the right reasons.

Playing for Rangers can bury players. There is massive attention on and off the pitch. Walter was always good at reminding us of what was required and how to deal with it. But some players just couldn't handle it, couldn't recover from the shock level of what exactly is involved when you play for Rangers and represent the club.

Lee could have crumbled, but he dug deep. That tells you so much about his character. Thankfully, with the support of Amanda and their sons and his parents, he came through the other side and it happened for him.

On a personal level, Lee was a massive help to me when I was captain. He had the trust and confidence of the younger players and they would confide in him. If he felt it was required, he would relay information back to me or deal with it himself. In that sense, he made sound judgement calls. He was my barometer for the mood in the dressing room. He'd let players know if they weren't up to the standards required, but do it in a nice way, for the right reasons, for the good of the club. He was also the life and soul of the dressing room, well liked and well respected.

On the park, as we sat in the dressing room before big games, it always gave me great comfort to see the likes of him, Allan McGregor, Barry Ferguson and Nikica Jelavić in the team, guys we could hang our hats on. I knew Lee was reliable and had my back covered. Those are invaluable assets.

He is now captain and is very proud. He is my friend, first and foremost, but I genuinely believe he should be captain. In fact, I would have made him captain as soon as I left in the early part of 2012. He was my natural successor.

Now that I've gone, I miss him. I was always in early at Murray Park for training, and I knew when Lee had arrived. He'd say 'morning' to everyone, from Stevie at Security to the girls at reception, and he would say it in a loud voice and in a genuine manner. So, I would hear about seven 'mornings' before

I got to see his face. He was loud and gregarious. We'd joke about that. He was funny, big-hearted and lit the place up. When he came in he made the training ground a better place to be. It's important to have a good environment every day at your work. That must have been invaluable during the critical period the club faced in 2012.

Not long after I left, he and others at Rangers had a lot to deal with. He wasn't the captain at that time but he was the natural leader. He co-ordinated with the PFA during the administration period to make sure every player was being looked after properly and given the best possible advice. People were fearing for their livelihoods and he made sure he gave up his wages to keep others in employment and keep Rangers functioning. That speaks volumes and confirmed everything I thought about him.

Now, with the club in the hands of new owners and coming out the other side, Lee has been a great sounding board for the young players at the club as it goes through a vital transitional period.

I still speak to Lee, Kris Boyd and Allan McGregor. We all have a bond and I think that will continue to be the case long-term. As a footballer, you may play for four or five clubs in your career and be team-mates with hundreds of other footballers, but, at the end up, you might only have a handful you keep in touch with. I'll have that with Lee, and he will have that with a lot of people because he's a great guy to know.

David Weir

1

MY MENTOR AND MY INSPIRATION

THERE ARE certain dates etched in my mind. 7 January 2005 when my eldest son Callum was born is one of those dates. His wee brother Jack came into the world on 14 March 2006. Happiest days of my life. My partner Amanda made me the most grateful man alive when she brought our boys into the world. We both look upon the birth of children as one of life's miracles. I really do find it truly incredible. I feel proud, privileged and blessed to be the father of two such wonderful boys. 11 July 2007 is another date that will never leave me. It was the day I signed for Glasgow Rangers. It took me more than a decade to start a relationship with Amanda because she was a stunner and I was too shy to speak to her, never mind ask her out, and Rangers took nearly twenty years to come and get me. Worth the wait on both occasions. I hope Amanda and Rangers feel the same!

In terms of my professional career, I have many people to thank for helping me get to where I am today. They will all be mentioned in due course but I must start with my dad. Had it not been for him I would never have the great job that I've had for nearly twenty years. He drove me on and was inspirational. I'm living my dream because of him. Yet, at times, I couldn't stand him for it. Could see him far enough. I felt he put too much strain and pressure on me from a very young age. He was doing it for the right reasons but when I was eight and nine years old it was hard to see it that way.

My dad was in the Navy for nine years during the 1950s and '60s and was a leading seaman as his life on the waves took him all over the world for Queen and Country. He always reminds everyone he is a certified 'Blue Nose' as he has sailed beyond the Arctic Circle and, at a special ceremony on board, had his certificate given to him by King Neptune, which is akin to the more popular and wider-known 'crossing the line' ceremony. He also served as a guard at Winston Churchill's funeral in London in January 1965 and was a guard at one of the Queen's garden parties. The period spent with the Navy really moulded his outlook on life and how he would raise his three sons, my two older brothers, Gregor and Wullie, and me. Mum would affectionately call him 'Popeye'. Maybe I could say he was like Uncle Albert from *Only Fools and Horses* as Dad liked to go on about how he sailed the Seven Seas and torpedoed the enemy!

He was also into his boxing during his Navy days. He would get up at 5.30 to run six or seven miles three mornings a week and then spend three nights in the gym. It must have been in there he perfected his right hook!

Dad has always been a stickler for discipline, manners and good timekeeping. He's always up at the crack of dawn; bed made, clean-shaven, hair combed, shoes polished and wearing a shirt and tie. Proper old school, although he's relaxed his dress code a little in recent years and will sometimes be seen wearing a casual shirt! He expected the same code of discipline and work ethic from me but I struggled to live up to it during my school days. Now, though, I'm very similar to him. There is a part of that in my make-up, my DNA. My dad's regimental discipline and the influence Billy Davies, Alex McLeish, Jim Griffin and Tom Forsyth had on me in my early professional years at Motherwell have helped to structure my career and my life outside of the game.

Dad would have me up early for school. He'd shout at me from the bottom of the stairs to get out of my bed. No kid likes to get out of a toasting hot bed to go to school, particularly when you're warm under the covers and it's the middle of winter. Dad would give me his two-minute warning and he'd come up and pull the blankets off the bed.

As I mentioned earlier, he was a real fitness fanatic. From as far back as I can remember he'd be out running. I think he used to like doing a four-mile run. I can remember lagging behind him, trying to keep up. I was in my early years at primary school at that time. Later in my childhood, he bought me running spikes. He'd take me sprint training and to sprint coaches at Motherwell College to give me an extra yard of pace in the hope it would help lead to a career in football. Dad played for the Navy football team and also represented Lanarkshire at athletics. He kept his vest from that event and I got him to sign it and framed it for him. He loves it.

He was delighted I loved sport and I was into a few things other than football. I was very keen on badminton and was proud to be selected for Lanarkshire. I was told I could compete at a high level in the sport but it clashed with football one day when I was due to either go to Meadowbank Arena for a Lanarkshire Doubles match or play in a Scottish Cup tie for Wishaw Boys Club. I had to choose. Football won. I also took part in athletics at the Lanarkshire Games and won the gold medal at the shot put. No matter the sport, Dad would encourage me to go for it.

I just knew, however, not to expect much praise from him. He'd rather bring up a negative aspect about my performance than a positive one. I longed for his approval, a small pat on the back. It rarely, if ever, came. But I did have tremendous support from him. Wherever we went for sport, Dad was always there. He never drove so we had to rely on public transport. He'd be well prepared and have the timetable of the buses to hand so we would never be late. Had he not been willing to sacrifice his time and always find the money for bus fares and football boots, then I'd never be where I am today.

When I started playing football at boys' club level he'd always be the loudest parent at the side of the pitch. He'd be shouting the odds at me. If I had scored four or five goals he'd be screaming at me to get another one. He never shouted at any other kids, not unless he was praising them.

He loved football and was the manager of Forgewood Boys Club. I played in his team, even though I was two years younger than the age group. He also took the school team at Wishaw Primary. I was in Primary 4 at that time and up against boys three years older. Sometimes I would get permission to get out of class for training or games, and that was a brilliant perk. The football link is in the genes, no doubt. My eldest brother Gregor was a good footballer but decided in his teens to pursue golf. Wullie was also a good player. He had a trial for Celtic when he was thirteen or fourteen. He was a striker and would rattle in forty or fifty goals a season. He just fell away from the game. That was a shame. Loads of people, even to this day, still say Wullie had much more ability than me when he was my age and I don't doubt that for a second.

I was always kicking a ball about. A lot of the time just on my own, for hours and hours. I didn't have a computer, and I didn't want one. I had everything I needed. Playing in our back garden in Wishaw was my favourite place. I'd dribble with the ball around clothes pegs and score a goal. Dad would watch me from the kitchen window. He'd be doing the dishes and I'd be scoring an imaginary goal for Rangers. He used to commentate to add a bit of drama and excitement. I loved it. The only problem was that I sometimes kicked the ball over the fence and into the neighbour's garden. It happened more times than I care to remember. On one occasion the neighbour kept my ball, refused to return it. He'd had enough. He said my ball was in his property and I wasn't getting it back.

I was upset. Dad came to investigate the problem. There was an exchange of words and it resulted in Dad hauling the neighbour into our garden. The neighbour still had my ball under his arm. 'Now,' Dad said. 'You're on my property and so is Lee's ball.' The ball was duly returned and everything was fine again. Dad told me the moral of the story was that I was never to allow anyone from stopping me playing football. That was one of his favourite sayings. His other one was when we used to argue he would say, 'Don't tell your da' how to make weans.'

Being the youngest child, it was almost as if I became the last chance for us to have a professional footballer in the family. But there was a danger I was going to ruin it all through a lack of discipline at school. I got suspended a few times and would often come home with a punishment exercise. When I told my mum she'd just give me a right hook to the jaw. Honestly, she had quicker hands than Muhammad Ali! My dad preferred to make me run round the block as a punishment and time me. I'd sometimes have to do it three or four times. I'd then get back in the house and would have to do a wee circuit of exercises such as press-ups, star-jumps, squats and sits-ups. My dad would be sitting in his big armchair with the remote control for the telly watching *Countdown* or whatever was on, but he'd be there counting me to make sure I competed my full set of press-ups. He'd count out loud. Maybe he just liked to try and keep up with Carol Vorderman!

But he cared and wanted me to succeed. He would wash and polish my boots for me when I was kid. He'd wash them twice and give them coats of polish and two buffs. They were the cleanest and shiniest boots in the whole of Lanarkshire. I had Patrick Milano and they were my pride and joy. I loved wearing them for Wishaw Boys Club. My managers there were Keith

Miller and Duncan Millar. Both were committed to the game and were excellent influences on us all. Keith was funny, class and knowledgeable.

When I went full-time at Motherwell James McFadden was my boot boy and he used to love it because I'd never ask him to shine my boots, just put a layer of polish on them and hang them back up on my peg. He said I was the easiest player at the club to look after.

The path I took to Motherwell was a long one and I had many clubs. My first game was for Bellshill Hearts when I was six years old. It was an under-10s team and Wullie played for them. They were a man short one afternoon and I made up the numbers. I didn't realise you had to change ends at half-time and thought we were shooting the same way. Thankfully, my knowledge on the rules of the game has improved. A little! I went on to play for Jerviston Boys Club at ten, eleven and twelve. We won the League there and happened to beat Mill United – with Barry Ferguson in the line-up – on the way. I then moved to Wishaw BC. I was playing in the centre of midfield and senior clubs, including Manchester City and St Johnstone, were taking notice of my performances. I was chuffed and it gave me an incentive to carry on and take it to the next level. Motherwell were also lurking around and there was an obvious attraction to going with my hometown team. I eventually signed a schoolboy form with the club when I was fifteen. I was delighted and I must thank Keith Miller and Wishaw BC for their guidance and encouragement during that stage of my early career.

The one setback I had came at Jerviston BC in a Scottish Cup semi-final tie that went to a penalty shoot-out against Petersburn of Airdrie. I missed my spot-kick and we lost the game. I was distraught. That moment has never left me and I still have a phobia to this day about taking penalties because of it. But kids are resilient, and I recovered from the trauma to continue my development as a teenager and into professional football.

To sign for Motherwell was a huge thing for me. I attended Knowetop Primary School, in the shadows of Fir Park, when I was in Primary 7 after we moved to the area. Tommy McLean was the manager at that time and my friends and I would try to sneak out of school to see the players arriving for training and get an autograph. The squad at that time had plenty of quality and had a fine crop of young first-team players such as Chris McCart, Tom Boyd, Fraser Wishart, Andy Walker and Ally Maxwell. John Gahagan – now Scotland's finest after-dinner speaker – was also there. But it was clear Motherwell gave youth its chance and it was a club I had a soft spot for.

The highlight of being at Knowetop was going through the entire season undefeated and winning the prestigious Hunter Cup at Fir Park. We won 5–0 in the final. I still have a video of the game.

There were some great times during those early years but some tough times too, especially Dad's fitness regimes. But I certainly learned a lot. Thanks, Dad. Love you.

2

GROWING UP WITH THE
BROTHERS GRIN

MY MUM, of course, played a role in helping me to get where I am today. First and foremost, she went through a testing labour to bring me into the world on 14 May 1978 at Bellshill Maternity. I was a big boy and tipped the scales at a healthy 12lb 12oz. My parents were told I was the biggest boy in the hospital for three years. I must have put my mum off having any more babies! I was the last of her three sons.

My birth wasn't straightforward and there were complications. I was born with a heart murmur and my parents were extremely concerned. I was put into a special unit for babies and Mum was in intensive care. Mum's sister came to visit and after she had seen me she went to see my mum and came away with a great line. She said, 'Iris, Lee's a big boy – I should have bought him a school uniform instead of a baby-grow.'

My brothers Wullie and Gregor were a few years older than me and needless to say they were big influences on my early life. I have several happy, funny and sad memories. From as far back as I can remember I didn't like it when they left the house in the morning to go to school. I wanted them to stay and keep me amused. As far as I was concerned, their education could wait. Or, at the very least, they could have folded me up into their schoolbag and taken me with them! Mum would probably have been delighted to see the back of me for a few hours as I'm told

I was quite a handful – hyperactive and more than occasionally disruptive. Like most toddlers, I was up to all sorts and couldn't be left alone for a second. Mum often tells me how much hard work I was. Being the youngest I would always get called 'the baby' so I would try and take things to the limit as I had a better chance of getting away with them. I'd hammer nails into my mum's sofa. You know, wee things like that, harmless stuff!

When Mum tried to enrol me into Pather Community Nursery, one of the teachers came to us for a house visit, basically to go through a few formalities and rubber-stamp my place. Valerie Watson was her name, and she was a neighbour so she knew I had a bit of a wild streak in me. She came to the door and told Mum there was a space for me and I could start the next morning. She was standing in the porch and all of a sudden I came flying out of the bedroom window – on the second floor – screaming, 'Suuuupermaaaan!' I had the full Superman outfit on. Clark Kent didn't have a look in! Thankfully I landed safely, but my daft stunt caused a bit of damage in other ways. Valerie called it off. She said the playgroup wasn't insured. Mum pleaded with her, her best line being that the playgroup was on ground level so I wouldn't have far to jump!

I was always busy, constantly on the go. Mum tried to get me into lots of different clubs to keep me amused. I was hyper and had to use up my energy, otherwise I would have driven my parents and brothers crazy. The janitor at Wishaw Academy had a wee after-school club and that was on every night. I think we paid 10p a night. We would play football and badminton. It was great fun and gave me an extra grounding.

When I got home, most nights I would be out playing with pals, using up whatever energy we had left before bedtime. Our favourite game was 'Grand National'. That involved starting in a garden at one end of the street and jumping through every hedge in every garden until we reached the end of the line. We were fearless. We'd be screaming at the top of our voices as we rampaged through the hedges. We wanted the neighbours to come out and chase us. If we got caught we got a clip round the ear, but it all was great fun. Still another childhood memory that makes me cringe!

We would do quite a lot of things as a family. Dad was always keen we attended church in Wishaw together every Sunday. He was a deacon in the Reformed Presbyterian Church. It is now defunct and that saddened my old man. The building is still there but is now used for different things in the community. However, Dad was extremely proud that his church had direct roots to the Covenanters and their many heroes. For attending church, my brothers and I would get a quarter-pound of Bonbons to sing songs and shake everyone's hand at the end of the service. So, in my eyes, it was a good deal. We went for years and Dad loved it. Dad is very religious. His grandfather was an Ulster Unionist follower and a strict Brethren. We'd also attend Sunday school and had some friends there. My cousin Victoria Mitchell also went. We were really close back then. She now works as a journalist.

My dad was employed in the Ravenscraig steelworks as a security guard working twelve-hour shifts and eventually got made redundant. It meant my mum had to work more and she held down two jobs. During the day she was a manager at JH McKenna bookies and at night she worked a shift in a pub, the Auld House in Wishaw. Mum was the breadwinner at this stage and my dad was the house husband. We didn't have much spare cash but any money my parents got they spoilt us in any way they could. They would never have liked to have lived a flashy life and never spent their earnings on stuff they needed. It all went on us, whether it was for new training shoes, football boots, school trips or golf equipment.

On one occasion we went abroad on holiday to Portugal

and we had a great time in the sunshine. But even when we were on holiday, Dad wouldn't let up on my training. He'd still make sure I was getting plenty of exercise, whether it was doing lengths in the swimming pool or running along the beach most mornings.

Dad put all his effort into getting the three of us into sport. At home in Wishaw, we stayed across the road from the old bus station and there was a park next to it where he would take us to play football. We loved a good kick-about. We also enjoyed the Super Bowl nights and we'd make an American football pitch in the house. We all had our own favourite team. I liked the Chicago Bears.

We were a close family and I shared a room with my brother Wullie. Gregor always had his own room. We would play pretend fighting, wrestling and tell jokes before we went to sleep. Gregor was always the cool one in my eyes as he was oldest and I looked up to him. Wullie would always look out for me and occasionally give me a slap if I annoyed him. Gregor played football too but then went into golf where my dad encouraged him and is currently playing off 6. Whatever path we chose our parents supported us and that's the type of parent I want to be to my kids. I don't want them to feel pressurised into doing anything. Just as long as they work hard and give their all, they can choose any career path they like.

I was fortunate in a way, in that I always wanted to play football. That was all there was to it. I flirted with other things like cars and badminton, but football was always top of my list. Although, when it came to leaving school, I had to look at a few options in case I didn't get taken on at a club anywhere. I did, however, go through a wee spell of wanting to work in the local sweetie shop in Motherwell. They had boxes and boxes of great sweets, like Bonbons, Cola Cubes, that kind of thing. I thought it would be great to work in there. I asked Mum to get me an application form, although she was reluctant as she felt I would go through my wages in the shop buying sweets. Thankfully, the football came good – but I've never managed to get rid of my sweet tooth!

As far back as I can remember I watched football on the television, especially back in the 1980s and '90s before live games on the box became the norm. It was a treat to see a full ninety minutes and that's why I loved the Scottish Cup finals. The whole day was such a buzz. I couldn't sleep the night before it, especially if Rangers were playing. My parents would give me money for sweets and I used to think about what I'd buy and the juice I'd drink. The Graeme Souness era was special and then the nine-in-a-row period under Walter Smith. I loved Ally McCoist, Richard Gough, Mark Walters, Davie Cooper, Brian Laudrup and Ian Durrant. But Paul Gascoigne was my absolute favourite, my hero. Sad as it may sound, I think I actually loved Gazza as a player!

My love for Rangers was probably because my dad was a diehard. He used to sing all the songs in the house at the top of his voice while making dinner or in the toilet, and if Rangers were on the telly and they scored, he went crazy. I remember a Cup final against Aberdeen that Rangers won on penalties. Dad ended up taking his celebrations too far and bared his backside to the telly. Yes, a full moonie! Mum was disgusted, hit him with her slipper and told him to grow up.

Mum also loves Rangers and was brought up in Motherwell. She lived close to the Orange Halls and would often go there for a night out and a bit of socialising. That area was known as 'The Globe'. Mum loved Rangers then and still does now. Same with dad, and their passion for the club was drilled into me and my two brothers. We thrived on it. It was a big part of our lives. Still is, of course.

Apart from supporting Rangers, there was no greater buzz than playing the game. Football gave me a focus and, to an extent, kept me out of trouble. I wasn't the greatest of pupils and I would give my teachers a hard time. They know who they are and I offer my sincere apologies for the bother I caused and any undue stress I may have brought on them. But my heart was in the right place it's just that my brain wasn't always! I was immature and too easily led astray. Football was always my thing and Mum often tells me that my report cards usually said that Lee just wants to be a footballer and isn't interested in school.

My first school was Wishaw Academy. I attended that school until Primary 5. I did get suspended from school and had a good few punishment exercises and that meant more trouble for me from Mum and Dad when I got home. Mum could tell by the look on my face when I came in from school whether I had been in trouble or not. On one occasion I had my mum's blessing not to do a punishment exercise and the school weren't happy about it. It was something out of nothing and it all blew up out of proportion. It ended up with me being taken out of school before I got expelled.

My pals at Wishaw Academy were wee James Campbell and Stuart Cadzow. The three of us loved a giggle and carry-on. We weren't nasty; we were just mischievous. I missed them when I left.

We moved house from 247 Stewarton Street, Wishaw, to Motherwell because my bedroom ceiling fell in on me and my brother during the night. It was caused by dampness. Half the stuff in the loft fell on top of us. My mum and dad couldn't believe I slept through it. Never even flinched, apparently. Wullie ran through to tell Mum and Dad the ceiling had caved in and their immediate concern was for my welfare. Why could they not hear me crying or screaming? They ran through, Mum and Wullie picked me up from under the rubble still sleeping, or knocked out, one of the two. Everything landed on top of me. They had to scoop me out. I was seven. We were on the list for a new council house and got one in Motherwell. My parents are still in the same house.

And from then on, I had to travel every day by myself to Wishaw Academy. It was a bus from the end of our street. I was Primary 6 and at the time enjoyed the bus. I then moved to Knowetop Primary for Primary 7 and had to meet new friends.

Believe it or not, I was a very shy lad. Was always very quiet around new people and would hide behind Mum. I'm still very shy. I have to be in my comfort zone to come out of my shell. I'm never going to change. Because I play football now people may well mistake my persona for arrogance or ignorance but I am genuinely just really shy.

Give me a ball, though, and I'm in my element. As a school kid, I would go out in the streets myself with my football and run around the roads or kick the ball off the garages pretending they were goals. I also used to have a kick-about at George Street Park. Usually between fifteen and twenty boys would get together and enjoy a game, and I still have friends from that period in my life. A lot of the boys were older than me and they were great. I looked up to them and they would look after the young ones as they were also from the same scheme. It made us feel safe and we always had a laugh with them.

For a few weeks during the summer – during Wimbledon – football would take a back seat and was replaced by tennis. We played on the roads, chalked out a court, and used a row of supermarket trolleys as the net. I loved being John McEnroe. He is one of my sporting heroes. I loved his temper but, more than anything, I admired his ability and work ethic. He hated to lose. You could feel his anger and pain bursting through the television screen when things weren't going his way. He is now the best tennis pundit on television. Thankfully, he doesn't do clichés. He tells it like it is and is also extremely informative. A perfect mix.

For the other forty-nine or fifty weeks of the year, football was the main sport. As I got older I loved the game more and more and gained confidence to play against the boys who were a few years my senior. We'd sometimes play ten-a-side down the park and when it was raining a game of 'hackarama' topped our agenda. It was wet and slippy and perfect for dirty big rasping slide tackles. Believe me, no prisoners were taken. The younger ones had to be tough because the older lads wouldn't hold back. I wasn't intimidated because I was big for my age. I was about eleven or twelve at this stage, and the older boys called me 'Tyson' after Mike Tyson. I had a stocky build and a really thick neck. I didn't mind the nickname but I'm glad it never stuck.

Dad would sometimes come and watch us playing. When the game was finished, the lads would head off for a juice or a sweetie, but not me. Dad would keep me behind to do some jogging and sprint work. I used to be raging with him for doing it to me but it was all part of his grand plan!

My close mates at the time were Chris Reid, Derek Inglis, Gerry O'Donnell, Stuart Beaglin, Paul Baird, Chris McEwan and my good mate JP Curran. Chris Reid was my best pal and still is. I'm still in contact with Derek and his family. Stuart is a Motherwell diehard and JP is a close pal. We didn't go to school together but were close and he has since moved to Dubai. I've been over a few times to see him and his family. I feel fortunate to have such good friends around me. We would do anything for each other and you can't put a price on that.

Because I chose to try and go down the career path of being a footballer, I did have to sacrifice a few nights out and different things. My social life was non-existent at times, but it has all been worthwhile. I've been proud that I started my career that way and still have the same attitude. In terms of preparation, I've never done anything in the game that I shouldn't have. I've never had a drink forty-eight hours before a game. I believe if I worked as hard as possible, made sacrifices, then I would be able to achieve pretty much anything I wanted to. Of course, I've had a bit of luck here and there, but I also believe that slice of good fortune is possibly a reward for dedication and desire.

Most young boys want to become footballers, but very few make the grade. Many teenagers have unbelievable ability but you need more than that for football to become your full-time occupation. When I was a teenager, still at school, many players my age had twice the ability I possessed, but they weren't totally committed and refused to make the necessary sacrifices by putting the hours in and walking away from any potential scenarios that would jeopardise a future in the game of football at professional level. They allowed themselves to be easily sidetracked. If I didn't have football then I don't know what I would have done in life. I appreciate every day how lucky I am and the people close to me don't let me forget it. They would quickly batter me down to size if there was ever a hint of getting carried away with myself. The friends I've had from school days would also not allow me to be arrogant or 'Billy Big-Time'. They know me as Lee from Wishaw Academy, Knowetop Primary and Dalziel High School.

Moving to high school was a nerve-racking experience. Thankfully, I was lucky enough to be in Chris Reid's classes. Both of us and Derek Inglis would meet most days with four or five of the other guys and hang about together. Andy Devlin was one of them. He was the school captain and is a good friend of mine and is a sports journalist. He helped me and my family deal with the media pressure when I joined Rangers. We remain close, and I've also a lot of time for his two brothers, Euan and Alan.

My first day at Dalziel High was one I will never forget. Dad bought me my uniform and a fake Raleigh schoolbag. I got a new pair of boots as well. My mates were all cutting about in Timberland boots and quality sports footwear but I wasn't. I had to settle with desert boots a size too big for me and my trousers were skin-tight. I was mortified, but what the hell. I decided to go the full ten yards and put almost a full tub of gel on my hair, which made it look really greasy, which wasn't my intention. I went to school looking like a teddy boy and my mates laughed at me all the way there. I was so embarrassed.

At least I felt safe at school as my brother Wullie was there. He was popular and would always look out for me. As we got older, sharing a room with him became quite an experience. He would go out and drink some weekends and come home drunk. At one stage I had a fish tank full of amazing tropical fish with all the glitzy trimmings, such as a little sunken ship at the bottom of the multi-coloured chips on the pretend seabed of plastic plants and little divers. It was my pride and joy. I had silver sharks, all sorts of fish and the best filter to keep it clean.

One morning I woke up to find Wullie vomiting. It was a disgusting sight but what made it worse was the fact he had the top of my fish tank open and was being sick into it. I was totally devastated. My heart sank. It was the only thing I had. I looked after those fish really well and my brother was killing them. I still haven't forgiven him.

My point to him was spew-up on the carpet or on your bed but not into my fish tank. His argument was that Mum would have gone mental if he had ruined the carpet or the quilt, so the fish tank was the safest bet. I had to clean it all. Luckily I didn't waste any time in getting stuck in and that meant none of my fish died. But my relationship with Wullie lost a bit of life. I didn't speak to him for months.

On another occasion he woke up with a hangover and some light-sticks he'd brought back home with him from the raves he used to attend. He was desperate for a drink to quench his morning-after thirst and cut the top off of one of these things with scissors. He mistakenly thought it was a flavoured twist'n'squeeze drink and swallowed the lot. His stupidity meant he had a glow-in-the-dark tongue. I laughed for ages and looked on that as being a score draw after the episode with my fish.

He was also really noisy when he came home drunk but was a sound sleeper. That meant I could get up in the morning and steal the change from his pockets to go out with my mates. Chris and I would meet up and first thing he would ask was, 'How much did you get from your brother?' I was paying the attempted goldfish murderer back bit by bit!

Chris has two big brothers and a big sister. His parents are fine people. His dad is full of patter and opinionated and his mum is always asking if you're okay and asking about your well-being. She prefers to ask after other people than talk about herself.

I had a much more steady and straightforward relationship with Gregor. I used to wear all his clothes and splash on his after-shave. When he left school he went to university and got his degree in Risk Management. He was also a part-time DJ. I would go into his room and have a shot on his decks but I wasn't the best. Gregor got me into all sorts of music, like the Stone Roses. Wullie got me into Pink Floyd and Dr Hook – hey, when you're in love with a beautiful woman, it's hard. To this day, I still listen to them all.

In my eyes, Gregor was always trendy and had all the clothes and seemed to go partying all the time. I used to watch him play in the Pro-Am at Wishaw Golf Club. He played for their team and I'd walk round with my dad when he was playing a match. I looked up to him and thought I wanted to be like him when I got older.

I also looked up to Wullie, but in a different way. Wullie played football and was brilliant at it. If he put his mind to something nothing would stop him succeeding. He won Joiner of the Year when he left school. Celtic also came in for him when he was at school. He went for a trial with them but it was only for one game and it didn't go to plan. He should have been given another chance. It was Celtic's loss. I've no doubt in my mind that if he'd stuck at football a little longer than he did and been a little bit more dedicated he would have gone to the top. So, in a way, I used to look at my brothers and wanted to be like them both. I was always in the corner looking at them thinking, 'I want to be like you two.'

They've been a huge influence on me and so have my parents. Dad drove me on as a kid and Mum would always stick up for me when I was younger. She is fiery and often speaks her mind. One example that will always stick with me is when she used to say to my brothers about bringing girls home. Her usual line was 'So-and-so isn't good enough for you. Look at the size of the arse on her.' We would slag my mum's backside but when we did, she would just look back at us and say, 'Not a bad backside after three kids. Wait till it hits your woman.' All good fun. She is also very stubborn and rarely backs down on anything, and absolutely nothing fazes her.

I grew up loving her mince and tatties. She is brilliant at making one of my favourite meals. Money was tight so we were never out for meals at restaurants. But there wasn't a dining-out culture thirty years ago like there is now. There must be at least 300 restaurants in the West of Scotland to choose from and thirty hotels, but that wasn't the case all those years ago. Kids nowadays want to go out for lunch and dinner, or have a fast-food drive-thru, but that wasn't in our mindset in the early and mid-'80s. It was all about what your mum was making for dinner. We were all happy with that. Our house used to have that whiff of homemade mince and tatties. As soon as I came in the door from school the smell would hit me. Beautiful. In saying that, I love all food. I love an Indian or a Chinese takeaway. My favourite dish is the South Indian garlic chilli chicken. Spaghetti arrabiata with extra chillis runs it a close second, but nothing will ever beat Mum's mince and tatties.

She would do anything for anyone and her kindness has always overridden everything else. When I was a kid she would go to ridiculous lengths to spoil her boys at Christmas. We used to have bin bags full of toys and clothes. She was also a 'chocoholic'. Her and Dad would rarely have much spare cash but she tried to give us a treat every day and I looked forward to her bringing me in a sweet from work. It was usually a King-size Mars Bar.

Yet, I must have driven her up the wall when I was younger. But according to my brothers, I'm her favourite son. They say I always have been and always will be. They reckon I got away with more than they ever did and most of the time they would get the blame for things and cop a sore one as a result. To this day, when we're all together at family dinners, they will remind me of this. However, for all they slag me off, I know my brothers are proud of my achievements in football.

3

£80 A WEEK BUT I FELT LIKE A MILLION DOLLARS

FOOTBALL CLUBS started to show an interest in me when I was around fourteen and playing for Jerviston BC. Jerviston had a good team and we were very successful. Our biggest rivals were Mill United. They were the established side in Lanarkshire but we managed to topple them. I was a central midfielder and sort of stood out because I was a bit taller and more physically developed than most of the other lads. Believe it or not, I had a decent turn of pace when I was a teenager and used that to good effect. I would take the free-kicks and the penalty kicks and I was often getting told I was going to make the grade as a professional footballer. My family came and watched me every week and were very supportive. We also used to get our games videoed and Dad would put my game on on a Sunday night when we got home. It became compulsive viewing in the McCulloch household. The sight of me and twenty-one other kids running around a red ash park, chasing a Mouldmaster ball was just too good to resist!

Motherwell, Rangers, St Johnstone and Hibs all showed an interest in me. By this stage I had moved on to play for Wishaw and then to Rangers SABC. It was then I decided to sign schoolboy forms with Motherwell. As I said earlier, they were my local team and had a good youth policy. It was also just two minutes from my front door so there wouldn't be any inconvenience or expense when it came to travelling. Motherwell were delighted to get me on an S-form and also allowed me to continue to play for Rangers SABC, the only stipulation being that I did not train with Rangers during the week. I had a successful two-year period with Rangers and we won the Scottish Cup in consecutive seasons. I left to join Motherwell for the Under-16 team.

Motherwell were fine with me being with Rangers. It was straightforward most of the time, but it turned a little bit messy one day. The Rangers team I played for were fortunate enough to be chosen to take part in one of the Champions League pre-match ceremonies at Ibrox. One afternoon we were on a public park practising what we had to do for the event and a few of us were carrying on. The coach made us do a few laps of the park as a punishment. Willie McLean – brother of Jim and Tommy – was Head of Youths at Motherwell at that stage and happened to be taking in another game when he spotted me doing laps. He mistakenly thought I was 'training' with Rangers and let rip, swearing at me and making me feel extremely uncomfortable and embarrassed. My parents weren't happy at Mr McLean's conduct towards me and a few phone calls were made to him just to let him know that they found it unacceptable. Fortunately the matter was closed after that and we all moved on.

I enjoyed my spell at Motherwell and the club looked after me very well. The only negative I can remember was Motherwell asked me not to play for my school team. I was happy enough to abide by that but I was gutted when five of my Rangers SABC team-mates were selected for the Scotland team to go down and play England at Wembley. Scotland won 2–1. I'd have loved the opportunity to have been involved in that memorable occasion.

By the time I reached Fourth Year at Dalziel High I was going through the motions with my schoolwork. To be truthful, I became a waste of space in the classroom. Some of the teachers at school were cautious and warned that I might not make the grade. When I was on S-form they told my parents that I shouldn't be taking football for granted and that I had to concentrate more on schoolwork. There was no chance I was going to do that. Football was all that mattered to me. But it did put doubts in my mind. It was just as well I stuck in and made the grade as a footballer because I left school with no qualifications. I didn't even bother turning up to do my Chemistry exam and opted to go golfing instead. Chris Reid and I used to have a competition in Chemistry to see who could write the least amount so the winner was the smallest dot on our jotters. It got so bad that the teacher just let us do our own thing, usually pouring a beaker of water over one another. Looking back, we were trouble and the teachers must have dreaded it when we were in the same class. We kept each other amused. Entertainment came first and schoolwork came a very distant second. On reflection, by rights we should have been given a good slap by the teachers, told to get our heads down and to stop being so disruptive.

I yearned for the weeks when we were allowed to go off on work experience. With me being an S-form at Motherwell it was simple enough for me to go there and see the workings of the club from the inside and get a taste of what life might be like as a professional footballer. I had asked Motherwell assistant manager Tam Forsyth to get me in and he sorted it with the school. I was already going in there on a regular basis, whether it was for a mid-week training night or to help out during the school holidays. To go there to 'work' was perfect for me. I couldn't ever imagine myself working in an office; I just wasn't interested in a nine-to-five lifestyle. That said, I'm sure it would have been much less demanding being in an office than working under Forsyth. He just never let up. It made no difference to him that I was a kid. He made me work and left me in no doubt as to what would be required as a young footballer trying to make the grade at professional level.

Tommy McLean was the manager. As a person he had a

reputation for being a hard taskmaster. I'm not sure if that was accurate or was actually more of a reflection on his big brother, Jim, and maybe that followed the family. I didn't find out for myself either way as I had very few dealings with Tommy. He stuck to the first team and had little to do with the youths.

Most of my dealings were with Forsyth. I didn't find it easy. Tam was a character and a strict disciplinarian. He took no shit from anyone, senior players or youngsters. Looking back, it gave me some extra mental strength at that time. Most important of all, though, he also knew the game. I learned so much from him in my early days and it stood me in good stead. He'd tell me where to run and when to run. But he did lack a wee bit of patience. If I didn't get it right first time he would lose the plot.

There is a great story about Tam after a training session at Smithycroft. When we were finished he asked all the YTS boys to collect the bibs, cones, discs and balls and put them on the trailer to take back to Fir Park. According to Tam, we were one ball short. He only counted nineteen balls and we had arrived with twenty. Nobody was allowed to leave until the missing ball was found. All the boys were hunting high and low, in the long grass and down by the trees. The rain was lashing down from the heavens. Ninety minutes later the search was still going on. The boys were tired, frustrated, wet and cold. Far from amused. A few were ready for chucking it and going back to the Park. One of the boys then demanded a recount. He asked Tam if he had counted the ball he had been holding under his arm for the past hour and a half. Needless to say he hadn't.

I loved being involved at a professional club and it whetted my appetite. The banter between the senior players was brilliant, but unforgiving. Apart from the ability to succeed, I knew I was going to need two things to survive in football: a thick skin and a huge pair of balls. Footballers can be cruel and they pounce on any signs of weakness. I was determined to make sure I didn't crumble.

24

During the holidays my job at the stadium was to brush the shower area, clean the urinals and the baths. Big Tam loved a bath, loved a long soak after putting the boys through a training session. I felt I had to try extra hard to get it clean for him. When I had hosed it and cleaned it with Jif and the cloths, he would run his finger up and down the tiles to check it was spotless. Most of the time I got pass marks. But a couple of times I was in a rush to get away early and tried to cut corners. He knew. So, he would call me back in and say, 'Right you, ya wee slack-arsed bastard. Come here. Stand in front of me and tense your fucking arm so I can give you two or three punches.' He'd leather me. It was extremely painful. His parting words when I didn't clean the bath right were: 'Remember, son, do your job right off the park and you will do it right on the park.'

Often when he was in the bath he would shout me through and ask me to run down to the shop for him because he wanted some chocolate, maybe a cake or two as well. His favourite saying for the chocolate run was, 'Take your time going, son, but hurry when you're on your way back.' Genius. Tam was hard but in general quite fair.

However, I remember on one occasion my dad lost the plot with him. We used to get free football boots from Motherwell but on one occasion I was told that the supply had been used up and there was nothing left for me. I went home and told dad he needed to go out and buy me new boots. He was having none of it. So, he marched up to Fir Park and demanded to see big Tam. He more or less got him by the scruff of the neck and told him it was unacceptable that I had to buy my own boots.

The following day I had my boots from Tam. And by the way, he actually gave me two pairs. Now, of course, with Tam being a Rangers legend as part of the 1972 European Cup Winners' Cup side, he works on match days visiting the Hospitality Lounges. I will sometimes bump into him. To this day, we still have a laugh about that episode and he always finishes with, 'Mind and tell yer da' I was asking for him.'

I played in the BP Youth Cup team when I was on S-form at that time and that was good. I also got called up for a few reserve games and had the privilege of playing and training with the late, great Davie Cooper. Davie used to wear a big black bin bag under his training gear every day and then at lunchtime he would not stop eating chocolate digestives. He was the star player at Motherwell at the time and I was in awe of him and his talent. When I was lucky enough to play in the same team as him, at training he would say repeatedly, 'Just give the ball to me.'

Like any busy young kid would have done, I followed him around, watching his habits and trying to copy him. He used to say to me that he thought I was a decent young player and that I had a future in the game. But he then told me he thought I was too fat and would have to keep an eye on my waistline. That was fair comment, I suppose.

I reckon I must have been a bit chubby at school as I never trained too much. So, Davie's comments more or less put me on a diet for life! It was a privilege to get that wee taste of life with him. It was tragic that he died in 1995 from a brain haemorrhage at just thirty-nine years old. But it was fitting that the North Stand at Fir Park has been named after him.

Tragedy has followed so many players at Motherwell from the 1990s. Jamie Dolan died in 2008 when he was just thirty-nine. Paul McGrillen took his own life at just thirty-seven. And there was Phil O'Donnell losing his life on the Fir Park pitch in 2007. Again, it was only right of Motherwell to name a stand after Phil.

The time spent on work experience was beneficial and I must have made a good impression. Motherwell offered me the chance to join their YTS scheme as an apprentice footballer. But by this stage, Manchester City and St Johnstone also made it clear they wanted me to join them full-time. I decided I was going to sign for St Johnstone. They had an excellent youth set-up and had players coming through the ranks such as Callum Davidson and Phillip Scott. My heart was set on going there and I was prepared to move to Perth and live in digs. And then, in the summer of 1994, I was introduced to Alex McLeish.

McLean and Forsyth had left Motherwell to take over at Hearts. McLeish was appointed as the new Motherwell boss. It was his first job in management after a hugely successful playing career with Aberdeen. John Park was Motherwell's chief scout at that time and I had informed him I wouldn't be accepting the club's offer of a YTS and was going to St Johnstone. Motherwell weren't best pleased and started to play funny buggers with me. Because I was an S-form with them they held my registration and weren't prepared to release me to move to Saints. It got me down and weeks of wrangling started. This was just before Big Eck McLeish was appointed.

I couldn't understand why Motherwell were making life difficult for me and a course of action I wanted to take was to stand outside the main entrance at Fir Park with a bottle of wine and twenty cigarettes to make me look like a no-hoper. I was going to act drunk and cause a scene. In my infinite wisdom, I thought that would make them ditch me. Mum told not to be so stupid and there would be another way to sort it out to my satisfaction. She was right.

John Park had spoken highly of me to McLeish but explained the situation to him. The new manager thought I was worth the effort and invited me and my parents into his office for a meeting. Our intentions were to tell him I was going to St Johnstone and there was nothing he could do to change our minds. We decided to meet him out of politeness.

Big Eck was very polite and made a fuss of us all, particularly my parents. He told them his plans for the club and that youth would be given its chance. He was convincing and charming.

Mum was putty in his hands. So was I. Within an hour I had signed a two-year YTS for Motherwell and it was all because of Big Eck. We were getting our pictures taken together and I was proud as punch. I think I was his first signing for Motherwell, although keeper Stevie Woods might have signed on the same day.

There's no doubt, looking back on it now, he had learned plenty from the Master – Sir Alex Ferguson. Big Eck's man-management skills in his office that night were different class. He concentrated on my parents, told them everything they wanted to hear and they couldn't resist. I was given £80 per week for my first year and £100 per week for the second year of my apprenticeship. Believe it or not, that was very good money back then for an apprentice footballer just out of school.

I felt like a million dollars when I walked into Motherwell on my first day as a YTS footballer. I was proud of myself and vowed not to waste the opportunity I had been given. And it was only a two-minute walk to the front door. I was given my 'duties' on my first day and I had to look after Billy Davies, Paul Lambert and the gaffer. I had to make sure their boots were spotless and shiny and that all their training gear was there for them every morning. I'd get in at 8.30am and was often there until 5 at night. I also had to clean the shower rooms every day, and in the winter months I had to make sure the huge kit hampers were put on the Fir Park pitch overnight to try and beat the freeze. Back then, we didn't have under-soil heating!

My eleven YTS colleagues were a great bunch and we had brilliant times together. Garry Gow became a close friend. He was a typical goalie – daft as a brush and great fun. He was very opinionated and argumentative but great company. He grew very close to my family as we'd sometimes nip home to mine during the day for a cup of tea. He moved to Australia a few years ago and is happily married to Brie. I miss him.

We were lucky to have a very good first-team dressing room. The senior players really took to us and looked out for us. They'd encourage the YTS lads – particularly Gowser and myself – to get involved in wind-ups, whether it was hiding the clothes of a team-mate or a set of car keys. We would mess about every day and verbally slaughter some of the first-team guys. We had no fear. Some of the senior pros loved our cheekiness, whether it was our patter or watching us having dance-offs to our rave music.

We also had a couple of scams on the go. One was that we'd wash the first-team players' cars for a fiver. We'd be hard at it with the buckets of water and the sponges but we found a huge hose at the other side of the ground and we used to drive the cars there. The first team, of course, were unaware we were driving their cars. Our little empire was going well until one day one of the lads crashed one of the cars into a taxi. The car belonged to Billy Davies and he was raging. The club got involved and it all got rather messy. Needless to say, that was the end of our venture into the world of business.

But Billy Davies and Paul Lambert were good to me. They'd give me a few quid every now and again and always looked after me at Christmas time. To be fair, I think I earned it. Both of them were a pain in the backside when it came to their boots because they demanded I Tipp-Exed different logos onto their boots to protect their sponsorship deals. I'd have to do that every week because on match days the Tipp-Ex would come off after about ten minutes.

One of the other wee scams we had going before I joined the YTS was with the match day tickets. We all got two tickets each. Craig Dargo also got two tickets but he stayed too far away to travel in. I used to get my big mate Chris 'Tiffy' Reid to go to the Fir Park ticket window and get Dargo's tickets. He had to sign for them with Dargo's signature. Then Tam Forsyth found out about it and he battered me all over the place.

We also used to get McDonald's gold cards. The league was sponsored by McDonald's and all players got given cards that allowed us to eat free at any of their restaurants. It was brilliant. We were there four or five times a week. I gave mine to big Chris and he'd go into MacDonald's with the ticket and would have to declare how he got the privilege tickets. He said he played for Motherwell. He was 6ft 4in, with really long hair and a big, hairy growth. A lady behind him in the queue heard him state he played for Motherwell and asked for her and her son to get a photo taken with him. The big man posed quite the thing. Absolutely no shame.

As the weeks and months passed in the YTS I had a lot of time for our manager. Alex McLeish was a fabulous guy and made me feel so welcome and very relaxed. He loved a laugh and a joke with the young guys but would also exert his authority every now and again if ever he felt we needed to be reminded. One afternoon he called me away from cleaning the showers and into his room. He was getting dressed – stood half naked in front of me, if truth be told – and had his serious face on. He kept asking me, 'Who am I?' and I kept replying, 'You're the gaffer.' This conversation went backwards and forwards at least half a dozen times. I had no idea where this was leading and I was panicking a little. He then pulled down his jumper from the peg and pointed to the logo on the left breast. He then asked me again, 'Who am I?' and I this time I said, 'You are the Boss.' He was wearing a Hugo Boss jumper. He said, 'That's right. I am the Boss. And don't ever forget it. Now, fuck off.' Then he started to laugh.

He was great for me and I have absolutely no doubt I would not have made the grade as a full-time professional footballer had it not been for him. He was an unbelievable influence on me and just perfect at that stage of my career. He knew the game of football inside out, but more importantly, he knew the personalities of the players and what made them tick, how to get the best out of them. Like I said previously, definite touches of Sir Alex about him. There is no doubt he was a huge influence on Big Eck when he was manager of Aberdeen.

I was also fortunate to have really good senior players at the club. The likes of Tommy Coyne, Rab McKinnon, Dougie Arnott, Lambert and Davies were very helpful. They could tell I was interested in learning the game and wanted to know what was required to keep progressing. Every day I would watch these guys train and it was an invaluable education, but it also left me with quite a bit of self-doubt and questions would gnaw away at me, most importantly, 'Would I ever be good enough to get up to their standard?' But I wasn't for feeling sorry for myself and throwing in the towel. Quite the opposite. It made me work harder, ask more questions and listen more intently. I had gone from playing against kids on public parks to training with talented and experienced professionals. It was a huge step up but I had to, and was desperate to, take the challenge on.

Tommy Coyne was very serious and analytical about the game. Young lad or not, he'd give me pelters if I didn't do something right on the park. He was doing it for the right reasons but I had to stand there and listen to him going off on one. I could either go into my shell or stand up and be counted. I chose to show I had the balls for this game. It gave me the determination not to get another rollicking from him, not to repeat the mistake again. Owen Coyle was also very helpful. He always had time for the younger players. It didn't surprise me he went on to become a very successful manager. His knowledge of the game is superb as are his man-management skills.

As much as I enjoyed it in the YTS and we had our laughs and bits of mischief, I never forgot what I was actually at Motherwell to do. My only objective was to get through the YTS and sign professional forms. At the end of my first season the twelve YTS lads were called in for a meeting in the gaffer's office.

Unfortunately eight of the lads were released. I felt for them but that's how cruel football is. I was kept on. I continued to work hard and tried to improve my fitness, first touch, my heading and my all-round game awareness. By this point I had a clear understanding of what I needed to do to try to make the grade.

I was rewarded a few months later when the Boss took me off the YTS six months early and gave me a professional contract. I went from £100 per week to £250 per week and also had a £250 bonus every time I played for the first team. I felt like a millionaire. It was brilliant. But just as rewarding was when the Boss sat the rest of the YTS lads down and told them that I was to be their benchmark. If they worked hard and showed the right attitude they'd be able to follow in my footsteps and get a contract. That was very humbling. At the same time, Big Eck sat me down for a heart-to-heart. He told me I would need to make sacrifices to continue to progress in the game. He laid it on the line and pulled no punches.

Away from football, I hung around with about a group of twenty guys, most of them from my school days. We used to get up to the usual stuff. Our meeting place, our 'local' if I can call it that, was the Fir Park café, just a free-kick from the ground. People used to come from far and wide to get their ice cream from there. We'd play pool there and the jukebox would be on.

When I was at school we'd also go to a wee den on weekend nights and get absolutely blotto. We were away from civilisation in our wee hideaway. We'd try to get into pubs and discos, Philleas Foggs and Bar One. We'd hang around the Civic Centre as well. Most of us would hang around with white trainers on but we weren't allowed entry into the disco with them on. One night, me, Tiffy and JP were so blitzed we decided to take our black socks off and put them over our trainers to make it look as though we had black shoes on. Needless to say, we were found out by the bouncers and chased away.

A few of the lads in the group of friends I hung around with were into drugs and other stuff. The Boss made it clear I had to distance myself from that and I knew exactly where he was coming from. It was an easy choice for me to make but it was a difficult one to go through with. I had to cut my ties with them. I know a few of my pals thought I was a Billy Big-Time for doing so and that I had suddenly developed ideas above my station. A few of them slagged me off behind my back. I found that hard to take and was very disappointed.

I knew my true friends would stick by me, such as big Tiffy and JP. I'd spoken to them about it and they backed my stance. They knew why I had to keep away. That's true mates for you. I've been vindicated and I'd advise any young player to do the same. Don't allow yourself any excuses. Even if it means you have no pals left, do the right thing. This was my time to truly become a man.

Big Eck agreed with what I was doing and decided to loan me out to a couple of Junior teams to toughen me up and prepare me for life in the big, bad world. I had a spell at Cumbernauld United and that was a bit of an eye-opener, but not too bad. The main thing I remember about being there was the guys in the team came up with my nickname 'Jig', and it has stuck ever since. All sorts of reasons for me being called this have been floated but the story behind it is this. I scored a few goals for Cumbernauld and it made it into the local newspaper. The headline would scream out across the page, 'Gigantic school kid scores again'. Now, because the first team used to always mention my 'package' then it all started from there, saying it's 'jiganourmous' then that was shortened to 'Jig'. So there you have it, and all rumours are put to rest!

Eck then wanted to send me to Carluke Rovers and it caused a major argument with him and my mum. Serious words were exchanged during a telephone conversation and I thought it was going to end my Motherwell career. Mum said that I would end up getting seriously hurt and that she wasn't going to stand back and allow this to happen. The Boss argued that the move would be the making of me. After a day or two of talks, the Boss got his way, and rightly so.

However, a few weeks later I broke my ankle in a game for Carluke. When the Boss phoned the house to see how my recovery was going he was given a right ear bashing from Mum. My God, she let him have it with both barrels. I thought I'd be shown the door. However, another few weeks later, I was given a new contract.

Deep down I think Big Eck probably admired my mum for being outspoken in that way. They hit it off the day he persuaded me to sign for the club and that fondness for one another is still there. If Eck had to walk into a room and see me, the first thing he'd ask is, 'How's Iris getting on?' Guaranteed.

Indeed I remember when he was Scotland manager and myself, Allan McGregor, Barry Ferguson, Kris Boyd and Alan Hutton had a drinking session at a hotel. There's no doubt we'd had a few too many vodkas. We phoned SFA official Richard Simpson to come and join us. He was delighted to get an invite, that's the kind of guy he was. When he arrived we poured a glass of orange juice all over him. Disgraceful behaviour. Appalling, in fact. He immediately went to Big Eck to report us, which, I suppose, was fair enough. Eck wasn't pleased, but, I suspected, not particularly bothered either.

He sat us down and had a word, telling Barry he should be setting a better example, that kind of thing. I was last in line and when he got to me, he looked straight at me and said, 'Well, big man, what do you think Iris would think of you for doing this?'

After I recovered from my ankle injury I started to play reserve games for Motherwell. I was progressing nicely. The Boss would pull me aside most days to tell me to concentrate, that I wasn't far away from the first team. He told me that the first-team guys were all nervous that I was going to take one of their places. He would come away with little gems to me, telling me not to blow my chance and to make sure I would go on to have a career for the next fifteen or twenty years. He said to me, 'Don't be the guy in the pub shouting at the telly. Be the guy on the telly getting shouted at.' I've never forgotten that.

I enjoyed mixing more and more with the first-team guys and it was great to be involved with them. They made me feel a part of it and never patronised me. It was another part of my education to see the working functions of a dressing room, from the nerves and excitement five minutes before kick-off to the tactical instructions at half-time and the rollickings or smiles at full-time.

One incident will never leave me, from one of my first games with the first team when I was just seventeen. Our central defender big Brian 'Buff' Martin had an absolute nightmare first half in a game. The strikers tore him to pieces. Big Eck went off his head at half-time. Buff was having none of it and, with a serious voice and straight face, he told the Boss, 'It's not my fault. Listen, I've told you before it takes me half an hour to get going in a game because my calves are so big.' Big Eck was speechless.

I made my European debut away to MYPA 47 in August 1995. I was seventeen. It was amazing. All my pals got tickets for the MYPA game. They were from Finland and we were expected to beat them, but they beat us 3–1 at Fir Park in the first leg. We had an uphill task but there was belief we could do it. We scored two goals through Alex Burns and Dougie Arnott to make it 3–3 but we still needed another goal. I came on for the last twelve minutes. Paul Lambert played me in and I struck a shot from twenty yards and it hit off a post. The BBC radio commentary claimed the ball had gone in. Now, the game wasn't on telly and BBC Radio Scotland was the only way of keeping tabs on our game. My dad was tuned in back home, listening to the game in my bedroom. When the commentator said I'd scored he jumped up and down on my bed in celebration – so much so, he broke my bed! But it was all for nothing. We went out on the away goals rule and we were devastated. MYPA were managed by Harri Kampman, who would later succeed Big Eck as Motherwell manager.

Dougie Arnott said to me after the MYPA game that I was unlucky not to score but told me to stick in. I played a few reserve games with Dougie and he pulled me aside after a few games and told me to go in and see the gaffer and tell him I was ready to play in the first team. I shit myself and didn't have the confidence to chap Big Eck's door. Looking back, I see where Dougie was coming from.

I continued to chip away at the first team and my big break came on 31 January 1998. I came off the bench with twelve minutes to go and scored two goals in a 6–2 win over Hibs at Fir Park. We were 2–0 down early doors but goals from Arnott, Mickey Weir and Eric Garcin got us 3–2 up at the interval. I then came on and within three minutes made it 4–2 when I received a pass from Tommy Coyne, dribbled past Shaun Dennis and then shot past Chris Reid. Tommy Coyne made it 5–2 and in the last minute I got our final goal of the afternoon when I headed home a Kevin Christie cross. The pitch was a bit damp and the ball was gleaming. It was dark, under the floodlights and I loved the nice, clean glaze on the grass at the time of year. My big brother Gregor and his wife Joanne were there and I waved up to them after my goals. Naturally, they were delighted for me. I felt amazing.

After the game Andy Watson told me the press wanted to interview me. Back then you were thrown into a room and told to get on with it. There was no media training, no advice on how to answer an awkward question without saying too much but talking a lot. I had no idea what was involved and what I was walking into. I was really nervous. I sat in the dressing room sweating. I was preparing a script in my head and decided I was going to go into the press room and not take any questions. All I was going to say was, 'Every dog has its day and today was my day' – and then bolt out. Thankfully, I never said it. I'd have got ripped apart.

It was actually just a one-to-one interview I had to do instead of being put in front of a few journalists. I was to be interviewed by Thomas Jordan of the *Evening Times*. Stevie Woods had told me that Thomas was a good guy and that I should not have been worried. Stevie was right. In fact, I don't know who was more nervous – me or young Jordan! But I was very shy. It was my first ever interview.

Later that night the game was shown on Sportscene. I was delighted. Some guys my age – such as Barry Ferguson at Rangers – were still playing reserve football and here was I on the telly and scoring goals. I felt it totally vindicated my decision to join Motherwell. If I'd gone to St Johnstone I might have struggled to make it because I doubt the players and manager there would have been as good as what I'd had at Fir Park.

But I was dealt a blow a few weeks later when Big Eck resigned to take over at Hibs. Two days after we defeated Hibs 6–2, the Easter Road side sacked their manager, Jim Duffy. They were bottom of the league and heading towards relegation. They looked to Big Eck and that was not surprising. Hibs are a massive club and Big Eck had carved out an excellent reputation for himself at Fir Park, taking the club to second place in the league behind Rangers in his first full season. I knew I was going to miss him and wondered if my career would hit the skids. Big Eck was an amazing guy and a perfect boss for me.

He was replaced by Harri Kampman. Things wouldn't be the same again.

4

FROM YTS TO WIGAN

I WAS disappointed when Alex McLeish left. He had faith in me and helped my progression from YTS player to the Motherwell first team in the SPL. But Alex had moved on to bigger and better things and I'm led to believe he had turned down offers in the past, one being to be part of Wim Jansen's backroom staff at Celtic when he took over there in the summer of 1997. So, I did not grudge Alex his move to Hibs. I wished him well.

Harri Kampman was appointed on 25 February 1998 as McLeish's replacement. In his first couple of meetings with the players Harri made it absolutely clear that he felt Scottish football wasn't technical enough and that our players had too many bad habits and were set in our ways. He wanted to get rid of several of the players and bring his own men in. He also left the young players in no doubt that we wouldn't be getting a sniff of first-team action. We'd have been as well packing up there and then and going on our summer holidays. Senior players' noses were also put out of joint very quickly by Kampman. From very early on, I did not have any good vibes and felt it was all going to end in tears for him and the club.

He didn't speak to me. I wasn't in the first-team squad. That's why I didn't like him. He wasn't willing to give me a fair crack of the whip.

Motherwell is a family club and is all about rearing its own.

He wasn't interested in that. He wanted to flood the place with foreign footballers, with a few of his targets being from his homeland in Finland.

One of the first things he changed was the eating habits of the players. He made immediate alterations to the dining room. He had all the salt and pepper shakers removed from the tables as he believed such things were not good for our diet. He said that all the players ate like animals and it was disgusting. He also said we ate 'monster' food. It was just one negative after another. The boys turned on him very quickly.

John Chapman and Bill Dickie ran the club at that time. They appointed Kampman and I suppose at that time it was fashionable to appoint a foreigner. All of a sudden Scotsmen weren't good enough. Kampman had also been in charge of the MYPA 47 team that had knocked us out of the UEFA Cup a couple of years earlier. But his appointment was a huge error of judgement. He was not a good man-manager. He never spoke to me and did not enhance my career one little bit. If anything, I went back the way and my confidence was knocked for six. He never took me aside to teach me anything about the game. No pointers whatsoever. The young players kept getting pushed further and further away by him. It seemed as though we were non-existent.

Some of the senior players – led by John Philliben, Jim Griffin and Billy Davies – held a few meetings to try and keep the place calm, basically to stop there being a full-scale dressing-room revolt against Kampman. The senior guys were not impressed with the way the younger players such as myself were being treated by Kampman and they kept a close eye on things. On a couple of occasions they would pull one or two of us aside and tell us to be patient and not to do anything silly. They told us Kampman's time would be coming to an end sooner rather than later. We just had to tough it out.

So, we had to bite our tongues and suffer his bull. Every

meeting he had with the players he would mention Jari Litmanen and the fact he helped carve out that particular player's career from his teenage years. There was no doubting Litmanen was a special talent and had a golden spell at Ajax, but Kampman seemed to live off of this. It became boring to listen to that chat after about the first fifty mentions. Indeed, after a few weeks the boys used to run a wee betting book to guess how many times he would mention Litmanen's name during a meeting.

At the end of his first season he released some good players and strong characters such as Philliben, Tommy Coyne, Willie Falconer, Dougie Arnott, Shaun McSkimming and Brian Martin. My good pal Gary Gow was also released. It was sad to see those kind of guys depart and, in many ways, the heart and soul was ripped out of the club. Personally, it was a case of keeping my head down and trying to stay positive. I could easily have let it all get to me – and many times it very nearly did – but I was also determined that this guy was not going to ruin my good work from the previous three years and force me out and onto the scrapheap. One thing I kept reminding myself of was the little pep talk Alex McLeish had with me when I signed professional about being the guy on the telly and not the guy shouting at the telly. Alex would always say that football was a game full of opinions and that the world is full of people that talk about how they could have made the grade and excelled in the professional game but luck wasn't on their side. Alex told me on several occasions to make my own luck by working hard. Although he was no longer my manager, Alex still had a real positive effect on me during the trying times under Kampman.

A bright light then appeared in the form of Brian McClair. He was one of the players brought in during the summer of 1998. Brian arrived from Manchester United. He'd had a magnificent career with Motherwell, Celtic and United. It was a real coup to get him back to Fir Park. Kampman also signed three Dutchmen

– Michel Doesburg, Jan Michels and Rob Matthaei. Scottish players Greg Miller, Jered Stirling and James McGowan joined, as did veteran English defender Shaun Teale. Two of Kampman's fellow countrymen arrived in the form of keeper Mikko Kavén and striker Kai Nyyssönen. On paper the wheeling and dealing might have looked good and whetted the fans' appetite. Truth be told, there had been no improvement, not because of the players though. Pre-season results suggested that to be the case. We went to Finland and performances and results weren't impressive. That was down to the manager.

I still wasn't being given a fair crack at it. I was being given five minutes here and there – at best – off the bench. I was starting to think I wasn't going to make the grade. I thought I was going to be driven out of the game by Kampman. At night I would sit and ponder what alternative employment was out there for me. Well, at least the sweetie shop was still operating! I was genuinely worried. I hadn't made a good enough name for myself for teams to come in for me if it was made known I was available. At best, I thought I might get a decent part-time side, even then I only thought that would transpire if I went on trial first to prove myself. It all left me depressed, no doubt about it. It was a horrible feeling to have day-in and day-out. I used to enjoy going to my work but Kampman totally changed that. I hated my job and it screwed with my mind.

When I got really down – and it was often – I would try to console myself and lift myself by remembering the pep talk from Alex: 'Be the guy on the telly, not the guy shouting at the telly.' I would say that over and over again. It became my own little personal catchphrase. Billy Davies was also a great source of comfort to me. He told me to keep my head up. He was like that with everyone. He would go to all the lads in the dressing room in a bid to keep morale as positive as possible. Jim Griffin was always asking me how I was and he helped me through it all.

But I was finding it increasingly difficult to contain my anger towards Kampman. Sometimes I would be standing at the dressing-room door, close to the long corridor to the left-hand side. You could hear the footsteps walking along the corridor from the dressing room. So, whenever Kampman was making his way along, away from the direction of the dressing-room door, I would pop my head out and shout, 'Ya fat bastard.' He had no idea who was shouting at him. It was totally infantile behaviour on my part, but it was a tremendous source of comfort to me at the time!

We were bought over by John Boyle in August 1998. He arrived in spectacular style and promised to make the club great again. He had been involved in the holiday business for a number of years and, according to the media, had built up a personal fortune of tens and tens of millions of pounds. John struck me as being quite flamboyant and fond of the spotlight and media glare. He talked a great game but also delivered. For instance, he made the pricing more enticing for fans and cut the entry fee to £5 for a few games at Fir Park. It worked a treat. Almost 10,000 turned up for a home game against Dunfermline and then more than 11,000 came through the turnstiles for a game against Dundee United. Considering that game was also live on television, that was a truly remarkable attendance. Results were decent to start with but then we hit a bad spell for a few weeks. We lost 2–0 at home to Ayr United in the League Cup. Then we lost games to Hearts and Dundee. The fans weren't happy and felt there wasn't enough attacking football on display under Kampman.

Brian McClair must have been scratching his head at what was going on under Kampman. After coming from Sir Alex Ferguson at Manchester United, it may well have crossed his mind why on earth he had left Old Trafford. Brian was also good to me. He would pull me aside now and again after training and tell me to keep my head up and that I had the ability to do well in the game. I was grateful then for that and still am now. He also offered me sound and solid advice when the club wanted to give me a new contract.

McClair was brilliant. I recall one time sitting next to him on the plane on the way back from pre-season in Finland to Glasgow. He read a book for most of the journey and didn't say a word to me. He was dry and gave the impression of being introverted, although, I have to stress, I did not think he was being ignorant. It was just his way. I was staring at him, in awe, really. He put his book down and as we made our approach to land he eventually looked at me. I said, 'You okay?' half sarcastically. He started to laugh. We then spoke for a few minutes and he must have regretted it. I must have rattled a hundred questions at him, from what were David Beckham and Eric Cantona like as footballers and people to how many sugars Sir Alex Ferguson took in his tea. I also thought he was a multi-millionaire many times over and asked him if he owned a boat and a private jet. His ears must have been nipping by the end of it, but he opened up and I sat with my jaw wide open listening to his insight into life at Manchester United. He must have taken a bit of a shine to me because I used to take him home after training and he also got me a signed Beckham shirt, which I still have to this day. I also had a copy of Brian's book and he signed it for me.

A bit later, he left to go back to Manchester United as their reserve team manager. I caught up with him a couple of times down there when I played for Wigan. It was great to be in his company again. Brian was good for my career. He played in the middle of the park for Motherwell and was good at keeping the game flowing, using his head while letting others use their legs.

There was excellent news on 15 October 1998 when Kampman was sacked by John Boyle. He won just five out of his twenty-one games in charge. It was the right decision to dismiss him. Most of the lads were delighted when Kampman was shown the door. Good riddance.

The word in the dressing room after Kampman was sacked was that Boyle offered the job to McClair, but McClair had rejected it because he didn't want to be a manager at first-team level. He was close to Billy Davies and there was a suggestion that McClair recommended that the job be given to Billy. And right enough, next thing Billy was made manager. It was the appointment of Billy Davies that took my career on to a new level. After the dark days under Kampman, I felt refreshed and optimistic when Billy was put in charge. I knew he liked me as a person and seemed to think I had the ability to make a worthwhile contribution to Motherwell Football Club. So, it was up to me to get my head right again and make my mark.

Very early in his tenure Billy pulled me aside for a one-to-one to say he knew I had the ability to play as a central midfielder, the way I had under Alex, but he thought that my future in the game was at centre-forward. He told me he liked the way I held the ball up and used my physique. Derek Adams was already at the club and played as a striker. Billy planned to bring in a few strikers to help me out and bring me on. He signed his brother-in-law John 'Spenny' Spencer from Everton for a club record fee of £500,000. Spenny was a striker of quality. Billy also added the experienced Don Goodman to the team. It was an indication that Boyle was willing to spend money and was going to give it his very best shot to make Motherwell a force in the Scottish game. The ultimate dream was to challenge the Old Firm, a tall order, but one Boyle felt was not totally unrealistic.

Spenny was a big influence on me. He'd been with Rangers, Chelsea and Everton and knew his stuff on and off the park. He gave me little pointers, pieces of education that were priceless. He told me about my diet, what I should be eating and avoiding, and warned me against going to restaurants as I would have no idea the ingredients a chef would use in his dishes. It was about making my own food and trusting my own judgement. Well, I couldn't cook and wasn't about to start, so I passed all the information on to my mum!

As soon as Billy was appointed he made a few changes. The alterations were all good and welcomed by the players – and they had a purpose; it wasn't change for the sake of it. He was only thirty-four but he made an instant impression. He was firm but fair and told us that we'd all be given a chance. The slate was wiped clean and the Kampman regime was well and truly over. We finished the 1998-99 season in seventh place in the SPL. I made thirty-two appearances which I was happy about.

One of the things Billy was really big on was diet and health. For example, he'd fine you £100 for every pound you were overweight. We were weighed at least once a week, sometimes twice. I'd have breakfast and lunch at the club and then two salad rolls for my dinner at home. I was usually quite hungry at night but I was scared to eat pasta or raid the cupboards for biscuits or crisps in case I went in overweight the next day. Simply, I couldn't afford to pay the fine and thankfully I was never once overweight. Sometimes it felt tough and unfair, but it was a great learning curve and education for me. Billy drummed in that I had to make sure my preparation for the entire week was spot on, that it didn't just start on a Thursday morning or a Friday lunchtime. He wanted every player to make sure that come kick-off time on a Saturday we had done everything to be in the best possible condition, both physically and mentally. Now that, of course, didn't guarantee we'd have a great game but it gave us a much better chance of performing to a high standard.

That triggered my whole outlook on fitness and diet along with, I suppose, my dad being in the Navy, where everything was quite regimented. From the age of nineteen or twenty it became an obsession. Still is. Because of it, I've always felt fit.

I've never really gone into a game feeling my preparation hadn't been good. Sure, sometimes I've felt low in confidence, but rarely, if ever, felt as though I could have prepared better.

Billy's training was tough but it was good. We trained twice a day two or three times a week and it was always enjoyable. It was good coaching and there was a big emphasis on technique. He wanted every player to finish each day feeling they had learned something new and improved their game. In my first year under Billy I performed well.

Off the park, things were also good. The players loved Boyle. I certainly had loads of time for him. He paid most of the players very good wages and offered brilliant bonuses. I have to say some of the money on offer for winning Cup ties was absolutely ridiculous but totally welcomed by the players. One example that springs to mind was a deal negotiated by the players with John Boyle during a winter break in Portugal in January 1999. A scheme was put in place that resulted in us getting £9,000 per man for beating Hearts and Stirling Albion in the Scottish Cup fourth round. We were used to a maximum of £400 for a win.

Billy also had other employees on a bonus for us doing well on the park. Office staff and other workers were on a bonus, not the same money as the players but a few extra quid for them come payday. It meant the whole club was pulling in the same direction; it was a proper team effort, from the dressing room to the laundry staff and groundsmen and beyond.

I enjoyed having a few extra quid. I treated my parents to a few nice things and bought myself a car, a Peugeot 306. Things were progressing and my performances under Davies were being noticed outside of the club. My game was going well and I was making a bit of a name for myself in Scotland. One day, sitting in the house in November 1999, the phone went and it was a Scottish journalist sounding me out about a possible move to Celtic. He told me that Kenny Dalglish, Celtic's Director of

Football, was very keen on me and wondered what my thoughts were about joining the club. Now, I was a huge Rangers fan and my family loved Rangers and had absolutely no feelings for the Parkhead club whatsoever. I was totally taken aback by the conversation with the journalist and told him that I would speak to Celtic if they had a bid accepted by Motherwell. Truth be told, I was really excited about it, mainly because the legendary Kenny Dalglish rated me as a player. I was told I would be kept informed and that Kenny Dalglish would speak to Celtic's Head Coach John Barnes about making a move for me.

As soon as I came off the phone I went into the living room and relayed the whole conversation to my dad. Well, the look I received from him . . . honestly, it was as though I'd just told him I'd been arrested for murder and was looking at a life sentence in jail!

As it turned out, Barnes was sacked in February 2000 after Celtic lost at home to Inverness in a Scottish Cup tie and nothing more ever came out of that conversation with the journalist. But I was making headlines. The newspapers had me linked with several big clubs down south during that November. It was reported that Leeds, Spurs, Portsmouth and Middlesbrough had all sent scouts to watch me. I never heard anything official about it but it was a nice feeling to think clubs in England were aware of my ability.

A concrete bid of £1 million arrived that month from Hearts. It was the third bid they'd made inside a fortnight after the previous two were turned down. I heard about it one day on the radio. In fact, the report stated I had signed for the Tynecastle club. I knew nothing about the bid, never mind actually becoming a Jambo. When the news broke I was on my way through to Fir Park to play against Hearts. I was twenty-one at the time and it felt very surreal to hear my name being talked about on the radio this way and to be valued at £1 million. Honestly, it was crazy stuff.

£1 million for me? Do me a favour. I felt it was ridiculous money. A packet of crisps and a can of Irn-Bru felt more appropriate. I went into the game in an apprehensive mood. My mind was all over the place, to be honest. It was live on Sky television and we won 2–0. I scored the first goal and it was a tremendous feeling.

As we walked off the pitch at full-time, Pat Nevin, who had come on as a sub but was also our chief executive, pulled me aside to say that I was not to worry because Motherwell wanted to keep me. That made me happy because I wasn't sure if Motherwell felt it would be good business to cash in on me. I didn't particularly fancy a move to Hearts but I would have gone if it was necessary for Motherwell to bring in funds. I felt Hearts wouldn't have been a step up. I had also set my sights on playing in England. Hearts boss Jim Jefferies later told me how disappointed he was not to have signed me.

John Boyle wanted to show how much he wanted me to stay by flying me to London the next day to discuss the offer from Hearts. I was told that if I really wanted to go then he wouldn't stand in my way. Over dinner, we discussed the offer but he made it clear that if I pledged my future to Motherwell he would double my wage packet immediately to £2,000 per week and I wouldn't even need to extend my contract. It was a no-brainer. We shook hands on the deal. It was yet another surreal experience for me being in London with John, at his home in Notting Hill to be precise. He showed me all the sights and took me to a few of the locations used in the movie *Notting Hill*. We even sat on the bench used in the film where Julia Roberts and Hugh Grant had a romantic moment!

Boyle opened up on his grand plans for Motherwell Football Club and it struck me how driven he was to challenge the Old Firm. The grand plan was probably to form a Lanarkshire United Football Cub. The impression I got was that he was considering trying to merge Airdrie and Motherwell together and possibly

Hamilton Accies, too. I was happy to be staying at Motherwell but Boyle told me he expected me to keep improving so that sooner rather than later the club would get a good transfer fee for me.

One other thing we negotiated on was me receiving a percentage of any future transfer fee the club received for me. Boyle didn't have a problem with that and we shook hands on it. We discussed a cut of around 20 per cent but my mum and dad were in a council house at the time and they were able to buy it for themselves for £18,000. I told Billy Davies and John Boyle this. They said they'd give me the £18,000 right away if I agreed a reduction to around 5 per cent of any future fee. I was happy to do that. Everyone was happy. My parents were now able to live rent-free. I was buzzing because it was great to be able to give my mum and dad something back after all the sacrifices they had made for me. I was very grateful to Motherwell for giving me that money at that time to help look after my parents. It was a lovely touch from Boyle.

I continued to work hard and I really wanted that move to England. Spenny kept telling me to be patient. My game continued to come on leaps and bounds under Billy. He was a great man-manager and also a very conscientious coach. Every now and again, after training he'd ask to have a word in private and he'd take me out onto the pitch and we'd walk around, asking me how I was feeling, how my parents were, that sort of thing. We'd also talk about the game, whether it was the previous Saturday or the next one coming up. He made me really think about my role on the pitch and what I had to do to keep improving. A couple of times a week he'd take me for one-to-one training sessions, just wee finishing drills where he'd talk me through movement into good areas when we had possession and when we didn't have the ball.

He created a togetherness in the squad. The lads loved playing for him and there was also a new attitude around the place. Boys volunteered to do extra training, whether it was with the ball or just a weights session. The boys wanted to have a six-pack they could show off! The football we played was really good and there was a real confidence at the club. There was also a good social scene and although the gaffer was teetotal, he didn't have a problem with the boys having a right good drink at the appropriate times.

We also had a great atmosphere inside the club. Wind-ups took place all the time, and I remember wee Spenny caught me with a cracker. The politician Tommy Sheridan was a friend of the gaffer's and Tommy liked a game of football. I think he fancied himself as being good enough to have made the grade. He came in for a training session now and again and back then I didn't know who he was. He joined in the warm-up one day and I asked wee Spenny who the new guy was. Spenny was on to it quick as a flash and sensed an opportunity to get one over me. He told me that it was a new trialist over from France and that he was a striker. Spenny introduced him to me as Pierre le Blanc and Tommy played along with it. I was trying to give it a bit of 'Bonjour, je m'appelle Jig McCulloch' and stuff and spoke very slowly, trying to make the bold Pierre feel welcome – even though he might have been there to take my place. That said, I didn't think he was up to much. I wasn't overly concerned. Then, ten minutes later during a wee game, Pierre shouted to me, 'Hey, Lee, any chance of passing the fucking ba' to me, big man?' I was done. Hook, line and sinker.

The boys had another good laugh with me during my 21st birthday party at one of the Fir Park hospitality suites. It was a surprise do organised by my parents. All of my family, friends and team-mates turned up. I had to go up and make a speech. I was really nervous and didn't want to take to the stage but I gave in. I took the microphone and thanked everyone for coming, especially my dad twenty-one years ago! And that was it. I walked off. My mates and brothers were in stitches but some of the family were a little bit embarrassed! Still, it was right good night.

But the best feeling was finishing as top scorer in the 1999-2000 season on twelve goals. We finished 4th in the league that season. Strides were being made on all fronts. Considering I wasn't a 'proper' striker, I was really chuffed with my goals return. I was given the no. 9 jersey to wear the following season, as some kind of reward, I guess.

In 2000-01 the football continued to go well and clubs monitored me. There was interest from Bradford City – Jim Jefferies was manager there at that time – but it was Wigan Athletic that showed the most determination to get me and a bid in excess of £700,000 – a club record for them – was accepted by Motherwell in late February 2001.

Billy had me in his office and told me he didn't want me to leave and that he wanted the club to reject the bid. But he was resigned to me going; however, he wanted me to get a few quid for myself from Motherwell because of the fee they were to receive. It was then I witnessed an uneasy relationship between Pat Nevin and the gaffer. The players had long felt there was tension between them. It must have been strange for both considering Pat was the chief executive and Billy was manager. It was obviously near to impossible to have a good working relationship as there would have been a conflict of interest in so many different ways. Billy and Pat had a bit of a ding-dong about my money, if my memory serves me. Despite the fact I had been given the £18,000 for my parents' house, I was also given £20,000 to go and another £20,000 a few months down the line once Wigan had paid the second instalment. I made fantastic money. I couldn't have been happier.

I owed a lot to Billy. He gave me the information and knowledge to play as a central striker. He taught me about movement, when to take the ball in, when to spin and when to lay it off. He taught me about how a target should play and also the defensive side of my game when playing as a striker. He gave me videos of Alan Shearer to take home and study. He urged me to bulk up my frame in the gym and get fast-feet drills going to improve my burst of pace over five or six yards. He also added mental toughness to my game. I've never, ever worked so hard on my game as I did during that eighteen-month period. It was brilliant. It was as if Billy had made me his project and he was going to make sure it did not fail. He wanted me to get a move to England and he seemed just as delighted as me when it happened.

I was sad to leave Motherwell, but, for a number of reasons, it was time to go. I needed to test myself at another level and Motherwell got good money for me. Indeed, Billy's parting words will never leave me. He shook my hand, wished me all the best and said that it was the right time for the club to sell me. They were going to get more than £700,000 for me and that would help pay for the club's new stand. Billy said he was going to call it 'The Lee McCulloch Stand'!

I did leave with a heavy heart and took ten minutes alone in the stand, looking onto the empty pitch. I recalled my first goals against Hibs and visualised all the great players I had played with, that had helped me become a professional footballer and that wonderful opportunity I was about to be given in England with Wigan Athletic.

I used to badger the likes of Alex McLeish, Andy Watson, Tommy Coyne, Rob McKinnon, Brian Martin, John Philliben, Owen Coyle, Dougie Arnott, Jamie Dolan, Jim Griffin and Phil O'Donnell into teaching me about the game, giving me a few minutes here and there to help me progress. In my early days I was just a teenager and impressionable. On reflection, they must have thought I was a bit forward and in their face, but I just wanted to show a desire to learn my trade. It all worked a treat.

I left the club having played twenty-nine games and scored nine goals for them in that season. My final game for the club was on 24 February 2001 and we defeated St Mirren 1–0. It was a nice way to bow out.

It was time for me to leave Motherwell. I loved the town and the club but I felt increasing pressure at Motherwell because all my pals supported the club and I never wanted to let them down. And it was difficult to please the fans. Anywhere I went in the town people would recognise me and want to speak to me. I was in the newspapers a fair bit by this stage and I felt the publicity was a bad thing for me. It was as though everybody wanted to scrutinise everything about me on and off the park and focus in on any possible negatives. The 'local boy done good' story fits well with a lot of people but some people, for whatever reason, don't want to see people prosper and move on. Maybe it's just a Scottish thing. Billy Connolly uses the analogy that if he walked into a bar in his home city of Glasgow and offered to buy everyone a drink then he'd be accused of being a flash bastard, but if he didn't offer to buy drink then he'd be a tight-fisted bastard. Colin Montgomerie said if he had a nice car parked in the street some people would rather run a key along the side of it than compliment the vehicle and how hard he'd worked and how dedicated he'd been to be able to buy it.

On a couple of occasions it caused problems for myself and my family. My brothers and close mates kept on top of things and looked after me and they were all very good for me at that stage of my life. It was the sort of thing where some guys would come up to me on the street and try to have a go, give me some verbal abuse. It was nothing out of order but it did make me feel uncomfortable. Had I retaliated in any way then there would have been occasions it would all have kicked off. It was good to know that my brothers and my big cousin, Derek Anson, always had my back and looked out for me. That was comforting.

5

WHELAN AND DEALING OUR WAY TO THE BIG TIME

MY MOTHERWELL team-mate Stevie McMillan was also going to sign for Wigan. It was a double deal. We were picked up at Cumbernauld Airfield in Wigan owner Dave Whelan's helicopter and flown down south. I felt like a movie star and it was all very exciting. But I was also nervous and constantly questioned myself if I was doing the right thing. I had spoken to a few people about moving to England and the feedback was mainly positive but reservations were expressed about going to play in the English Second Division. The game in the English third tier was more physical and no prisoners were taken. The skill level wasn't as high as the SPL and that's probably why a number of people said to me I was taking a step backwards by going to the old English Second Division.

I understood why people with no knowledge of the workings of Wigan and their plans for the future would think that way. But I knew what the ambition was. My good friend Ged Brannan had signed a few weeks earlier from Motherwell. We were close. He kept me in the loop and raved about the club. He told me in no uncertain terms to make sure I joined him at Wigan. To be fair, I didn't need a lot of convincing.

A 25,000 all-seater stadium had been built and Dave Whelan was going at it full tilt. He wanted to get into the Premiership as quickly as possible and was willing to throw millions and millions of pounds to realise his dream. On arrival the helicopter hovered over the stadium to show us the ground and then we flew on to the training ground. We then landed on the JJB grounds next to the stadium and got down to talks. Whelan and the club's general manager John Benson gave me the sales pitch and I totally bought into it. They spoke to me for an hour or so and by the end of the meeting I felt like it was Manchester United I was signing for.

I was to be given a signing-on fee of £100,000, split into two payments of £50,000 during the course of the year. I'd never had money like that in my life. It was an incredible feeling but also quite scary to be handed such a vast amount of dosh.

I was also going to more than double my earnings to £4,750 per week. Or so I thought! I was told that was going to be my weekly wage but for some reason it later turned out that there was something different written in the contract. As this was all new to me, I had an agent helping me out to make sure it went smoothly. However, things didn't exactly go as planned and somehow I ended up getting less than I'd expected.

As I later discovered, the deal that was discussed with me verbally was not what was written into the contract. However, when I was given the contract to sign on the dotted line, I duly did. I trusted everyone involved. But when I took a good look at the contract in finer detail, I was on less per week than what I was originally told I was getting. I was on £4,500 per week. Maybe not a huge difference each week, but it all adds up. I don't know how this happened but it was another lesson for me. You need to know exactly what you're signing, read the fine print and trust your own judgement. It doesn't matter what club or advisors or agents or whoever you're dealing with, you need to personally make sure that everything is as it should be. Otherwise you only have yourself to blame.

This lesson was to come up again at Wigan, when a London

agent asked if I'd be interested in moving to Charlton Athletic and that he could sort it for me and double my wages. I told him I played it with a straight bat and told him I'd consider all offers if a club agreed a fee with Wigan. The next day at training the manager Paul Jewell called me in and ripped me to shreds. 'You want the fuck out of here, do you? Well, there's the fucking door.' I was distraught. The agent went straight to the manager and repeated our conversation. He was out of order. He approached me, tried to drive it on, then twisted it and knifed me in the back. So, I've been turned over a few times. As far as agents are concerned, I've little time for some of them, although I totally accept there are good ones out there. Bottom line, I've learned to trust myself more than any agent, advisor or whoever.

Many footballers like to have agents as some kind of security blanket, but too many agents tell players what they want to hear and it's a great ego boost for the client, whereas, when needed, they should be telling their client a few home truths. Also, part of the job of an agent is to have good working relationships with as many clubs as possible – from the owner to the chief executive to the manager to the chief scout. That can help get his client a move to a particular club, a move that sometimes suits the agent more than the player. Many footballers have the talent to sell themselves and they will never be short of offers, but others are not so fortunate and need to be marketed by the agent. Some agents do it right and others can't see any further than the next pound sign. I prefer my destiny to be in my own hands.

Apart from the weekly wage, there was more upheaval on day one at Wigan. Bruce Rioch was the manager but he was sacked the day I signed. I never even got to meet him! In fact, I never spoke directly to him. The closest we came to dialogue was through a third party and that was about football stuff a few days before the move. Colin Greenall took over from Rioch for a few games and that was fine. He gave me my debut in a home match against

Swindon Town on 3 March. The boys seemed to like Greenall, but Dave Whelan had grander plans and he enticed Steve Bruce to the club as manager for the final eight games of the season in the hope of securing promotion. We finished in sixth position and got to the play-offs but lost out 2–1 on aggregate to Reading. That was a major disappointment.

Steve Bruce was a good man. I liked him as a person and as a manager. He was the kind of person that put the lads first. He arrived as a big hitter, not long finished in the game as a player and captain of Manchester United. He had a huge presence and had the respect of everyone at Wigan. He lost his temper with the boys once or twice after games and we were left in no doubt about what he expected and exactly who was boss. He could be intimidating when he wanted – and felt he needed – to be. He was also relaxed and funny, had a good sense of humour.

Off the park, I found out it was a weird experience moving away from home. I'd hardly been out of Motherwell. I'd only ever been away abroad once on holiday with the family and that was to Portugal. I was useless on my own. My parents really worried about me when I moved away down south from their home in Motherwell. I found the first few weeks quite difficult, as did Stevie McMillan. We felt as though a number of the players were set in their ways and didn't like 'outsiders' coming into their club. We'd also arrived for a huge transfer fee and they must have been wondering the type of contracts we'd been given. I think there was a little bit of resentment, but they were subtle about it; it was never blatant. But it was definitely there.

It was good to have Stevie for company. We knew each other well and had each other's backs covered. He was well aware of my faults and how naïve I could be. One example he was all too familiar with was when we were away on Scotland Under-21 duty in Austria. I was seventeen and, like I said, had only been on holiday to Portugal. At the team hotel we found visa forms in our room but there was no need for us to fill them out. I was sharing the room with Stevie and he told me to fill it in; it was stuff like passport details and any immigration stuff. It didn't apply to us, but I got a pen and got on with it, at Stevie's behest. I filled it in to the best of my ability and then phoned home to speak to Mum. I was excited to tell her I was in a great hotel with a beautiful, swish room. We had a huge double bed each, free shampoo, coffee and biscuits. I told her I felt like royalty. And then I said, 'Oh, and another thing. I've just filled out this visa form. Will come in really handy if I get time to go shopping, eh?' Stevie nearly fell off his bed and since then I've never lived it down.

Stevie's partner moved down to Wigan with him and they moved into a nice estate. I found a nice three-bedroom house only a few doors away. Ged Brannan and Matt Jackson, the Wigan skipper, were both a huge help to me in the early weeks. They took me around, showed me potential areas to live and places to go and the places to avoid in Wigan. But I still missed the comfort blanket I had up the road from my mum and dad. I'd get letters through the post and it would be asking questions about telephone lines, gas and electricity, direct debits and Council Tax bills. My head was thumping with it all. I hadn't a clue, didn't know where to start. It got to the stage where I'd phone my mum and read the letters out to her. She would then come down the following weekend and sort it all out for me. Goodness, when I think about it, two and a half hours on the train down for her just to read a letter out to me!

I lived alone and felt as if I was in a mansion. I was lonely. I missed home. A lot of the time the only company I had was the microwave oven and the Dolmio pasta dish I used to throw in it. Nowadays, at almost every full-time club, you get breakfast and lunch at the training ground. We didn't have either at Wigan back then, so it wasn't unusual for me to only have one really good meal per week. I was living on microwave food and takeaways. It was either that or I starved.

When Steve Bruce left after two months to go to Crystal Palace the job was given to Paul Jewell. He became the fourth manager in three months, but it all got much better under him. He got rid of a few players in the summer and brought a few in. One of the players that left was Roberto Martinez. He joined Motherwell on a three-year contract and it was very unfortunate for him and everyone else at Fir Park that the club went into administration in April 2002, just over a year after I had left. John Boyle had thrown millions at it and eventually had to hold his hands up and say enough is enough. It was horrible that nineteen players were sacked on the spot. Some of them were good friends. Other employees also lost their jobs. It wasn't a pleasant time to be there and the uncertainty lasted for almost two years.

With new faces in, the dynamics in the Wigan dressing room changed quite quickly. It was like a fresh start for everyone, new friends to be made and all grudges buried. Jewell made it clear he would not tolerate any big-time attitudes and was very big on having a good harmony and togetherness. Peter Beagrie was one of the casualties. He'd had a good career at Everton and Bradford and had made a few quid. He wasn't shy at telling the boys and he would often use his now legendary line to team-mates: 'Hey, you got change of a million pound note!'

We were regarded as a huge club in the Second Division because of the money we were paying and that meant most teams wanted to beat us, looked upon as a bit of a scalp. So, it was important we were all in it together. Nothing was going to be achieved playing and behaving as individuals.

Yet, not everything had the air of money about it. The club's training ground was far from what people would have expected. It was very basic. We used to share the JJB pitch with the rugby team and that made the surface heavy and not conducive to good football. We also shared the training ground with them. We had no canteen and no chef. We would have jugs of diluting orange and blackcurrant set out on a table and sandwiches with butter and jam, that kind of thing. We just helped ourselves and got on with it. We also had to wash our own kit. We didn't have any laundry facilities. It was an eye-opener. Big time. I hated washing my kit every night. I used to do it in autopilot mode – forty-degree spin cycle and then onto the clotheshorse! It eventually made me a better person, helped me grow up and stand on my own two feet, but I didn't see it that way at the time.

But whenever I felt a little bit down, I had the consolation of knowing I had a few quid in my pocket to spend. In my first few months I changed cars a few times and seemed to never be out of the fancy showrooms. I felt it was crazy money for a twenty-two-year-old to have, but I loved it. I felt like a multi-millionaire, a proper Jack the Lad. I was often bored after training and in the evenings so I spent money to keep me amused. I bought an Audi TT then got a Jaguar and then a BMW. Honestly, Jeremy Clarkson wasn't a patch on me back then. It was total daft boyness!

But I was paid to be a footballer and help Wigan become successful, although it just didn't happen for me in the first few months. In fact, my first full season was stop-start. I had one or two injuries and never got into my stride. My game lacked consistency. I was also moved around to a few positions and that didn't help. The fans also looked upon me as a prolific striker. I signed as a centre-forward and they thought I was going to hit at least twenty goals and, being the club's record signing, be the main man to win us promotion. But that was never my game. I was a link-up man, a target man for others to feed off of in the final third, in and around the opposition penalty box. I would chip in with at least ten or eleven goals but I would always get plenty of assists, but until the fans started to appreciate and understand what my game was about it was a difficult period for me. I felt they were on my back a little bit and didn't really think I was an asset.

As team-mates, we helped each other out and would try to gee each other up if and when required. After a few months we had a few Scottish players at the club and another few who were non-Scots but had played in the SPL. Big Stewart Kerr arrived from Celtic. He moved into the same estate as me and I used to drive him everywhere as he didn't have a licence. He was a good laugh and we had a lot in common, like our love of boxing. He was also as daft as a brush and had good patter. Typical goalkeeper. His career was cut short through injury and I remember he collapsed in pain one day at training and an ambulance came onto the pitch to take him to hospital. Unfortunately that signalled the end of Stewart's career. What a waste, as he was a very good keeper.

Gary Teale signed too. We played Ayr United at Somerset Park in a pre-season friendly and Gary played very well. Wigan signed him a couple of weeks later. It proved to be a great bit of business. Gary and I have been close from the day he signed. A gentleman and a top footballer on his day. Michael O'Neill was there and so was Jason de Vos. Brian McLaughlin and Derek Stillie were also there. We had a wee contingent from Scotland down at the club and it was good. We kept each other going a lot of the time. We'd sometimes meet up to watch the Old Firm games and that was always an interesting afternoon. The allegiances weren't long in bubbling to the surface. Andy Webster also signed for us but he only played a couple of games and then moved a wee while later to Rangers. We were a wee clique, to be honest.

Paul Dalglish was a close friend from our time there. He came on loan when Bruce was manager and then stayed on for Jewell's first full season. I was sorry to see him leave for Blackpool. He really looked out for me in my early days at Wigan. Indeed, he felt sorry for me at my first Christmas on my own and obviously didn't want me eating microwave grub so he passed his mobile phone to me one day after training and his dad, Kenny, was on the other end of the line. Kenny asked me to their house on Christmas Day to join him and the family for dinner. It was an amazing gesture. Due to commitments at my end and at my own family's end in Lanarkshire, we couldn't spend Christmas together so I had to go to King Kenny's residence for my turkey 'n' trimmings.

I wanted to look the part so I went out and bought a whole new outfit. Nice trousers, shoes with a glare you could brush your teeth in and a lovely shirt, one with a big collar and cufflinks. On Christmas afternoon I put a tub of gel in my hair and brushed my teeth at least half a dozen times and off I popped to the Dalglish house in Southport. I arrived with a bottle of wine for The King and a bunch of flowers for Mrs Dalglish. As I've said before, I'm naturally shy and I was very nervous about eating with them and being in their company. When I arrived at the house, I lost the power of speech for a wee while. Every time I went to join in on the conversation or start a new one, I froze. I was just in awe of the King. Or maybe it was because I was so full up with all the lovely food Marina (she insisted I didn't call her Mrs Dalglish) put on for her family and guests. I was absolutely stuffed. Paul noticed my nervousness and had a wry smile on his face but there must also have been a part of him saying, 'Come on, Jig, get a grip of yourself.'

After dinner we watched *Only Fools and Horses* and then went to the bar in the house. It had a pool table, a dance floor and around 1,000 bottles of bubbly – I kid you not. I think they were all Man of the Match champagne! When I did find the courage to speak I asked Kenny about his career, the European Cup and League Championship successes and how they celebrated such victories. I'd also read his autobiography and asked him a few things about that. I felt much more comfortable talking to this footballing genius about football.

It was a great day and I'm still grateful to them all for making me feel so welcome, but I cringed as soon as I got home and got ready for my bed – I had left the plastic cufflinks on my new shirt. I didn't think to cut them off and get proper ones. It looked horrendous. I put it down to pre-dinner nerves!

From the New Year onwards, we were expected to seal our move up to Division One but it never worked. We just never found a true level of consistency. On a personal level, I was disappointed with too many of my performances and the lowest point came in a home match against Tranmere Rovers in March 2002 when I was given a straight red card after just twenty-five minutes by referee Mike Riley for a disgusting and shameful tackle on Jason Koumas. I flew off the ground with both feet and was never going to get near the ball. Thankfully, I didn't make contact with Koumas. We lost the game 2–1. I was just frustrated with myself and was hurting knowing we were really struggling to live up to the expectation levels and win promotion. Unfortunately season 2001-02 was a big disappointment and we finished in tenth place. Jewell wasn't happy with a number of the players and I'm sure he felt too many Scottish players were at the club and down to enjoy the money rather than getting their sleeves rolled up and helping the club become successful. Although the Wigan fans were expecting more from the team and from me, they continued to support me and it's something I'll never forget. They were amazing.

Changes were made for the following season and people within the club and the dressing room became more ruthless. The team prospered and we won the Second Division Championship in 2003 with 100 points. Jimmy Bullard signed for us for £275,000 from Peterborough United midway through that campaign and proved to be an important addition. He was bubbly and talented, great for the lads off the park and an asset on it, where it mattered most. But the main man was Nathan Ellington. He scored some phenomenal goals, and defences in that division just could not live with him. He signed on deadline day the previous season for £1.2 milllion from Bristol Rovers. He was the missing link we needed and he was an absolute bargain even though it was a lot of money to splash out. I genuinely believe we would have struggled to win promotion without him.

We celebrated by going round the town in an open-top bus and it was nice to be able to do that.

Shortly after that my career at the club took off. It all changed during the pre-season as we prepared for our first season in the old Division One, now known as the Championship. Jewell told me he was going to play me as a wide left midfielder with a licence to come inside and play almost as a central midfielder. He also wanted me making diagonal runs into the area to support the front two. I wasn't to be an out-and-out winger, hugging the touchline. That was never my game. I would cut inside onto my right and play the ball down the line for the overlapping Stevie McMillan or Leighton Baines. Stevie was really unlucky with injuries and because of that his career at Wigan never got going as it should have. He was cruelly denied so much more out of football. I felt for him, I really did. Leighton was an outstanding full-back and got into the team as a seventeen-year-old, and from day one played with the brains of a veteran.

In the forward areas we had Ellington and Jason Roberts. They were a formidable partnership. They had pace and power. They could take the ball into feet and didn't mind a ball over the top. But we could also be direct. The pair of them loved to mix it up with the central defenders. They weren't shy at leaving a bit on the opposition. We had Jimmy Bullard in the central midfield area and Gary Teale on the right.

But we blew it when it mattered. We finished in seventh place, yet we were top of the league after eighteen games. But we faded and didn't have quality or bottle or stamina – call it what you want, maybe it was a mixture of all three – and we won only three of our last ten games. West Ham defeated on us on the final day of the season with a last-minute Brian Deane goal and that resulted in us slipping out of the play-off places into seventh spot. Naturally, we were distraught.

I think a lot of people expected to return for pre-season with a hangover but we were the exact opposite. There was a steely determination not to miss out again. We knew how deflated we felt at the end of the previous campaign and weren't going to subject ourselves, or our supporters, to that again.

In 2004-05 we got off to a flier and we were unbeaten in the opening seventeen games. We went straight up as runners-up to Sunderland. We got 87 points, 16 points better off from the previous twelve months. It was a rise to the top that probably arrived quicker than everyone expected. But we weren't complaining.

I thoroughly enjoyed our time in the Championship. It was a tough league but it was brilliant. I found it great preparation for the Premiership. It was full of huge clubs with brilliant grounds – Nottingham Forest and Leeds United spring to mind right away. There was absolutely no let up in that league.

Wigan was the making of me as a footballer and helped me mature as a person. I was a shambles as a man until then and I was far too immature. I think what helped me off the pitch was escaping the 'local boy' tag at Motherwell. I was able to be anonymous in Wigan town centre. Nobody knew me and nobody wanted to know me. It was the same if I went shopping in Manchester and Liverpool. The Wigan Warriors rugby league players were the celebrities in the town centre. They had an excellent tradition and had been extremely successful over decades. They attracted crowds of around 20,000 to the JJB Stadium – compared to us getting 7,000 or 8,000 in my early days at Wigan – but they were earning less than a fifth of what we were. They were winning every week and gave the town hope and something to focus on. They shared the training ground with us and I think there may have been resentment about what we were earning compared to them. I could see their point.

I went along now and again to see them play. It was decent stuff and I learned about the game. My dad enjoyed it more than me; he liked to go and see them when he could. The football team overtook them in the popularity stakes once we got into the Premiership. The roles were reversed and that gave us a good feeling. Whelan supported the football and the rugby but there was no doubt the football club was his priority. Eventually everyone bought into us and we overtook the rugby team in terms of popularity with the local community.

We enjoyed some great games on our way to promotion in season 2004-05 but it was a tiring campaign. Sometimes we would be close to seven hours on the team bus to travel to away games such as Queens Park Rangers. We also had journeys to Plymouth and Ipswich. When we had so far to travel we would report to the stadium on a Friday morning and head off. We would stop off close to London to break up the journey and have a training session. It saved us from spending almost all day Friday sitting on our backsides.

There was no respite in the Championship. We had forty-six league games to play plus Cup games. It was Saturday–Tuesday, Saturday–Tuesday. It never stopped. Whenever I felt it getting on top of me, I would dangle a wee carrot and tell myself, 'It's Vicarage Road and Ninian Park just now but it won't be long until it's Old Trafford and Stamford Bridge.' When we got into the Premiership, we would then go by train and hire a first-class carriage. It's the best way to travel. I loved it on the train.

We had some key games to get us into the top flight. A few stick out for me personally. We played away at Nottingham Forest towards the end of the season. There was pressure on us to win the game. I scored our goal but they equalised late on to draw

1–1. It was a full house at the City Ground and the atmosphere was brilliant. I loved that game; it just sticks in my mind. Walter Smith was Scotland manager at that time and attended the game. I played well, thankfully.

We played Preston North End at Deepdale and that was another cracking game. Memorable. Billy Davies was Preston gaffer at the time and I always seemed to score against them. The game was live on Sky and I scored with a header. A win would have taken us up but then they levelled late on to spoil the party.

It came down to the last game and we had to beat Reading to go up. We won 3–1 and I scored. I also got Man of the Match. It was a brilliant day and one I'll never forget. It was the biggest game in the club's history. This was our moment and a chance to give the fans something to really shout about. We finished runners-up to champions Sunderland on 87 points. My dad and some of my family were down for the game and it was special to share it with all of them. We each received a £100,000 bonus for winning promotion.

I scored fourteen goals that season and was also given the tremendous honour of being voted the Players' Player of the Year. It was at that time I was getting into the Scotland team under Walter Smith. Things were good. Nice little financial rewards came on the back of it all. Puma offered me a contract to wear their boots and wear some of their other merchandise. I signed a two-year deal and earned £150 per first-team appearance; £150 per goal; £1,000 for every Scotland cap and £5,000 worth of clothes and equipment at cost price every year from their factory. I was on a bonus of £25,000 if I played in a Champions League final and £50,000 if I won the Ballon d'Or (I think their money was safe with that one!). We'd get all the latest PlayStation games and equipment sent to us for nothing. I also had a deal with Audi cars that allowed me 20 per cent discount. I had that at Wigan and Rangers but they took the privilege away when we were removed from the SPL to go into SFL Division Three.

It was a great journey from Division Two to the Premiership. It was a real squad effort but I don't think any players made a greater contribution than Ellington and Roberts. They were phenomenal. Any side outside of the top eight clubs in the English Premiership would have loved to have had that pairing. We also benefited from the gaffer allowing us to go out and express ourselves.

Jimmy Bullard, Matt Jackson, Leighton Baines, Graham Kavanagh, Gary Teale and John Filan were also all huge for us. We were a close group, almost like brothers. We'd go for dinner and a couple of drinks. We loved to go to the driving range or have a game of golf. It's the closest dressing room I've ever been a part of. The manager treated us like adults and let us get on with it. He loved to see us getting on so well. I am absolutely certain we would not have won the two promotions if there wasn't such a togetherness. It played a huge part in the club's success story over that three-year period.

That said, it wasn't like we had a 'Tuesday Club' or a 'Sunday Lunch Club'. We enjoyed ourselves and loved a carry-on but we weren't ones for hammering the bevvy. We were fairly sensible when it came to that, but we were very close.

As well as improving on the park, the club was much more professional off the park. We got a Boot Room built, had a full-time kit man and washing machines put in. We had a full-time chef and canteen. We got a Jacuzzi put in, ice baths and a gymnasium. In my first couple of years there we just had a couple of large Portakabins and they were used for a variety of things – treatment room, office staff headquarters and the weights room. The weights area comprised of a couple of dumb-bells and a bar. The Portakabins were also freezing – there wasn't any proper central heating in them. We'd be on the treatment table in there and we would be chittering during the winter months.

There was no drainage on the pitches and it used to be ankle deep in mud for a number of months. It really sapped our energy and on a few occasions some of the lads took cramp at training. But Whelan also improved all of that and got a proper drainage system and upgraded the pitches. The training ground I walked into on the day I signed was totally unrecognisable compared to the place it became three years later. So long as we were going well and winning promotion, Whelan promised to spend money to upgrade our facilities and make us much more professional. He was true to his word. He was also conscious of every penny. It was well known in the dressing room he would make sure the lights were turned off at the training ground and then he got sensors put in to save a few quid. We all had a wee chuckle at that.

Whelan was very hands-on. When I signed a new contract he called down to the training ground and told the office staff to tell me to get to his office at JJB HQ. His office was plush, state-of-the-art. It was like JR Ewing out of *Dallas*. I sometimes found it quite daunting to be in his company on a one-to-one basis.

He was also so passionate about Wigan and totally loved the club. He was at the training ground every day and would be in the dressing room on match days before and after games. He liked to entertain and used to bring celebrities to the stadium for games. He brought Ruby Wax one day as she was doing her show in Wigan. He brought her into the dressing room and she interviewed me for her show as I'd scored a goal that day.

Whelan was a good guy and I never felt he interfered with the manager and players. Some owners have been known to overstep the mark and meddle in things they should keep out of, but Whelan got the balance right. He is a very loyal owner and always stands by his managers. From my vantage point, he appeared to have an excellent working relationship with Jewell. There was mutual respect there.

Being successful at Wigan meant the financial rewards were excellent. It allowed us to live a good lifestyle but I made sure I never took anything for granted. I bought a nice house in Warrington and lived in the same estate as Kerry Katona. My good friend James McFadden – who was with Everton at that time – was also in the estate. Graeme Park, the legendary DJ, was next door. I really enjoyed living in Warrington; it's a lovely place, nice and peaceful.

When my partner Amanda and I got together in due course, we both liked living there. Then, for her Christmas in 2005, I bought Amanda a new house in the estate, just a few doors along the road. She had told me a couple of months earlier she really liked the house and it was slightly bigger than the one we were already in. I blindfolded her on Christmas morning and took her into the car and drove around for about ten minutes to try and put her off the scent. When I parked the car for some reason she thought we were at a stables and that I had bought her a horse. She got out the car, back to just fifty yards from our house, and I opened the front door for her and then took the blindfold off. It was a lovely three-storey house. It was beautiful. We had many happy memories in there and we were really sorry when we had to leave.

6

MY FAMILY

AMANDA IS my partner and soon to be my wife. I'm extremely lucky to have her and we're both very fortunate to have two lovely sons together, Callum and Jack.

Amanda also went to Dalziel High School in Motherwell. If I had my way I would have asked her out when I was fifteen, but it took me the best part of ten years to pluck up the courage. She was the vice-captain at Dalziel High and I was two years below her. Me and my mates always used to talk about her and her best mate Suzy Russell. Both of them were the school babes, the ones we all fancied like mad. Amanda was tall and blonde, I was spotty and shorter and lacking maturity. I was always scared to speak to her. For some strange reason, I thought she'd be arrogant and wouldn't want to speak to me. We did converse a few times at school sports days but that was probably only because I was winning a few competitions and that gave me a swagger for all of about five minutes, and then I'd go back into my shell! I always wanted to ask her out and time after time I'd convince myself to have the courage to speak, but my bottle would always go and I'd clam up. I'd end up walking away, scared. Around my mates I was always up for a laugh and never short of something to say, but the big blonde always left me speechless. Over the years I've managed to massage the facts of the story and say that she actually chased me for years and I eventually gave in!

We bumped into each other in the Cricklewood Bar in Bothwell in June 2002. I was at Wigan and Amanda happened to be living in Manchester as she was working at Christie's Hospital as a research assistant in gene therapy. We were both single so decided to meet up down there a few weeks later for a drink.

But now I'll let Amanda tell her side of the story.

'After school I studied at Glasgow University and graduated with first-class Honours degree in Experimental Pathology. I then went to Australia to travel for a year in 1998 and came back. I landed a job as a genes research assistant at Christie's Hospital in Manchester in 2001.

'When Lee and I met again all those years after school it felt like it was "meant to be"! We had only seen each other a couple of times since we had left school and then we found ourselves both living and working within twenty miles of each other in England.

'We met on the night of the Queen's Jubilee in June 2002. We bumped into each other at the Cricklewood Bar in Bothwell. We had a chat and it was nice to catch up. We arranged to meet up the following month when we were both back down in England. We had our first official date on 22 July 2002 in Warrington.

'We clicked and got on well from our first date. We became inseparable, mainly because we were down there on our own. Lee would get impatient in the afternoons, asking me to leave work early to come and join him as he would be finished training. But some of us have to work real hours! We moved in together six months later and got our first 'baby' – Sasha, our dog.

'Lee and I both wanted children and talked about having a family from early on in our relationship. We were both extremely excited when I found out I was pregnant and, although he never said too much about it, I knew Lee was desperate for a boy. He had bought a little Wigan strip with "Daddy" on the back before Callum was born and was so proud the first day Callum wore it.

'Callum was born in Warrington General Hospital on

7 January 2005 at 11.35am. He weighed 9lb. It was a long labour. I needed an epidural to ease the pain but it took longer because the anaesthetist was too busy chatting to Lee about playing for Wigan Athletic and getting his autograph. Meanwhile, I was bent over, having contractions. Lee has assured me he is indebted to me for the rest of his life after what I went through that day.

'Almost before we could blink, I became pregnant again.

'Callum was only six months old when I found out I was pregnant with Jack. We were delighted but it came as a bit of a shock. I'm epileptic and I took a fit in the middle of the night on 22 July 2005, in my sleep. It was the first time it happened to me since I was at secondary school. I was at secondary school when diagnosed with it. I went on medication, had to take it every day. I came off it when I was in my mid-twenties. I only started to get symptoms again after I had given birth to Callum. Lee had never seen a seizure. We were out that night for dinner in Manchester to celebrate the anniversary of our first date together. Thankfully, Lee's parents were down and Lee shouted for his mum to phone an ambulance. Lee tried to help by putting his finger in my mouth to stop me swallowing my tongue but that is the worst thing he could have done. I bit down on it and he was in agony. I woke up with two ambulance guys in the room with their orange jumpsuits on.'

It was a Saturday night so as you could imagine the hospital was mobbed with people encountering problems on a night out. After Amanda was examined, the nurse asked if she was pregnant. We said no, no chance of that. A wee while later she came back and said, 'Oh, just to let you know you are pregnant.' It was a major shock!

Jack was born on 14 March 2006 at 11.25pm at Warrington General Hospital and weighed in at 8lb 11oz. That was an easier labour for both of us!

Amanda had three or four seizures in the first few weeks after Jack was born. By then I knew how to deal with it. The doctor had put Amanda on a high dose of medication and she told me she felt like a zombie most of the time. It was hard dealing with a dog and two babies, especially when I was on the road with Wigan. There was also the added complication and frustration of Amanda not being allowed to drive for a year because of her epileptic fits. We definitely needed support because she was told not to bathe the kids on her own in case she took a fit and they slipped under the water. Things like that. It was quite frightening. She'd have to walk everywhere. She couldn't just pack up for the weekend and drive up the road, and it was too much trouble getting a train. It was like a flitting with two young babies, just not worth it. Thankfully she had good friends around her and both sets of parents were down a lot.

Now that we're back in Scotland it's great that the boys can spend lots of time with their grandparents. The boys are great together and with them only being fourteen months apart they are good friends. They both enjoy football but I've never pushed them into it. They can choose their own paths in life and all that Amanda and I will drum into them are family values, good manners and a good work ethic. Amanda and I feel strongly about that.

Amanda is a great mother and a brilliant partner. She has given me the freedom to concentrate on my career. She doesn't care much for football and isn't interested in coming to watch me playing but she understands what's required and it's been good to always have her backing on that front. She has the patience of a saint and that's something that's really helped me with my career.

Now, the next big step for us as a family will be when we get married. I know Callum and Jack will enjoy the moment when they see their mum and dad finally getting married.

Amanda: 'We got engaged on 10 November 2010. It was a mid-week and Lee had played for Rangers and came home after losing the game to Hibs. He'd also hurt his knee and was in a bit of pain. We had just moved into our new house in Bothwell and the kids were away at their grandparents' so we could get on with getting the place in order, unpack boxes, that kind of thing. It was the first night we were to stay in the house together and that was the night Lee chose to propose.'

I'd been planning it for weeks. We had been together for almost a decade and the time was right. I got a magnum of champagne and got her ring sorted. I got Amanda a lovely solitaire ring when she had Callum. It wasn't an engagement ring but it was a sign of my commitment. I knew she wouldn't have wanted a new ring when I proposed so I had to come up with a plan. I told her I was taking the ring to get cleaned and asked a jeweller to put some new diamonds on it. I'd asked Amanda's dad Gavin for his permission. Her mum Joyce was delighted, but I was nervous the night of the proposal. We lost to Hibs and I had injured my knee. I was in agony driving back to the house from Ibrox.

Amanda: 'Lee was acting strange, seemed on edge, when he came back from work that evening. We had a glass of wine and he started to read out a list of things that he loved about me. He was fidgeting in the breast pocket of his Rangers suit jacket. It was from there he eventually produced a ring. He got down on one knee, clearly in pain with his knee injury, and proposed. I was shocked but absolutely thrilled. It was lovely, a moment I'll never forget.

'It means we are set for a busy period over the next year or two. I will graduate in September 2013 after studying for three years to be a midwife. I'm looking forward to it. My mum was a midwife so it's nice to follow in her footsteps. I get a lot of pleasure and satisfaction from my job, dealing with beautiful newborn babies and happy parents. After that, I hope we can share a lot more time together and enjoy a nice holiday. Due to our commitments with work and studying, I've rarely been off at the same time as Lee. We've managed a short break here and there with the kids but that's been it. I suppose, however, the main thing is to make sure I've got time to plan our wedding. I'm looking forward to it. Lee is a fine man and a wonderful dad. I'm incredibly proud of all he has achieved and how he has dealt with everything in the past eighteen months. Rangers have become a massive part of our lives. The recognition Lee gets has been quite difficult for both of us to adjust to as we are quite private people, but we have learned how to deal with it and embrace it in the right way.'

I'm really looking forward to the future with Amanda and all the good times ahead that we'll have together.

7

SCOTLAND:
THE VOGTS OF CONFIDENCE

DESPITE THE FACT I was playing well for Wigan, I never expected it to lead to a Scotland call-up. Wigan, I felt, was still regarded as an unfashionable club by most people in Scotland, and some cynics may well have been along the lines of, 'Well, it's only Wigan. Any player could get a game for them', which had been said, but we had quality on the pitch and the club was growing. So, I must admit, it was a surprise when I was called up by Berti Vogts for a friendly against Trinidad and Tobago at Hibernian's Easter Road Stadium in May 2004. The call-up was a nice reward for the way I was playing for Wigan. I was extremely proud.

The game took place on a Sunday afternoon, and it was a roasting hot day. We were winning comfortably, 4–1 up at the time, and as is the way in such fixtures, many substitutions were being made by both managers. Berti seemed to be throwing everybody on except me. I was the last outfield player waiting to get on. As the clock ticked down, I became agitated, maybe even embarrassed at the thought of not managing to get on when everyone else did.

I remember with about ten minutes remaining I was sitting beside James McFadden. He had been taken off by this stage. I told him I was desperate to get on but didn't think I had any chance. Yet, pre-match, Berti assured every player that they would play at some stage. I was raging as I voiced my anger in the conversation with Faddy. He took the bull by the horns and said, 'Right, fuck this. I'll make sure you get on.'

Next thing I knew he shouted to a player, who was playing in the centre of midfield, 'We need a favour. Throw one in. Say you've got a sore calf and need to come off so we can get Jig on.'

I think my face was crimson but, to my amazement, the player said he would do it. Less than two minutes later he was over at the touchline, in front of the dugout, and told Berti he had to come off as he had a calf strain. Berti turned to me and told me to get stripped – I was going on. Smiling ear to ear, I gave Faddy a high-five, took my warm-up top off and put my shin guards on. I puffed my chest out, ready for the fourth official to hold up my number. I was so excited.

Then, the fourth official appeared and said we weren't allowed to make the change as we had used up the agreed allocation of substitutions. I was gutted. Honestly, my world collapsed around me. I couldn't believe it. I sat back down. Faddy was in fits of laughter. He couldn't control himself. In contrast, I was in a huff, and my petted lip came out. It was one of the lowest points of my career. Looking back on it now I can see the funny side. But, at the time, it was anything but a laugh for me.

For friendly games the players don't receive caps, they are given pennants. I was given one at full-time by the SFA but it's the only time I've never wanted anything after a game. Faddy gave me a run home that day and he loved winding me up. I struggled to see the funny side of it.

I did make it into more of Berti's squads. However, he was clearly reluctant to play me and I don't think he really fancied me. That said, I was determined to get on that pitch and represent my country. I eventually made my debut for Scotland away in Moldova in October 2004 in a qualifier for the 2006 World Cup to be held in Germany. It was a vital game and the feeling of the nation was that Berti had to win it. Pressure was growing on him after some poor results, none more so than the 4–0 defeat to Wales in a friendly. Lots of people in the game felt he was lucky to survive that one.

He used to video our training sessions and then he'd make us watch them after our evening meal the night before the game. Interestingly enough, what also happened on those evenings was that the players were allowed to drink alcohol. White wine, red wine and rose wine, plus a few cold beers, would be there for us. Some of the boys had a beer or two. I didn't. I've never been one for drinking the night before a game, but it seemed to make a few of the lads feel relaxed, take any tension away. I have to say a nice atmosphere was created partly because of that, whether you had an alcoholic drink or not. We'd also be watching edits of some of the funny bits from training, some of the sitters and some of the bad first touches!

The game itself was no laughing matter. We drew 1–1 that night. Another poor result. I came on as a sub and it was great to finally make my Scotland debut. Happy days.

Although I came on as a sub, Berti must have had some faith in me and obviously thought I might be able to get a winning goal. I was extremely surprised to get the nod. I was on for fifteen minutes and thought I played fairly well in my role of centre-forward. I had a few touches and managed a couple of shots on goal. But we didn't win. The result was a disaster and yet another nail in Berti's coffin. Our chances of qualification disappeared.

The Scotland fans went mental at time-up. They gave it tight to Berti. I felt for him. We were flying back to Glasgow that night and the SFA Head of Security, Willie McDougall, warned the players as we got to the airport to be on our toes as there was a nasty atmosphere inside the airport. They were still gunning for Berti. The fans were throwing things, mainly at Berti. The players were on edge. That was his last game in charge and he was sacked the following month.

There's no doubt he made many mistakes and results weren't up to the required standard. The SFA had no choice but to sack him. In the post-mortem of his time as gaffer he was accused by some of handing out Scotland caps like sweeties and that may well have been a fair criticism. He capped dozens of players in his two and a half years in charge. I was fortunate enough to be one of them so you won't hear me criticise him for that.

My view on it is that when he came in he had to start again as several players had retired or were nearing the end of their international careers. They had served the country and Craig Brown well by getting to Euro '96 and France '98, but it was time for change after Brown and a fresh eye was needed on players and the set-up of our national game. Berti certainly made changes but he wasn't successful enough.

I always found Berti to be a players' man. He put us first, and players appreciated that. Some players did want to play for him. I was sorry for him when he was sacked by the SFA, but I felt it was the right decision. His time was up and a new man was needed to try and take the country forward.

The search was on for Berti's replacement and there appeared to be just one man in the frame from the outset – Walter Smith. The Gaffer. I was delighted when he got the job. I thought it was a great move by the SFA, but I was uncertain about my own future for Scotland with him in charge. I'd never worked under Walter at any stage but I was in a good period at club level for Wigan. I had scored fourteen goals and was awarded the Players' Player of the Year. I thought Walter wouldn't be interested in a Wigan player. So, I had sort of written off my international career and thought I was going to have just one cap.

His first squad get-together was in February 2005. He decided against taking on a friendly game and opted just to have a gathering for a couple of days in Manchester. Sir Alex Ferguson allowed him to use Manchester United's excellent training facilities at Carrington. I wasn't included in that squad. My disappointment was short-lived, however. The following month we had to play against Italy in Milan in a World Cup qualifier and fortunately my name was in the Gaffer's frame.

To play in the San Siro was an exceptional experience. We lost 2–0 with Andrea Pirlo scoring with two free-kicks. Kenny Miller missed a couple of half-chances and he also came out after the game and said he was to blame for the defeat. He was being harsh on himself. Yes, he had two half-chances, but they weren't sitters. We were disappointed to lose but it was a solid enough performance and we were well organised. We were also encouraged that Italy didn't manage to beat us in open play! There was also some positive coverage from the press and that was welcomed by the players and the SFA, especially after some of the headlines and comments Berti had attracted.

We knew plenty of hard work was ahead. We weren't silky and we were never going to out-pass teams and win comfortably. It was about hard work and giving your all for the jersey. We all wanted to do well for Scotland. We knew we'd have to grind out results. I played on the left wing most times and I knew I just had to work my backside off, get up and down the pitch, win high balls and try to bully the full-back. It wasn't rocket science. It wasn't pretty, but we tried to be effective.

We also won silverware during Walter's stewardship when we lifted the Kirin Cup in Japan in May 2005. It was a three-team tournament with Japan and Bulgaria and we were proud to finish first. We drew with Japan and thrashed Bulgaria 5–1. But there was also drama off the park. We had a night out in Tokyo to celebrate and Gary Teale ended up in jail. He got arrested for jumping along a few taxis at a rank. As he was being led away, he shouted, 'Jig, remember to wipe my footprint off of that car!' We had to bail him out a few hours later and then run to the airport to catch our flight home. It was crazy stuff. Teale was so relieved and we were pleased for him, although it was a pretty daft thing to do but obviously funny.

We were singing on the team bus on the way from our hotel to the airport and some of us were still under the influence after a heavy session celebrating the night before after Scotland grabbed a tournament win for the first time in many years. We drew a large penis on Faddy's head when he was sleeping. He had no idea and no one brought it to his attention. He was walking through customs with the drawing still intact and then Walter pulled him. He had the 'Walter stare' on and said to Faddy, 'Listen, son, get to the bloody toilet and get that off your forehead,' or words similar to that! Faddy did manage to see the funny side.

Walter was brilliant at handling such situations. He loved a laugh and a joke and that's why he was so fond of Billy McCulloch, the Scotland masseur. In any of the games that came down to do-or-die scenarios, Walter would say his piece and then hand over to Billy. Billy was at Chelsea full-time and is adored at Stamford Bridge. He is also a passionate Scotsman. He has a great sense of humour and can make anybody laugh at any given time. Billy would do a wee stand-up routine for us at some point in the build-up to kick-off on a match day. He'd have us in stitches. He is hilarious and it definitely helped us relax.

The highlight under Walter's time in charge came in a Euro 2008 qualifier against France in October 2006. We played France at Hampden Park and I played for fifty-eight minutes. The thing about that game was I hadn't played or trained for Wigan for four weeks. I was out injured. But Walter included me in his squad. He made his intentions known to me as soon as we arrived at Cameron House a few days before the game. He knew I was going to be a wee bit short of match fitness but told me to give it my all for an hour and then he'd take me off. I was only too happy to oblige. Yet, after fifteen minutes I was breathing out my backside. The wee right-back for France, Sagnol, just kept flying past me, but I managed to hang in there.

We won 1–0 thanks to Gary Caldwell's goal. Sir Alex Ferguson was in the dressing room after the game and shook us all by the hand. He was the happiest guy in the place. It was a fantastic experience and a memorable day to beat such a talented team with players such as Patrick Vieira, Claude Makélélé and Thierry Henry in their line-up.

To be perfectly honest, that result didn't come as a major surprise to me. We had a decent squad of players but our main strength was our team spirit. It was very similar to a club atmosphere and we would all have given anything for Walter and his assistants, Tommy Burns and Ally McCoist. The three of them worked fantastically well together. To be given the chance to work for my hero, Ally McCoist, was special. I admired him and looked up to him when he was a player. I didn't know Tommy but everyone told me he was a gentleman and a good football man. After spending some time with him in the Scotland set-up, what struck me most about Tommy was his enthusiasm and sense of humour. Great patter. He was brilliant with the one-liners. I was a victim of it once or twice. It was a major loss to the game when Tommy sadly passed away in May 2008. He's missed by all.

During a training routine, one of my first sessions with the squad, wee Faddy whipped in a cross that was perfect for me to go and attack. I'd connected with the ball, on the volley, less than two yards out, but somehow managed to put it over the crossbar. I held my head in my hands. My face must have been beetroot. All the boys looked at me, wondering what the hell was going on and all laughing. I was laughing at myself too!

Quick as a flash, Tommy shouted over to me, 'Hey, Jig, for fuck sake. What was that? We've already got boys here that can do that. We're needing something a wee bit different!' Even now, I still can hear him shouting it to me. Everyone was in stitches. That was typical of the banter in the squad during that period. It was just like a club atmosphere and it helped us get to fourteenth in the FIFA rankings. It was some turnaround.

8

PLAYING IN THE PREMIERSHIP: 'THAT'S FOR YOU, JIG' – MIXING WITH THE BIG BOYS

IT WAS good to be a part of such good times at club and international level. I knew doing well for Wigan at a higher level would keep me involved in the Scotland set-up. As soon as we got into the Premiership we were well aware that plenty of people expected us to be relegated and go straight back down to the Championship. We knew people were shooting the club down. We were ridiculed and people were out of order. We knew we were a good team and that we'd have to win over other people, prove we deserved to be in the Premiership. But that didn't mean the lack of respect and ignorance – collectively as a football club and individually as human beings – was justified. We were determined to make our detractors eat their words.

Some were more outspoken than others, such as Rodney Marsh. Basically, he said that our team was too old to compete and that there was no point in us being in the top flight. Paul Jewell was angry. We all were, but we used it as part of our motivation. Marsh was the most outspoken of them all. To me, he enjoyed a very good career as a footballer but he wasn't much of a pundit. That said, although none of us agreed with him, I suppose he got people talking and reacting to his opinions and that's what that business is all about. It gave us an incentive, that's for sure. What also helped was the fact we were to be given a bonus in the region of £100,000 per man to stay in the league. That was on top of £1,500 per win. Dave Whelan was very generous, that has to be said.

On the downside, we lost Nathan Ellington to West Brom for £3 million. I couldn't believe it when 'The Duke' left. I was gutted. The squad had to be strengthened and the two headline names that arrived were Henri Camara from Wolves for £3 million and Stéphane Henchoz from Liverpool on a free transfer. Both had been at Celtic on loan the previous season and neither proved to be a huge success in the SPL, but they were experienced and we were going to need calm heads in the months ahead. Pascal Chimbonda arrived for £500,000 from French club Bastia. He was a right-back but very much an unknown quantity.

Henchoz was a quality international defender for Switzerland. As is the case with new signings, there is always an interest in how much they are earning, especially since we were now in the Premiership and the bulk of the lads that got the club promotion remained on Championship wages. Some players were obsessive about it. Using various sources inside the club and agents in the know, the boys had heard that Henchoz was on around £40,000 per week. I didn't have a major problem with what any player was earning, each to their own and good luck to any footballer who can command that kind of money. The only slight problem I had – and that the rest of the core of the lads from the previous season had – was that no player was on more than £20,000 per week. Jimmy Bullard wasn't for holding back and assured the rest of the lads he'd get to the bottom of it. Henchoz turned up for his first day in his red Ferrari and was introduced to the boys. He was very pleasant and didn't appear to have any sign of an ego. Jimmy introduced himself and then came right out with it in front of the rest of the squad.

'Stéphane, do you mind if I ask you a question, big man? The boys are all quite close here and we tell each other what we're earning. How much are you on a week?' I curled up in a corner with embarrassment. Most of the lads stared at the floor, but Jimmy looked Stéphane right in the eye. Our new signing was totally taken aback but realised at that moment that Jimmy was very influential in the dressing room. He was a wee cockney wide man but I had so much time for him. A great person.

Henchoz told the lads he was on around £40,000 per week at Liverpool and had a similar deal at our club. He said he would tell Jimmy in private the exact amount. They immediately stepped outside and Jimmy was back less than two minutes later to tell us the big man was on £38,000 per week. He had a huge grin on his face as he broke the news. Jimmy wanted us all to go and see the gaffer to see if we could try and get a bit of parity for the rest of us. His rallying cry was, 'Let's go and kick the gaffer's door down, troops. We ain't having this shit.'

Ellington had received a huge wage rise and others considered that might be the route to go down – look for a move to another club to cash in on the fact people in the game were taking notice of us and knew we must have something to offer. It was at this time I was told by someone – albeit with no direct connection to Wigan or Rangers – that Alex McLeish was interested in taking me to Ibrox. My ears pricked up at the thought but nothing came of it. It's hypothetical, of course, but I think I would have wanted to stay at Wigan at that point to sample the Premiership with them. But it was good to know McLeish had followed my career and knew I was doing well. Again, it made me think of the phrase he told me: 'Be the guy on the telly . . .'

It had taken me more than four years to get to the Premiership with Wigan and I was really looking forward to getting stuck into this fantastic challenge. Our first game was at home to José Mourinho's Chelsea and their multi-million pound squad of superstars. They were the Premiership champions and showed their class and willingness to play to the very end when Hernán Crespo scored the winning goal in the 94th minute to defeat us 1–0. It was heartbreaking, but a valuable lesson was learned about the quality and desire in the league we were now operating in. We lost 1–0 at Charlton the following weekend. We kicked on from there and took 25 points from our next nine games. Our next defeat was to Arsenal, 3–2 on 19 November. It took another five games for our next victory to come along when we beat Charlton 3–0. Then I also scored my first Premiership goal in a derby match against Bolton Wanderers. It's a strike I'll never forget. The ball came across and from about fourteen yards I caught it on the half-volley and rattled it into the bottom corner of the net. Match of the Day here we go! I was glued to it that night.

We also had a nice distraction throughout that period as we got to the semi-finals of the Carling Cup after wins against Bournemouth, Watford, Newcastle and Bolton. We were fortunate to be drawn at home in every round. The game that sticks out for me in that run was when we beat Newcastle 1–0. I played up front that night on my own. I was really pleased with my performance and I was involved in the winning goal when I helped get us a penalty kick with a couple of minutes to go. David Connolly kept his nerve to tuck it away in front of the Sky cameras. I got Alan Shearer's top off of him that night too. Newcastle had a strong team and it was a real achievement for us to beat them.

We then beat Arsenal 1–0 at home in the semi-final first leg. I remember that game well. I came off within half an hour with a hernia injury and my groin seized up. It was an on-going problem I'd been having for months and the medical staff and myself tried as best we could to manage it, anything we could to avoid going under the knife.

Arsenal had a strong side out and there was no doubt Arsène Wenger was desperate to win the tie and make it to the final. He often used the League Cup tournament as one to play his younger players in the squad but there was a clear determination to do well that year. He expected his team to beat us and so did the Arsenal fans.

After the game it was decided I had to go in for an operation. It was going to do more harm than good if I tried to play on. I was in too much pain and I had to admit defeat. I wanted to avoid an operation so I could play in the return leg and help us get to the final to play in the showpiece game at Cardiff's Millennium Stadium but there was no way I could keep playing through the problem.

On the day Wigan went to Highbury for the return game, I was getting my operation done in Manchester by Mr McClelland, one of the top surgeons in his profession. I came out from theatre and went to my room. I watched the game on television and was probably still feeling a wee bit drowsy – full of drugs, basically. But I came alive as the game wore on. The boys left loads of messages on my phone, saying they hoped my op went well and that they were going to go out and win the game for me. That perked me up, for sure. I appreciated the gestures of the lads and I knew they meant it 100 per cent.

Wenger played Thierry Henry, Robin van Persie, Dennis Bergkamp, Sol Campbell and Robert Pirès. Henry scored to give them the lead and the game went into extra-time. Van Persie then scored with a brilliant free-kick to put them in front but we never gave up, and Jason Roberts scored our goal in the 119th minute to take us through on the away goals rule. He ran to the Sky cameras to celebrate and was joined by Jimmy Bullard and the pair of them screamed into the lens that the goal was for me, 'That was for you, Jig!' It gave me an amazing feeling. I filled up and came close to tears. But the real hero that night was our keeper Mike Pollitt. He was sensational. He made a string of superb saves, including a penalty from José Reyes. Mike is a great guy and we still keep in touch.

I vowed there and then in the hospital that evening that

nothing was going to stop me from playing in the final against Manchester United. I spoke to Mr McClelland the next day and told him my target. He said it would be unlikely but not impossible. That was all I wanted to hear. Mr McClelland said if I made the final then he'd love my jersey from the game.

The negative from that semi-final was that Stevie McMillan picked up a serious knee injury in the first leg at the JJB Stadium. He would have played in the final but wasn't fit. He tried so hard to make a comeback and worked himself into the ground day after day to get going again, but it wasn't to be. He had to admit defeat in February 2007 when he retired from the game aged just thirty-one. It was a tragic end to the career of a dedicated and talented footballer.

I had just over three weeks to prove my fitness to the gaffer and I gave it my all. I pushed myself in rehab, kept my upper-body strength going and then got into some light jogging very quickly. I pestered the Wigan physio, the legend that is Alex Cribley, and the medical team every day, non-stop. They must have been sick of the sight of me and my moaning and my constantly voiced concerns about whether I'd be fit or not for Cardiff. But it paid off and I was passed fit to play and was given a place on the bench by the gaffer. I was chuffed to bits. Obviously I would have preferred to start the game but, considering the previous few weeks I'd had, I had no complaints.

There was Cup Final fever around the town and a real demand for tickets. It seemed as though everyone wanted to go to the Millennium Stadium. Our preparation couldn't have been better. The club looked after us really well. But there was a shock for me on the journey to Cardiff on the team bus.

People from a certain era will remember a television series called *Fun House* which was popular with kids from the ages of between eight and fourteen. It was hosted by Pat Sharp, a popular guy with the kids, and was set inside this wacky warehouse where all sorts of ridiculous games were played and challenges handed out to the two teams, one dressed in yellow outfits and the other in red. The researchers came to our secondary school to look for kids to appear on the programme. They held auditions. I was in first year and our school randomly picked out pupils to attend the auditions. We had to sit in a circle and then stand up and say three jokes. My crackers were: What do you call a dog with no back legs and metal balls? Sparky; and a guy went to the doctors and said, 'Doc, I feel like a cowboy.' Doc asks, 'How long have you felt like that?' Guy said, 'Almost a yeee haaaa.'

I can't remember my other joke but it's safe to say I'm never going to threaten Billy Connolly or Kevin Bridges! That said, my classmates loved it and were all in stitches. We were sent back to class and I thought nothing more of it. Next thing, I got called to the head teacher's office to say I had been picked and my partner on the show was my cousin, Donna Spence. I was taken aback at the time as I heard the jokes from my uncle Les. It was all his fault!

We travelled to the studios and were put up in lovely hotel. It was great. We recorded the show the next day and we were the yellow team. Let the embarrassment begin.

Firstly, I was on a snooker table full of slime with a small pool cue on my nose. I had to go on my knees and attempt to pot balls into the pockets. I won. We then had a question and answer round and we were asked: Which elephant packed its trunks and went to the circus? I stuttered 'Nelly' in a squeaky voice. Donna then made a brilliant contribution and caught loads of different items in her dungarees. The last part was the go-kart race and we were well ahead going into the final round. We collected plenty of tokens as we drove round the track but they fell out through the holes at the pedals. So, we ended up losing and didn't reach the Holy Grail – getting into the Fun House for all the prizes.

Anyway, since I became a footballer I was always anxious to keep this episode of my life under wraps. I was scared it would ever get out. And then it did. On the team bus on the way to Cardiff. Unbeknown to me, someone at the club had got a hold of the tape and put it on the telly on the bus. Paul Jewell was also in on it and made sure he didn't miss me during the team meeting that night. He let the boys rip into me. It was all part of the team bonding but I've never lived it down!

The Carling Cup Final didn't go to plan either. Chelsea had quickly become the benchmark in English football and Manchester United were trying to keep up with them. Normally, they would have fielded a few 'squad' players against us in a final but they had to get some silverware on the board in an attempt to dilute Chelsea's dominance so put out a really strong team. We were 1–0 down at half-time when Wayne Rooney scored in the 33rd minute. Louis Saha then made it 2–0 in the 55th minute and four minutes later Cristiano Ronaldo added another. Rooney made it 4–0 on the hour.

A couple of minutes later I came on as a substitute and played centre midfield. It was a struggle and we tried our best to keep the score down. We didn't want it to get out of hand and end up losing by six or seven goals. United were in full flow but they didn't score again. They played unbelievably well and we just couldn't live with them on the day. Sir Alex Ferguson's men gave us a wee slap and put us in our place. Of course, it was said that it was a great achievement for us to get to the final, and that was very true. But we wanted more than that. We wanted to go there and win, write another new chapter for the Wigan history books. This time, it wasn't to be.

My dad and other family members were at the game. They were in the posh seats with other family members of the Wigan players and the Manchester United players. Dad wasn't coping well with the scoreline and in the final few minutes of the game he started to shout for Chelsea and declare his love for them. It was his way of trying to noise up the Manchester United people but I dare say the Manchester United WAGS were not amused by my dad's infantile behaviour. Chelsea and José Mourinho may have been the supreme team at that time but that day Manchester United really showed their class.

We went back to the hotel in Cardiff and stayed the Sunday night. Amanda was pregnant with Jack at that time and she stayed over. I had a right good bevvy and made the most of the night. The gaffer got up and made a speech and it was nice to reflect on the whole journey from beating Watford in the first game all the way through to the final of a major competition. Our fans turned out in huge numbers and we wanted to send them back up north with a win. I felt we had let them down.

I still have my medal from that final. It was one of three I got from my time at Wigan. I also have the Second Division Championship-winning medal and a beautiful medal from being runners-up to Sunderland when we made it up to the Premiership.

The run to the Carling Cup Final was great but our aim throughout the season was to make sure we stayed in the Premiership. We tried to never lose sight of that. The fact we had such a good start in the league gave us breathing space. That was invaluable. We reached the magical '40 point' figure by mid-February and stayed in the division, effectively, with eleven games to spare. I played in thirty-five games. Jason Roberts finished top scorer with fourteen goals in all competitions. Camara notched a respectable ten. We ended the 2005-06 season in tenth place on 51 points. It remains the club's highest ever position, and with the strength and depth in the Premiership these days, that won't be easy to beat any time soon. And we really deserved that finish.

Everyone worked ever so hard to achieve it. Everything

was really thorough. It had to be. Jewell and his assistant Chris Hutchins worked hard all season on team shape. We'd spend ages on where to be when we had possession and where we had to be when defending. A lot of the time we'd just be walked through different scenarios, took our time over it all. In previous years the tactics were all about ourselves and what we would do to the opposition, but this was a different ball game now. We were the underdogs and we had to be 100 per cent aware of the damage the opposition could cause us. From that point of view, it was interesting to watch the gaffer and Hutchins grow into their roles in with the big boys. They handled it well. Very well.

If you make a mistake at SPL level and Championship level you will have a fair chance of getting away with it. Not the case in the Premiership. One mistake, a split second of loss of concentration, and you get punished. Simple as. You had to be on it for ninety minutes. There was no let-up in that environment. Most players had pace and power and had the capabilities of inflicting physical and mental pain. In a few games I felt like walking off the pitch because I was so frustrated and felt I was contributing nothing. I rarely got a sniff of the ball when up against Sol Campbell and I hated it. Papa Bouba Diop was also massive. He had thighs like tree trunks. I could never get close to him when we played against Fulham. I came up against him a couple of times in the middle of the park and he blew me away. He'd take a touch and I'd try to nick the ball and then this big Inspector Gadget arm would come out and just hold me off. He totally put me in my place. That was a lesson. But I had to get up, dust myself down and try to get on with it. Now I feel the better for it now, it definitely improved my all-round game knowledge. The uncomfortable and frustrating experiences stood me in good stead.

A lot of teams used to say we were a nightmare to play against purely because we would work so hard, run ourselves into the ground for the cause. We had to have unbelievable amounts of energy and the Prozone stats often showed several of the boys in the team running around 13 kilometres per game, and sometimes we had three games in eight days. It was honest graft but we had no option. We wouldn't tolerate slackers in the team and we couldn't carry passengers.

We were the new team in the Premiership and we had to scrap, fight, pull, push and run our bollocks into the ground to get even just a point from a game. We were brilliant at stopping teams playing. We didn't give the top players a second on the ball until we were in their faces.

It meant we were also dedicated off the park and myself and the lads were not ones for going to the pub and having major sessions. I preferred a glass of wine or a beer in the house, or we would meet at one of the lads' houses with the wives and partners for food and a couple of drinks. I can't speak for the rest of the guys, but I know on a personal level that if I was out a couple of times a week, even once a week, for a right good kick at the ba' then I would never have survived in the English Premiership. I would have been found out very quickly. My body would have packed in. To be honest, when I came off the park after every game in the top flight, particularly away from home with the travelling built in, I was absolutely knackered. I felt as though there wasn't an ounce of energy left in my body. I just wanted to go home and relax. I never had a problem with being disciplined off the park because from my early days at Motherwell the importance of preparation was drummed into me.

For home games we were allowed to stay in the house, but the kids were young and I preferred to go to a hotel the night before a game to make sure I got a good kip. Leighton Baines was the same. So the two of us would go for something to eat, go to the movies and then go to a hotel in Haydock. The hotel was just five minutes from my house so I wasn't far from home in case anything went wrong with Amanda or the kids. I liked to be close by because of the kids and also because of Amanda's epilepsy. It meant she was not allowed to drive for a year and I had to be there for her as often as I could to make sure she could get around and we could go to the supermarket and take the kids shopping, all of that kind of stuff. Amanda not having full freedom wasn't easy on either of us – it's amazing how you take having a car for granted – but the most important thing was that she got back to full health, which she did.

I would miss Amanda and the kids when I was away from home and even more so than when we were on away trips, purely down to the fact I had Jimmy Bullard as my roommate. To put it in the nicest possible terms, he was totally unpredictable. We'd have two beds in the room but there was one occasion I woke up and found him naked beside me in the 'spoon' position. When I asked him what the hell he was doing, he just smiled. 'Come on,' he said. 'You know I've always fancied you, big boy.' He was obviously joking with me but I got out of bed, grabbed him and threw him out into the corridor. Jimmy was brilliant that season. He took to the Premiership without a hint of a problem and looked as though he'd played in it for years.

I felt I made a good contribution to our campaign. On Boxing Day 2005 I scored in a 4–3 win over Manchester City at home. They had a good team, David James in goals and Joey Barton in midfield. We beat them 1–0 on their own patch in March 2006 and I scored the winner. I ran away to the cameras to do the 'baby celebration' as Jack had just been born.

One of the few times I felt I let everyone down was away to Chelsea at Stamford Bridge on 10 December 2005. We had a great chance to score and missed it. Then I was to mark John Terry from set pieces and he scored a late-headed winner from a corner kick. Jewell tore me to pieces in the dressing room at full-time. I had to take it from the gaffer and sat with my head bowed.

It was good to stay up in the Premiership with time to spare and I looked forward to us kicking on the following season, albeit I was under no illusions that bettering 2005-06 was going to be a difficult task. Near impossible, truth be told. Our case wasn't helped when we sold Jimmy Bullard to Fulham for £2.75 million and Jason Roberts to Blackburn Rovers for an undisclosed fee. Both were major players and an integral part of the success we'd enjoyed in the previous two years. I knew we'd not be the same without Jason's goal threat and I knew we were going to miss Jimmy's ability and leadership on the park. I missed Jimmy. The place wasn't the same without him. We used to fight like cat and dog on the pitch. Jimmy would never hold his hands up for anything. Even if it was blatantly his fault he would point the finger at someone else. It used to really annoy me and I would give him pelters for it. We came close to blows a few times and then when I'd still be fuming, he'd shout over at me and then blow me a kiss.

The squad needed to be strengthened and we signed Emile Heskey from Birmingham City for £5.5 million. He was an established striker of the highest calibre and it was a great coup for us to sign someone of that ilk with such an outstanding CV, having played for Liverpool and England. We also signed Antonio Valencia on a season-long loan from Villarreal. Wigan also offered me a new contract and I signed it. It tied me to the club until the summer of 2009. I was happy with my wage rise but things were still eating away at me.

Second-season syndrome can apply to most teams in the top flight and we certainly suffered from it. After a flying start the previous year, we stuttered this time and only had 22 points from our first twenty games. We went on a run of just three wins from fifteen league games between December and February. We were relegation material. I wasn't contributing as much as I should have been. In December 2006 I picked up a three-match ban from the FA for punching Sheffield United defender Chris Morgan in the face in a game at the JJB that we lost 1–0. The referee, Peter Walton, missed the incident but I was caught by the television cameras. Morgan's right eye ended up badly swollen but, as far as he was concerned, the matter was closed at full-time when I offered a sincere apology. The FA, though, weren't as forgiving and I missed the games during the festive period against Chelsea, Manchester United and Watford.

To make matters worse, I'd done in the medial ligament on my left knee. It was twisted not torn. For about six months I was taking painkilling injections to enable me to play for Wigan and Scotland. I was never in any doubt about taking the injections. I just wanted to play football. But I was nervous about getting a needle into me. I'd rub an ice cube into the part of my knee for a few minutes before it to numb that part so I wouldn't feel it. I hate needles and I also have a phobia about people pressing into my knees. All of it gives me the heebie-jeebies for some strange reason.

I didn't want to miss out on playing for Scotland either. Things were going well and the country was on a high as we were doing well in the qualification campaign for Euro 2008. But the positive results with Scotland meant Walter Smith was in demand. Rangers and Paul Le Guen parted company in January 2007 and the club wanted Walter to go back and take over from the Frenchman. It was a job he couldn't turn down. When Walter left to go back to Rangers a few of the boys phoned me up to say to get myself ready as he'd want to take me with him. I wasn't so sure. I didn't expect the call to come, but I was hoping it would.

Alex McLeish took over from Walter. He had Andy Watson and Roy Aitken alongside him as Ally McCoist had gone to Rangers to be Walter's assistant and Tommy Burns stepped down. There was pressure on him to keep producing the results we'd had under Walter.

I think that move by Walter back to Rangers turned my head, not that it would have taken a lot to distract me at that stage. I also had a wee nudge from a third party the previous month when I was informed that Paul Le Guen was interested in signing me for Rangers. Things were never to be the same for me after that. I wanted to go – and even more so now Walter was manager.

Overall, there was just something missing at Wigan. I felt things weren't right; the dressing room wasn't as good as it used to be, just not as infectious and the camaraderie wasn't the same. We sold Gary Teale to Derby County in January 2007 and that was another close friend away. Off the park, we started to get ripped apart. Our close group stayed together for a few years but eventually we all got dragged our separate ways, and it was sad when our 'core' broke up. It was out with the old and in with the new.

9

CLASH IN THE LATICS: HOW I GOT MY DREAM MOVE TO IBROX

THERE WAS talk of me going to Rangers less than a year or so earlier when Paul Le Guen managed the club. Sir David Murray was the owner at that time and he pulled the strings. I was doing well for Wigan. A Scottish agent who was close to Murray called me to say Rangers wanted me. I didn't pay much attention to it and didn't say a word to anyone because I had my doubts it was true.

The interest from Rangers reared its head again. Le Guen was still in charge and it rumbled on to when Walter Smith replaced him. I wanted to go and I made Wigan aware of my feelings. I asked to meet Dave Whelan. I wanted him to hear it from me.

As it turned out, this dialogue between Dave Whelan and myself was to become a bitter bone of contention. It was just the two of us in the meeting and there was no one else to confirm what was or wasn't said. From my side of it, I came away from the meeting thinking that we had agreed that the club would let me go on a free transfer if I played there for the rest of the season and we avoided relegation from the Premiership into the Championship. Whelan, however, had a different view, as I was to discover later.

Dave Whelan, as I know well, is a good businessman and club chairman. He and the club looked after me well when I was there and in return I always did my best for the club and, I think, delivered for them. But the end of my time there was soured by the dispute that stemmed from that meeting. How we could have come away from that discussion with such different conclusions I will never know. All I know is what I thought had been agreed between us if I played on to the end of the season.

That all happened in December 2006, just before the transfer window opened in January. I'd got an agent to write up a transfer request for me. He told me to hand it in to Jewell the next morning. That night, however, I read on *Sky Sports News* that I was planning to ask to leave Wigan. Someone had leaked the story to the television. I know who it was, and once again had to learn my lessons.

So, the next morning I was nervous at going in to give this official request to the manager. Obviously with the news being on the television the previous evening, Jewell was ready for me, and I wasn't up for a fight. I felt like a little boy being summoned the see the headmaster.

I had the transfer request stuffed down my pants. I didn't want any of my team-mates or other members of staff to see it, so I walked around the training ground with it inside my shorts for half an hour.

At 8.30am I chapped on the gaffer's door. I was shaking.

I took the transfer request out of my pants and told him I had something for him. It was my transfer request. He took it from me and said, 'Okay. Now, fuck off.' I was still shaking. I was scared of him, frankly. He was an old-school manager. Jewell called a press conference that day and absolutely slaughtered me. He told the media that I took the transfer request letter out of my pants and handed it to him. He said that I didn't even have the decency to keep it in my pocket, instead it was tucked down in my private parts. It was a fair point he made. But, I was all over that place that morning. My head was gone. But he also told everyone I hadn't even written it out properly. The agent wrote it out for me, e-mailed it to me and asked me to print it off. It was a nightmare and I felt embarrassed. It was also the last thing Jewell needed as it was pretty clear, even at that midway stage of the season, that we were going to be involved in a relegation scrap.

There's no doubt it was a selfish thing to do and I knew it wouldn't go down well with the manager and other people at the club. I didn't want to let my team-mates or the fans down, but I desperately wanted to go to Rangers. I took advice from an agent on how to handle the whole thing, but, with the benefit of hindsight, I should have handled it differently and just been myself.

I played in games during the month of January but wasn't at my best. Far from it. I totally let Wigan Athletic down during that period. The club transformed my career and enhanced it. The fans were amazing and all the people at the club were professional and kind to work with, but I knew it was time. It was at the end of the window when the chairman pulled me about a transfer and I got my head back together. I knew I then had something to play for and believed there was light at the end of the tunnel. It was less than four months; I had to stick it out. It shouldn't have been a problem. I owed it to Wigan to be focused for them during a critical period and, after all, I was contracted to Wigan until the summer of 2009. I was buzzing again at the thought of getting away and imagining the finishing line in my head. 'Not long to go now,' I'd say to myself when I got up in the morning and before I went to sleep at night.

On the last day of the season, 13 May, we needed to win to stay up. Nothing less would be good enough. It was a tall order as we hadn't won a game since a victory against Manchester City on 3 March. We were at Sheffield United and it was a very tense and anxious period in the build-up to the game, a match that was worth more than £50 million to Wigan. The players were also on £96,000 per man to stay up. United also needed to win to have a chance of staying up. It was the year they went down and West Ham stayed up, albeit in controversial circumstances when they had Carlos Tevez and Javier Mascherano in their team. More than 32,000 fans packed into Bramall Lane to see the game. There was some atmosphere; it was electric.

I played up front with Emile Heskey. We were a powerful partnership and we both linked up well that day. Emile was a class striker and valued highly by his team-mates. I got booked early doors for dissent because tensions were running high. It was so hard to keep a lid on it all. We took the lead in the 14th minute through Paul Scharner. Jon Stead equalised in the 38th minute. We got a penalty in first-half stoppage time and David Unsworth – a spot-kick specialist – kept his nerve to put it past Paddy Kenny. We were looking a safe bet to get the win but then with fifteen minutes to go, I caught Michael Tonge with a late tackle, only by a fraction of a second, and I was given a second yellow card by referee Mike Dean. I felt Tonge made the most of it but I was sent off.

I was in tears as I sat in the dressing room all alone and wondered if I had cost the club the chance of staying up. It then crossed my mind that I had blown my chance of the free transfer I thought I would be getting. I watched the rest of the game from the tunnel. Heskey moved back to centre-half but the final whistle blew and we stayed up. I was buzzing. It was the best feeling ever. It's very hard to explain the emotion involved after such a game. There's more relief than joy. Leighton Baines was first over to hug me and I sat in the dressing room in tears for a good half hour after the final whistle. Sheffield United captain Chris Morgan came into our dressing room and shook hands with every one of us. I thought it was a terrific gesture from him and spoke volumes for him as a person.

I got back on the bus after the game and asked the gaffer if he was going to fine me for getting sent off. He told me he wasn't and not to ask him such stupid questions on a joyous day. We went out that night and most of us got into quite a state. The adrenalin was still pumping fast and it only took a few beers to be totally light-headed. It was enjoyable all the same. I was pleased for big Heskey that he played his part in us staying up. He scored eight goals.

We were in the next morning and the gaffer called a meeting. He told us that we had all been brilliant for him but he was stepping down as manager. The club had reluctantly accepted his resignation. None of us saw that one coming. It took us all aback, came right out of the blue. Jewell felt he needed a break and I totally understood why as the pressure a manager is under when they are fighting relegation must be unbearable. Perhaps part of the reason he resigned was because he sniffed the break up of the team. He put a jigsaw together over three years and then he could see pieces disappearing. The time was perfect for him to go and the time was right for me to go in a different direction.

Chris Hutchins, Jewell's assistant, was appointed as Wigan manager and I went to see him straight away. I told him I wanted to leave to move back up the road and join Rangers. He told me he would think about it and that I should go away and enjoy my summer holiday. I had a good relationship with Hutchins. I was confident he would help get me out. He was a good no.2 to Jewell and they were a good partnership. Hutchins was an extremely good football man and also had a good rapport with the players. He was very approachable and I felt more at ease in his company – less intimidated is the best way I can describe it. I really didn't want to do it on my own and I wasn't comfortable. But I had to do it. By this point I had ditched all input from agents, so there was nobody to hide behind.

After that meeting I went away to Italy on a family holiday. I was constantly by my mobile phone, hoping for it to ring with news that a deal had been agreed to allow me to leave

Wigan and move to Rangers. I couldn't really relax. The whole thing had taken over my thoughts day and night. Phone calls were constantly going back and forward about my situation, and I still thought that I'd be allowed to leave on a free after the conversation that had taken place with the chairman six months earlier and the impression I'd come away with from that discussion. But it then became clear Wigan wanted a fee for me. I immediately phoned Hutch about this and told him the situation as I saw it. When he got back to me he told me the chairman had a different recollection of things to me and that I wasn't to be given a free transfer. I didn't know what to think but I was angry and very disappointed. Ever since the meeting with Whelan it was what I'd been working towards – firstly helping make sure Wigan survived in the Premiership and then heading off to Ibrox to play for my boyhood heroes.

We had a face-to-face meeting on the first day back for pre-season and I confronted Dave Whelan in front of the manager. He said there was no way he'd ever let me go on a free. He looked me in the eyes and said, 'Do you think I'd let you go on a free?' I was totally gobsmacked and it put all my plans in jeopardy. I felt like I'd been done in, like I'd given my best for the club and not got the reward I thought I was due. Whelan's recollection of that meeting was clearly different from mine and I felt really let down. I just couldn't believe what was happening.

I thought long and hard about my plight and a strategy to deal with it. I decided to leave the chairman alone. He ultimately would be the man to decide whether I stayed or departed, but it was best to get at him through the manager. So, Hutchins became the man I had to piss off. In my wisdom, I decided to fuck up Hutchins. It was my only way to get to Rangers. I knew Rangers wanted me. I would just need to finalise the wages and length of the contract. At this point I didn't have an agent and was happy to represent myself. But one or two agents angled to get involved in the negotiations and went to David Murray. I'm glad I sorted it on my own because I negotiated a better deal than what they claimed was on offer from the Rangers owner.

Some agents in football think they run the show, from owning the player and the clubs they are supposedly going to be transferred to. I've had experiences of agents telling me that Club A is the best to go to when really it may well have been the worst possible option, but they would have got a bigger financial reward for me going to that certain club. I have been told that I was going to be the highest paid player at a club when I was really going to be in the bottom tier of the salaries. I've had agents go directly to a buying club to tell them that they represent me when they weren't employed by me at any stage. It has led to some arguments and some things getting heated and nasty between clubs, agents and myself. It's not easy being caught in the middle and there were times I felt intimidated.

For a young professional it must be a nightmare. Any kid that shows a glimpse of promise is chased by twenty or thirty agents, all promising the earth. Youngsters and their parents are offered all sorts of incentives by agents. I think young players need to realise – and I will be telling my kids the same if they ever go down the football route – that it's not the agent that gets players the move, it's the player that gets the move. Simple as that. You have to be good enough for another club to want you and pay money for you.

So, having been deceived a couple of times, I was happy to sort out any deal with Rangers on my own. Knowing I was wanted by the club I love and that I was going to be extremely well paid for the privilege, I had to do my bit and get away from Wigan. I phoned Hutch and reminded him that he was just a new manager and needed the players fully behind him. He had to hit the ground running and the last thing he needed was a disruptive influence. I phoned the day before we were due to report back for pre-season and told him I was going to be his worst nightmare, that I would boot every single ball over the fence at training so that no work could get done. And I told him I would happily fight him if he wanted to confront me. I was not scared of the new manager but I was concerned about the reaction of the senior professionals in the dressing room would be if I had to start behaving this way.

So, I spoke to Mike Pollitt, Leighton Baines, Matt Jackson and Chris Kirkland. They basically ran the dressing room. They didn't have a major problem with my plan. In fact, they found it quite amusing, although they were concerned they wouldn't get any training done. I genuinely loved Hutchins and wanted him to succeed as Wigan manager. To be honest, I was bluffing with him and, thankfully, I never needed to actually put my threats into practice.

Of course, I was also aware I was taking a massive gamble. If this move to Rangers did not happen then I was throwing away a career in the Premiership, but it was a chance I had to take. I'd never have forgiven myself had I not.

I did make life difficult for Hutch in the first few days. It wasn't pleasant for him and, genuinely, I took no satisfaction from the way I behaved. During my summer holidays in Italy, I spent time at a detox place and came back in great physical shape. But I didn't want Wigan to know this. So, for example – and it shows the state of mind I was in at the time – I stood on scales at the weigh-in on the first day back and had a five kilo weight hidden inside my training top to make me miles overweight. I wanted the manager and backroom staff to think I had chucked it. I just wanted to play for Rangers and nothing was going to get in my way.

When I got into my car after training, I'd take a deep breath and be grateful it was over for another day. It doesn't come naturally to me to be a horrible person. Eventually, Wigan had had enough and they phoned Rangers and asked to start negotiating my transfer. It went on for a few days and they settled on £2.2 million, a fee that was ridiculously high for me. I know I was a Premiership player and I still had two years left on my contract, but I felt Rangers paid well over the odds. Still, I was very grateful to them for doing so.

I've still never been back to Wigan. I've never had a chance to say cheerio to the fans. I've been invited down a few times but just never managed it. I will be back down soon. The Wigan fans were always very good to me. They thought I was going to be a prolific scorer for them when I first joined and the relationship was a real slow burner to begin with. Once they realised my game wasn't about goals, they appreciated me and chanted my name in several games. To receive that recognition from them really helped improve my confidence I was sad to leave them behind as well as the players and the office staff. The staff were all lovely and considerate people.

One of the biggest accolades I received from my six years there was recently being voted by the fans into the club's All-Time Greatest XI. I was proud and privileged.

Over the piece, the Wigan fans were very good to me and treated me well. They would sing songs about me and I will always be grateful for the way they accepted me and my family as their own.

The Wigan fans' Greatest Ever XI is: al Habsi, Chimbonda, de Vos, de Zeeuw, Baines, Valencia, Liddell, Bullard, McCulloch, Roberts and Ellington. Not a bad line-up!

10

HOW I PAID THE PENALTY
FOR JOINING GERS

SIR DAVID MURRAY got the deal done and I've no doubt he was encouraged to do so by Walter Smith. Walter had given me his word a few weeks earlier that I would become a Rangers player and he mustn't have wanted to let me down.

When the fee had been agreed, I was phoned by Wigan and told to go to Murray Park. I jumped in the car and drove up to Glasgow. Such was my desperation to get up the road and get it all signed and sealed, I was caught speeding and given three penalty points. When I arrived, I was told to go to the club doctor's surgery in the west end of Glasgow. The doctor, Paul Jackson, was there to meet me, along with Walter. I went through some tests and then on to Ross Hall Hospital for routine scans. The deal was concluded very quickly, in a matter of hours. I was delighted. I signed for Glasgow Rangers Football Club on 11 July 2007, the proudest day of my career.

It was hard to take in that I had gone from being a wee boy that went to Ibrox with my dad and brothers to watch the club during the Graeme Souness era to now develop into a man that was going to play on the famous turf in front of 50,000 Rangers fans every other week. It's a struggle to put into words exactly what it all meant to me.

I went out and bought all of my family Rangers jerseys and

went back to my brother Wullie's house. Gregor and Wullie and my parents were there. We all had a few drinks and were absolutely delighted. This was a dream come true for all of us. Between sips of his lager, my dad just kept saying, 'You've just signed a four-year deal with Rangers. You're now a millionaire. In fact, you might even be a multi-millionaire!' I think my dad's pals were filling his head full of nonsense. I played it down, but I could see he was so proud of me and that meant so much.

My first taste of the Old Firm rivalry came less than twenty-four hours after I signed. I was at the supermarket with my parents, packing the bags into the boot of the car and a guy shouted, 'Why don't you fuck off back to England, ya orange bastard.' It's always nice to have well-wishers and be made to feel welcome back in my own country! It was a real eye-opener because even though I'd been a Rangers fan I had never been subjected to anything from Celtic fans, but I suppose I knew that was going to be part of the deal. However, through most of my Rangers career the Celtic fans have been great with me and I have had chats with them about both clubs.

Being a footballer has given me so many highlights and happy memories, but my first day at Rangers was just so special. I remember thinking the club was enormous and that I'd have to really work hard to earn the right to play for this magnificent institution. I was brought down a peg or two though. Because I thought that I'd be able to leave Wigan for nothing I informed Rangers they'd be able to get me for free in the summer. I was delighted. As were Rangers. But when it didn't work out as I'd expected, Gers had to pay £2.2 million for me. I remember seeing Ian Durrant for the first time after I had signed and he looked me up and down and said, 'You're the most expensive "free" we've ever had at this club. £2.2 million for you . . . !'

My first pre-season game was in Germany. I was sharing a room with Andy Webster. I was nervous on the match day because I was worried about the Rangers fans' reaction to their club signing me, especially for that amount of money. The game was at night and late afternoon I got my head down for a sleep. Webby also went for a kip. Our room door then started to batter down. It was Barry Ferguson and Kris Boyd. Boydy ran in and started to say that I was on the front page of the papers back home. He told me there was a report about how Rangers fans didn't want me at the club. He had his laptop with him, to give the impression he had looked it up on the internet.

Fergie stood behind him, laughing. I knew it was Fergie's idea of 'welcoming' me to the club.

I was in meltdown. I was gutted. Boydy and Fergie then left the room. I didn't get a wink of sleep after that. I knew they were at it but I was disappointed. But I suppose I was nervous and slightly fragile at that stage. Some may argue I was possibly a touch paranoid. Maybe that was the case.

I made my debut that evening and it was roasting hot, almost unbearable heat. We overcame the sweltering conditions to defeat SV Lippstadt 4–2. I scored two of our goals and played well. It was a great feeling to finally pull on a Rangers jersey and the goals were a lovely bonus – that settled me down.

But I had niggly problems off the park. I found it really hard to be accepted by some of the boys in the dressing room at Ibrox. Ian Murray, Chris Burke and Stevie Smith were very close to each other. I wanted to come in and speak to all of the boys, be friendly with them, but the dressing room was divided. It had cliques and was far from ideal. I'm guessing that was still down to some of the things that had gone on under Paul Le Guen the previous season when everyone knew Ibrox was not a happy place during that period for many reasons. Ian Murray, Stevie Smith and Chris Burke were all a right good laugh; their patter was always entertaining, but I think they were wary of me. Again, though, maybe I was paranoid.

I got changed in the locker next to Fergie. I wasn't for being associated with any of the cliques although I was close with Barry and Boydy. I wanted us to all be together, so that made it hard for me. However, the most important thing was to make an impression on the park. The rest would, hopefully, fall into place after that.

11

INTO THE LYON'S DEN: MY CHAMPIONS LEAGUE DREAM 2007-08

IN TERMS OF my game, I enjoyed pre-season and was on the right track. I made my European debut for Rangers against FC Zeta in a Champions League qualifier and scored in it. I played on the left-hand side of a four-man midfield. It was a position I played many times for Wigan, where I also had a licence to come inside to a more central role or push on diagonally to join the strikers. At Rangers, however, I was left midfield, more of a left winger, told to stay close to the touchline. I was to attack long, diagonal balls and the strikers were to get on the end of my flick-ons. It was quite good in the beginning.

We played well against FC Zeta, a hardworking side from Montenegro. I scored with a header after Davie Weir had given us the lead. The only negative was Alan Hutton got sent off, harshly, in my opinion. We won the return leg 1–0 through a DaMarcus Beasley goal. Zeta apologised after the game for racist abuse aimed at DaMarcus Beasley and Jean-Claude Darcheville. Disgraceful that kind of thing still goes on in this day and age.

Red Star Belgrade provided the opposition in the final qualifier and they stood between us and the £10 million jackpot the Champions League would bring to the club in revenue. They were a good side and we had to be ready. It was going to be a massive test. I played on the right of midfield and the game plan was to hit diagonal balls to me so I would win flick-ons and we could perhaps get some joy from the second balls. The manager's tactics worked. In the final minute of a tense and anxious evening, I flicked one on for Nacho Novo to score. There was a stat from that night – I won forty-one headers from forty-three high balls.

We were happy to take a 1–0 lead to their place but the atmosphere in Belgrade was very hostile. We got a police escort from our hotel to the stadium and our bus got pelted with bricks and bottles. It wasn't pleasant, but it only drove me on. I wasn't going to be intimidated by them. There was too much at stake. I was ready for the battle.

The stadium was packed from the moment we arrived. The fans also turned on us inside and threw lighters and coins at us, but we kept our heads, stayed focused and played really well. We drew 0–0 and I nearly scored, but their keeper made a really good save. Still, we were through. It was a fine achievement.

We were in the Champions League and I was excited. It was going to be my first time. I had been to games at Ibrox and Old Trafford but never played in them. I felt privileged I was going to be a part of the best club competition in the world. When we were drawn against Barcelona, Lyon and Stuttgart the talk outside of our dressing room was that we'd finish last and we should go out and enjoy ourselves. I didn't take any notice of what people said. My plan was to take it one game at a time but the thought of playing against Barca at the Nou Camp absolutely thrilled me.

I felt we had a decent team and would be able to cope with the demands. The signing of Carlos Cuellar was huge. I could tell right from the off he was a solid and capable central defender. He and Davie Weir hit it off to form a terrific partnership. The other plus point was the emergence of Allan McGregor as our first-choice goalkeeper. He had been at Rangers since the days of Dick Advocaat and then Alex McLeish and Paul Le Guen but he was never given a proper chance to establish himself under their time. Walter, though, put him in and Allan repaid him. Big time.

Our opening fixture was against VFB Stuttgart at Ibrox but I was gutted to miss the game through suspension after two yellow cards in the qualifiers. Thankfully, we won 2-1. We set up with a five-man midfield and Jean-Claude Darcheville up front on his own. The Germans had a terrific side at that time with Sami Khedira and Mario Gomez. Gomez gave them the lead in the 56th minute. We opened up a little bit after that and Charlie Adam scored a brilliant goal to equalise. Alan Hutton won us a penalty in the 75th minute and Darcheville scored. Hutton was fantastic that night.

Our next game in the group was Lyon away, leaders of the French league at that time. They had a brilliant team. I played on the left of midfield in a game that goes down in history as one of the best results on foreign soil for Rangers. Gary McAllister – also a Motherwell boy – was at the game and pulled me before kick-off to wish me all the best. It was a nice touch from him. The stadium was first class and there was a great atmosphere, our fans got right behind us to cheer us on. We won 3–0. I scored the first goal with a header from a Beasley corner kick. Daniel Cousin and Beasley got the others early in the second half. Lyon had a few chances and hit the woodwork three times but we were in control. We had a right good celebration afterwards in the dressing room and that night was possibly the happiest I can remember Walter Smith and Ally McCoist being after a game. They were ecstatic.

We were at home to Frank Rijkaard's Barcelona in the next game. They had Lionel Messi, Ronaldinho, Thierry Henry, Iniesta and Xavi. Not a bad team, I suppose! Barcelona was a huge game and on the morning of the tie we had a brief training session at Murray Park and then went upstairs for our video briefing on them – strengths and weaknesses, that kind of thing. Coisty and

Kenny McDowall would go through it all with us and when the heading for 'Weaknesses' came up on the PowerPoint, I just had to blurt out, 'I can't wait to see what you've got for this part of the analysis.' We all had a good laugh. It basically came down to the fact that they rarely swung a corner into the box; they preferred to take it short.

Ibrox was a sell-out and the atmosphere was electric. I loved the line-up three minutes before kick-off when the Champions League anthem belted out. The hairs on the back of my neck stood up. I wish I could have bottled that moment and savoured it forever.

We scraped a 0–0 draw. Needless to say we defended for the whole match and rode our luck at times. Ronaldinho hit the crossbar and Messi had one cleared off the line but we had a great chance in the final minutes, which Cousin wasted. Overall, it was yet another great experience for myself and the boys. That's when I knew Rangers were the real deal as a football club! After the first three games we were flying in the Champions League group section and had amassed an excellent seven points. We were brilliant. Everyone seemed to take it for granted we'd be in the last sixteen and the expectation level started to rise after the opening three ties.

The next game was Barcelona away at the Nou Camp, and although we lost 2–0 it could have easily been four or five. Henry and Messi scored. Apart from being mesmerised by some of their play, the lasting memory from that night was the backing we received from the travelling Rangers support. They were outstanding. They never stopped singing for the entire ninety minutes. We didn't create any chances for them to get excited about but we tried our best. Barca were an awesome team and went on to win the trophy that season. We left with a bonus, which was guaranteed UEFA Cup football – at least – after Lyon lost to Stuttgart.

We were on the road for our next game and it was another tough test – Stuttgart away. I got injured and had to come off in the 23rd minute. We lost 3–2 in a ding-dong battle. They scored a late winner through Marica. Charlie Adam and Barry Ferguson got our goals. We felt aggrieved not to leave Germany with a point, but we were still in a good position because we'd got off to a good start by getting seven points from our first three games. We only needed a point from our final game at home to Lyon.

However, the French side were clearly hurting from the hammering we gave them on their own patch and came to Ibrox with a determination to succeed. They went a goal up early in the game. We had a good few chances. Darcheville should have scored from about a yard out – an incredible miss – which would have made it 1–1 and would have made a difference but they went on to dominate and comfortably won 3–0. We were gutted. I really thought we were going to make the last sixteen. It was so disappointing to miss out but we didn't deserve anything from that game. Karim Benzema totally ripped it up that night. They out-passed us and outplayed us. They gave us a real going over and they couldn't be grudged their victory. Sidney Govou and a double from Benzema gave them the win. Darcheville was red carded in the final minute. It consigned us to third place in the group and that enabled us to enter in the Europa League. I was desperately disappointed to miss out on the knockout stages of the Champions League, especially when we'd got early points on the board and I'd thought it was in the bag.

Gers in the Champions League

13/07/07
Champions League Qualifier 1st leg – Rangers 2 Zeta 0

07/08/07
Champions League Qualifier 2nd leg – Zeta 0 Rangers 1

14/08/07
Champions League Qualifier 1st leg – Rangers 1 Red Star Belgrade 0

28/08/07
Champions League Qualifier 2nd leg – Red Star Belgrade 0 Rangers 0

19/09/07
Champions League Group stages – Rangers 2 Stuttgart 1

02/10/07
Champions League Group stages – Lyon 0 Rangers 3

23/10/07
Champions League Group stages – Rangers 0 Barcelona 0

07/11/07
Champions League Group stages – Barcelona 2 Rangers 0

27/11/07
Champions League Group stages – Stuttgart 3 Rangers 2

12/12/07
Champions League Group stages – Rangers 0 Lyon 3

12

THE LONG AND GRINDING ROAD
TO MANCHESTER

WE KNEW the title race with Celtic was going to be really tight and all our thoughts and efforts were on that. But the UEFA Cup was not to be sniffed at, although very early on we may have regarded it as a bit of an unwelcome distraction, truth be told. We decided to take it a game at a time and it soon grew on us. When we entered it in the last thirty-two, not for a minute did I think it would lead to us going all the way to the final in Manchester. Our plan was to keep it tight in the home games and not do anything silly. Funnily enough, we were drawn at home in the first leg in every round. We drew every game at home and then managed to sneak it when we travelled away. Our style was to frustrate the opposition and see what damage we could cause on the break. Some people thought the brand of football was hard to watch, low on entertainment value, and we should have been more adventurous, especially at Ibrox. But we received unfair criticism too, and I reckon it stemmed from Messi's comments after we drew 0–0 against Barcelona. He said we played 'anti-football' and we were unable to shake off that tag. But what was he expecting? We couldn't try to beat them at their own game. We had to defend for our lives and double up in the full-back areas. Messi played on the right and he was directly up against me and Saša Papac. We played with one up front and we rarely managed to cross the halfway line. But we were under

119

no illusions we were going to pin that great side back and have them sweating inside their own box. That was just not going to happen. A lot of people jumped on the bandwagon after Messi's comments. Some people made ludicrous comments.

One player who made an excellent impression for us during the campaign was Alan Hutton. He was outstanding against Barcelona and also played very well for Scotland in the games against France. He caught the eye of several big clubs and he left us in January 2008 for a fee in the region of £9 million to join Tottenham Hotspur. He left a huge void for us on the pitch.

We were drawn against Panathinaikos from Greece in the last thirty-two. We drew 0–0 at home in mid-February. It was a tight game and we defended well. Steve Davis had just signed on loan from Fulham and made his debut for us. It was clear he was a very good player and was going to be an asset in the middle of the park.

For me, the away leg was a weird one. I had a sore ankle and had no chance of playing, but I travelled to Athens to get treatment every day from the physios and medical team. The night before the game we went up to Allan McGregor's room for a game of cards. I think it was me, Kris Boyd and Barry Ferguson. I took a couple of sleeping tablets and a couple of glasses of wine during the card game. I received permission to do so as I had no chance of playing in the game. I was used to taking the tablets the night before mid-week matches, especially in Europe – they were given to us by the club doctor if we wanted them – because I felt it helped me get a sound sleep. In the morning we'd get up for breakfast and I'd still feel a wee bit groggy. We'd then go for a walk, get some fresh air and have a team meeting about tactics and shape, and then we'd have a few hours to spare in the afternoon. I liked to sleep and there may well have been still a trace of the tablets in me so it helped me relax. I was used to it. I felt it was great preparation for me. Come three hours from kick-off I felt refreshed and raring to go. But I'd never mixed the pills with wine. Well, what a hit it gave me that night in Athens. When I got up from the table, I could hardly walk straight. On the way down the corridor to my hotel room I was bouncing off the walls. I was all over the place. Never again!

Thankfully the boys were in a better condition than me and we got a great result, with Nacho Novo and Kris Boyd up front. The intention was to have a go at our Greek opponents and it eventually paid off when Novo scored a late equaliser to give us a 1–1 draw and take us through on away goals. Allan McGregor was brilliant that night, but he saved his best for the next tie.

The last sixteen paired us against Werder Bremen. They had a good team and, like most German sides, were solid, organised, athletic and technically very competent.

I came on as a sub with ten minutes to go in the 2–0 win over Werder Bremen. Daniel Cousin and Davis scored. I played up front. Walter asked me to go in that role and try to hold the ball up, kill a bit of time. Charlie Adam played a long, diagonal ball, I managed to spin off the centre-half and I cracked in a drive on the half-volley. It was blocked by the keeper but went through his legs. Yet the pace had been taken off it. The ball was crawling towards goal and I chased it in. I should have slid in to make contact and get it over the line but I just kept running and, as I was about to shoot, a defender came from nowhere and blocked my shot. I was only three or four yards out. I was gutted and angry at myself for not sliding in. I collapsed to the ground. One of the lowest points of my career – I blew a chance to put us 3–0 up. But what happened to me that night typified what was going on in my career at that time, it just wasn't going to plan. I wasn't playing to the level and standard I knew I was capable of. It was so frustrating, and there was worse to come.

After the game someone sent me a letter with a betting slip. The person had Cousin for first goal and us to win 3–0. My miss cost the guy a few hundred quid. He let me know in the letter he was far from happy. I showed it to Barry Ferguson. He burst out laughing and told me to put it in the bin. I was gutted. I wasn't sure whether to contact the guy and send him a signed jersey or something. He probably would have thrown it in the bin if I had.

We went to the away leg and they absolutely battered us. I was on the bench. Diego scored to put them one up after 57 minutes. It was then backs-to-the-wall stuff for us and I came on with twelve minutes to go to help shore things up. McGregor made a few brilliant saves. One of the saves was just ridiculous. It came with minutes to go and he sensationally turned Sanogo's effort onto the crossbar – the save of his career. We called McGregor the 'Mad Monk' after the crazy goalie in the movie *Mean Machine*, the one with Jason Statham in it. On the coach on the way to the airport I told him he had the game of his life and he said, 'Thanks.' His attitude was that it was his job to do that kind of thing. He never looked for praise and more often than not got embarrassed if any plaudits came his way.

And all of a sudden, before we knew it, really, we were in the last eight of the competition. We played Sporting Lisbon at home in early April. It was yet another tight affair and I almost scored late in the first half when I spun on the edge of the box and pinged a right-footed shot towards goal, but Rui Patrício got down superbly to palm the ball round the post. We tired towards the end of the game and they got a grip of the game. Liédson and Tonel came close with efforts. It was during that game, and as we analysed it afterwards, that I felt the legs were starting to go. We were also mentally tired. We were under no illusions it was going to take a huge effort to carry on and be able to produce good enough performances to win us games.

We soldiered on to the return leg a week later in Lisbon. We knew it was going to be vital to get an away goal. The surface on

Sporting Lisbon's pitch was first class. It was incredible. I think it's the best surface I've ever played on. We thoroughly enjoyed playing on it and we knocked the ball about in the first half hour like a top continental team. We were full of confidence and felt we were going to win the game. Darcheville put us one up on the hour and then Whittaker scored a terrific individual goal, a thing of beauty, in the closing seconds. Davie Weir and Carlos Cuellar handled Liédson superbly that night. We were in the last four of the UEFA Cup. It was unreal.

Fiorentina were our next opponents and we drew 0–0 in the first leg. I broke my foot the previous week against Celtic and McGregor also got injured that night so we both missed the semi-final. The visitors dominated possession for long periods but struggled to create clear-cut chances as Rangers held firm. Neil Alexander made good saves from Martin Jørgensen and Adrian Mutu. Novo chipped over from forty yards as we improved in the second half. Again we didn't manage to score, but we had been in this scenario before and we were quietly confident.

That said, we were rightly underdogs going into the game in Florence. They were expected to make it to the final but we had a bit about us. We weren't there to simply lie down. We had a European final in our sights. I was injured and sat in with the fans to watch the game. The Italians had most of the possession but Alexander wasn't overworked in goal. Saša Papac cleared an effort off the line and that was about it. We were dealt a blow when Cousin was sent off late on. Then it went to a penalty shoot-out.

Novo fired home the winning spot-kick after Christian Vieri drove his kick over.

I went to the dugout to watch the drama unfold. I was able to hobble over to congratulate Nacho along with the rest of the players. I think the Fiorentina players lined up at full-time to clap us off the pitch. As we walked up the tunnel the atmosphere was brilliant, we were on such a high. There was a slight lull, a split second of opportunity for someone to grab, and Kirk Broadfoot seized it. He shouted at the top of his voice, 'What the fuck is going on? This time last year I was playing for St Mirren and now I'm going to a UEFA Cup Final with Rangers.' It was perfect. Brilliant from big Broaders. He had a very good season for us and handled it all very well.

There was no real celebration after the game. No champagne. No singing and dancing. It was job done. Showered. Changed. Flight back to Glasgow. Prepare for the next game of a gruelling schedule. We had no time to party. But what wasn't lost on us all or our supporters was that Glasgow Rangers were in their first European final since they lifted the European Cup Winners' Cup in 1972. We were to meet Dick Advocaat's Zenit St Petersburg side at the City of Manchester Stadium on 14 May. Zenit had thrashed Bayern Munich 5–1 on aggregate so we knew it was going to be one helluva task to leave Manchester with the trophy.

The players received £50,000 bonus money for reaching the final. That was the same amount we were on for making the Champions League. We were also on £10,000 per win in the group stages. The money in the Champions League is off the radar. But the most important part of it all is the glory that comes with the success on the pitch. That's all that matters. The bonuses are secondary. I was thrilled we were in the UEFA Cup Final and I was determined to be fit to play my part.

Apart from my personal fight for fitness, the club was embroiled in a battle with the football authorities to extend the season to give us a better chance of preparing for the UEFA Cup Final and for the SPL run-in against Celtic. There was a fixture pile up to contend with and we faced eight games in twenty days during the month of May – six league matches, the UEFA Cup

Final and Scottish Cup Final. The club pleaded with the SPL and SFA for an extension to the season. We needed to be given some leeway and after discussions the league season was extended by four days.

Other SPL clubs protested and said it wouldn't be fair. From the players' from the other clubs view, if a lot of them had booked family holidays for the day after the season ended – as many of them do – then it wasn't fair on them to take a financial hit to cancel them. So, there wasn't too much that could be done. The slight extension wasn't ideal but it was something. Still, we were on our knees. It was going to be a schedule too far. It was far too punishing. But it was exciting.

We were on such a high and our fans were in wonderland. It was great to be a part of it all and help bring so much joy to many hundreds of thousands of people around the world. Everybody wanted tickets; it was relentless. Officially, we were given four comps and the opportunity to buy sixteen tickets. But I could have been given 300 tickets and still wouldn't have scratched the surface. It was a stressful time because I tried to accommodate everyone but it was impossible. I felt I let a lot of people down by not getting them tickets but there was nothing I could do. I tried my best.

Obviously I made sure my family were catered for. I hired a stretch-limo for them all to travel down to Manchester for the game. Dad was in his element. He still talks about it to this day. He loved going down the M74 onto the M6 and seeing all the cars, vans and buses decked out in red, white and blue, with plenty Happy Bears aboard. In the early afternoon on the day of the game, they found a massive grass area close to the stadium and sat down and soaked up the sun. They had a few beers and a few sandwiches, enjoying an old-fashioned picnic. And then a football appeared from nowhere. Before they knew it there was a game of football going on and it ended up about twenty-a-side, between the Scots and the Russians. Dad reckoned it was a great way to prepare for the game. And his team won.

On the team bus heading from the hotel to the stadium, I remember being quite overwhelmed by the number of Rangers fans that had made the journey to Manchester. It was an incredible sight, to see every pavement and road packed with our fans. It was an amazing experience. Going into the game, I kept thinking how good it would be to win it for them. But I knew it was a tall order.

Zenit had a brilliant team – Andrei Arshavin and Anatoliy Tymoshchuk were world-class players at that time. They were without their top striker, the suspended Pavel Pogrebnyak, but they were still confident. We had our team shape for the final. That was the way we were for every European game. Walter would walk us through it on the training ground for a maximum of five minutes. He much preferred to pull individuals aside and have a word in their ear, remind them of any specific job they might have been given. We'd watch videos of the opposition, their strengths and weaknesses, and how they went about their business for set-plays.

I was named as a sub. It was the best I could have expected considering I had broken my foot a month earlier. I had about two training sessions and no game time before the final. Manchester City's stadium held happy memories for me as I had played there twice with Wigan. We won both games and I got the winner in the first game, but three-wins-in-a-row it was not to be. It would have been the perfect thirtieth birthday present as well.

We lost 2–0. Zenit dominated the first half without seriously threatening us. Jean-Claude Darcheville forced a good save and Barry Ferguson's shot hit a post. But they scored in the 72nd minute through Igor Denisov. Konstantin Zyryanov side-footed home in the closing minutes to give Zenit their first ever European trophy.

I came on for the last ten minutes as a replacement for Brahim Hemdani. We had a go at them to get an equaliser but it wasn't to be. Unfortunately, we couldn't deliver. We gave it our all, though. The hysteria before and after the game took its toll. There's no doubt being involved in the UEFA Cup Final also cost us the SPL title. Of that I'm absolutely certain. Celtic only had SPL games to concentrate on week to week, but we had a pile up to get through.

Boydy and myself raided Jimmy Bell's room after the UEFA Cup Final. I think we filled a bin-bag each. We got T-shirts, balls – you name it. I didn't exchange jerseys with any of the Zenit players and kept both of my tops. We then went back to the hotel in Manchester and the Gaffer told us we were allowed a few beers but to be mindful of the fact we had a game three days later.

That particular game was away to Motherwell in the SPL. We were dreadful that day. We drew 1–1. Christian Dailly scored with a header for us. Mentally, I think we were finished by then. I felt it had caught up with us. That was the day we lost the SPL title. To be honest, under the circumstances, getting a point at Motherwell was a good result. Motherwell had a few Celtic fans in their team and that was an extra incentive for them. Because of our busy schedule, we hardly had a training session worthy of the name for six weeks. It was just play, then rest and recovery. Teams were fresher than us and, really, should have been beating us, especially on their own pitch. We were falling out of our beds and rolling onto the pitch. We had gone. I felt as though I was on autopilot.

I was nowhere 100 per cent fit at this stage. I hadn't properly recovered from the foot injury I sustained against Celtic five weeks earlier. I should have given it more rest to heal properly but it was too important a stage of the season to miss out. We beat St Mirren 3–0 at Love Street on the Monday night. We went to Aberdeen in second place on the Thursday evening. Celtic were in the driving seat. They only had to defeat Dundee United at Tannadice to lift it. We lost 2–0. Celtic won 1–0 to take the title by three points. It was a quiet journey back down the road from Aberdeen. I hated how I felt and I vowed not to feel as dejected as I did ever again. I used that feeling of dejection to spur me on for the following season. I think we all did.

We played Queen of the South less than forty-eight hours later in the Scottish Cup Final. It was farcical. We all needed a lift. We were down after losing the League. Boydy decided to grow a big Burt Reynolds moustache. He was shaving one day after a shower and kept a 'tache. He had asked me what I thought and I told him to keep it, that it was the type of thing Jimmy Bullard would have done. That was all Boydy needed to hear. He loved my Bullard stories. So if he scored in the final we agreed we had to do a moustache tribute to him. Boyd rattled one in from thirty yards. We went 2–0 up but we collapsed after an hour and they came back to 2–2. Then big 'Burt' popped with a header to win the Cup.

I can't recall a Cup final that we won with a bit of style, where we really trounced the opposition. It was similar in semi-finals at Hampden. We did play well against Celtic but they beat us in injury time; that was in the League Cup Final in 2009. We won the League Cup in 2008 when we beat Dundee United on penalties after a 2–2 draw. I was told to take a penalty but was reluctant to do so. I missed one when I was kid and it left me scarred for life. I spoke to Davie Weir before I was to hit mine and told him I didn't know where I was going to put it. He laughed and said, 'Just put it in the net.' I went down the middle and the keeper saved it. It was a horrible feeling but, thankfully, my mates McGregor and Boydy rescued me and came up trumps in the shoot-out.

It meant we won the two domestic Cups in 2007-08. It promised so much more. We played sixty-eight games that season. I started forty-two, and made eight substitute appearances. Overall it was a brilliant experience, many ups and quite a few downs. I have to give special mentions to Cuellar and Weir. They were exceptional in the centre of defence. McGregor was absolutely solid behind them and that was his first full season as a Rangers goalkeeper.

Gers in Europe

13/02/08
UEFA Cup – Rangers 0 Panathinaikos 0

21/02/08
UEFA Cup – Panathinaikos 1 Rangers 1

06/03/08
UEFA Cup – Rangers 2 Werder Bremen 0

13/03/08
UEFA Cup – Werder Bremen 1 Rangers 0

03/04/08
UEFA Cup – Rangers 0 Sporting Lisbon 0

10/04/08
UEFA Cup – Sporting Lisbon 0 Rangers 2

24/04/08
UEFA Cup – Rangers 0 Fiorentina 0

01/05/08
UEFA Cup – Fiorentina 0 Rangers 0

15/5/08
UEFA Cup Final – Rangers 0 Zenit St Petersburg 2

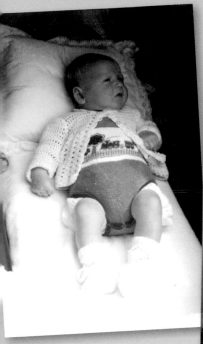

My first pic as a nine-day-old baby after tipping the scales at a healthy 12lb 12oz when I was born in 1978.

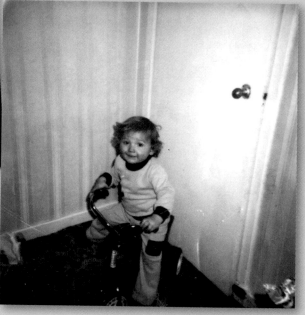

I used to love playing around our house in Wishaw as a toddler when I was just 14 months old.

I was Wishaw's Player of the Year and top scorer at Under-11s.

My first senior goals came in a thrilling 6–2 win for Motherwell against Hibs in 1998 at Fir Park. I came on late in the second half but still bagged two goals.

Scoring for Well in a 3–3 draw at Fir Park in 2000.

I must have impressed against Celtic when I faced them as I'd heard their manager at the time, Kenny Dalglish, was interested in signing me from Motherwell.

My first goal against my heroes at Ibrox in 2000 – what a great feeling!

© PA IMAGES

e and the boys at Wigan romped
r way to the old Division Two title
2003, finishing the season with
impressive 100 points.

I scored the opener and won the
Man of the Match award against
Reading in 2005 on the last day
of the season as Wigan sealed
promotion to the Premiership.

© PA IMAGES

ved mixing with the big guns
the Premiership and they don't
me much bigger than Michael
allack at Stamford Bridge!

The biggest stage in club
football in the Theatre of
Dreams as I help Gers
to a memorable 0–0
Champions League draw
at Old Trafford in 2010.

© PA IMAGES

© PA IMAGES

One of the greatest nights in Scotland's football history as we beat the mighty France 1–0 in Paris in 2007.

It's a dream start to our Euro Qualifier against Ukraine at Hampden as I score to put us 2–0 up after only ten minutes in 2007.

I faced up to ex-Rangers legend Rino Gattuso during a European Qualifier in Italy in 2008.

Celebrating my 100th career goal on my first day as Gers captain. What an amazing feeling.

© WILLIE VASS

It's party time at Tannadice in 2009 as we celebrate our first SPL title in four years with a brilliant 3–0 win.

© SNS PIX

Clydesdale Bank

PREMIER LEAGUE CHAMPIONS 2009/10

Clydesdale Bank PREMIER LEAGUE

RANGERS FOOTBALL CLUB

SEASON 2009/10

Two in a row in 2010 as big Davie Weir leads the sing-song at Ibrox.

Another title, another incredible feeling, as I lift the SPL trophy at Rugby Park in May 2011.

© SNS PIX

© SNS PIX

At Hampden lifting the League Cup trophy with Davie after we win in the final against St Mirren in 2010 – and after being reduced to nine men

Barry Ferguson and I sit dejected as we wait to pick up our losers' medals after the UEFA Cup Final in Manchester.

I learned so much from one of Scotland's greatest ever gaffers.

© SNS PIX

My two boys Callum (left) and Jack (right) sharing the joy as they get their hands on the SPL trophy in 2010.

vital point
Parkhead
2010 as my
ualiser stuns
home fans.

Happier times for
Scotland in 2006 as
we lift the Kirin Cup in
Japan after a 0–0 draw
against the hosts.

My footballing hero Gazza,
looking fit and well as he
returns for a visit to the
Ibrox dressing room.

The McCulloch clan love getting together for big family events.

My brothers Gregor and William and m[...] with our kids. Left to right: Gregor holdin[g] Jack, William, my nephew Mathew, me, a[nd] my nephew Dylan holding Callum. Love[d] hanging out with these guys!

I owe so much to my mum and dad, Iris and John, who were both instrumental in developing me as a player and a man.

Nothing beats spending family time with Amanda and the boys.

Amanda and I enjoy the sunshine in Portugal.

13

THE NIGHT SCOTLAND STUNNED THE WORLD

AS WELL AS Rangers doing well in Europe and winning respect back on that stage, the national team also had some brilliant moments. Walter Smith set the ball rolling on that front and then it was carried on by Alex McLeish, his successor. The highlight of McLeish's tenure was when we beat France 1–0 in September 2007. Just four days before that game we defeated Lithuania 3–1 at Hampden Park. I missed a sitter that day, but we won the game. I missed from three yards when the keeper saved my header. I was gutted. Quite embarrassed, actually. I had put a lot of pressure on myself to get my first international goal and I started to become anxious before and during games because I was still to break my duck.

McLeish subbed me that afternoon and I thought my chance of starting the game in Paris was gone. The night before the match, just as we were walking down the tunnel for our final training session, I pulled the manager to tell him that I wouldn't let him down if he chose me to play the following night. I actually apologised to him for being rotten the previous Saturday. I assured him I was mentally and physically right to play and help get a positive result against the French. Perhaps I sounded desperate, I'm not sure. Frankly, I didn't care. I wanted to play. The manager told me not to worry. He didn't give me any assurances, but I felt quietly confident. He made four changes for the France game and I wasn't one of them. Game on.

In the build-up to that game I was using Faddy's boots to train with. They were nice and comfortable. I felt good in them. I had decided to ditch my own footwear and wear the pair Faddy had given me. I trained with them for the previous two days, but in the build-up to kick-off, he asked for them back. He now wanted to wear them against France. I was gutted, but I couldn't refuse his request as they were his to start with. He also seemed nervous, which was unusual for him. Faddy then swallowed a few ProPlus tablets. I'd never seen anything like it. The wee man obviously was on edge, but six ProPlus? Incredible.

We set up in a 4-5-1 formation and I played left wing, but I was more like a left-back, doubled up to help Graham Alexander to try and keep Lassana Diarra and Franck Ribéry quiet. It was a shift and a half. We were constantly under pressure and only got out of our own half now and again. But the respite was always only for a couple of seconds and then they'd have won back possession and were coming straight back at us. But our defending was heroic and Craig Gordon made at least four outstanding saves. You always have a chance of sneaking something when the game is level. Every team always gets one moment during a game. Ours was a stroke of genius from Faddy. He had the ball inside their half and I remember shouting to him to pass the ball back to me but he took a touch and then rattled it in from the best part of thirty-five yards past Mickaël Landreau. It was unbelievable. What a goal. I'm glad I allowed him to have his boots back! We only had twenty-six minutes to hold out after the goal. No problem!

I feel so proud to have been a part of that team that night. Yet, we really should have been beaten. Trounced, in fact. The France team couldn't believe they lost the game. Our backs were to the wall for almost ninety minutes. Due to their pressure and pressing the ball, we were very poor at keeping possession and that allowed France to come at us in waves of attacks. It was non-stop and there wasn't a second to draw breath. It was such a relief to hear the final whistle. On the bus from the stadium to the airport, it was all very quiet, fairly subdued. We were all too tired to celebrate. I think there was also a feeling of 'did that really just happen?' Faddy offered to give me his boots from that night but I told him it was best he kept them. I think they are now in the SFA Museum. Fitting.

The 'well done' texts arrived from Coisty and many others. We became national heroes and our result made headlines all over Europe. The victory also gave us a really good chance of qualifying for Euro 2008, which was to be held in Switzerland and Austria.

The SFA showed a lovely touch by sending all of the players a beautiful, chunky silver medal with the names of the starting XI engraved around the edges as a memento of the occasion. I have it framed in my house along with my jersey, cap and team photo.

On a personal level, the following month was also special as I scored my first goal for Scotland in a game at home to Ukraine. It came from a set piece we had worked on. The ball came into the box and at the very last minute I lost track of it. That wasn't part of the plan, I must point out. I was unsighted, my view blocked by a Ukraine player. But I knew where the goals were. I made contact with the ball and managed to bend it into the top corner. I ran away and went mental. We won 3–1 for another important victory. Kenny Dalglish phoned me that night to congratulate me. What a feeling!

We took it to the last game of the campaign and we had to beat Italy at Hampden Park. The build-up to the game was incredible. Our base at Cameron House was buzzing all week. The whole country was up for it and tickets weren't available for love nor money. Qualification became a national obsession and there was a lot of pressure on us to deliver. But, hey, we only had the World Champions to beat!

When we got to the stadium, we were visited in the dressing room by Scotland's First Minister, Alex Salmond. He came with a book that had good luck messages and signatures from famous Scots people from all over the world, every one of them a legend, from Billy Connolly to Sir Sean Connery. I felt like stealing the book. Sir Alex Ferguson also came to wish us all good luck before the game.

I was in the team and wanted to be part of an historical occasion. We lost an early goal through Luca Toni when too many of us switched off at a throw-in and Italy punished us. We kept our composure and had the backing of the Tartan Army. The noise they made inside Hampden Park was unbelievable. I had a chance cleared off the line in the first half. Barry Ferguson equalised in the 65th minute and we were back in it. I was involved in the goal. A free-kick came in from Faddy and it was deflected into my path. I tried to shoot but didn't connect correctly with the ball. My first touch wasn't good enough, really. Luckily, Gigi Buffon spilled my shot, the ball broke to Barry and he scored from close range. Brilliant. We then lost a late goal. And another controversial one, too. They were given a free-kick down near the dead-ball line. In my opinion it was a soft award by the Spanish referee, Manuel Gonzalez. We thought Alan Hutton had been fouled and we should have been given the award.

That said, we didn't pick up their men in the box and Italy scored through a Christian Panucci header. It was a huge anti-climax. We lost 2–1 and we were out. The Italians and France qualified from our section. We finished third. Yet another glorious failure.

That evening, I thought about quitting the international scene. Maybe it was time to move on and let one or two of the younger guys progress. I spoke to Faddy about it. At that time, he was the golden boy of Scottish football. The whole country looked to him to produce a piece of magic in every game. I think he got the nickname 'The Fadiator', a name by which I still call him. Faddy told me not to be so stupid and to stay involved. He is a very good friend and I took his advice on board, but there was no doubt I retained a small niggle at the back of my mind. Faddy is like myself and we have a lot in common. He is a top bloke and he is also blessed with a great family.

Although we never qualified, we received some positive coverage throughout that campaign. The win in Paris put us on the map and Alex McLeish's stock rose because of it. Sure, he'd had a successful time as Rangers manager, but a win of that magnitude on the European stage gave him tremendous kudos. A few clubs down south wanted him and he chose to take over at Birmingham City. He attended the draw in South Africa as Scotland boss for the 2010 World Cup qualifying campaign but then flew straight to the Midlands for talks with City. He was gone as national boss a couple of days later. It was a sore one to lose him. Personally, I felt I had a bond with McLeish, from our days going back to Motherwell when he sold me on his ideas for the club. He also told me never to let anyone or anything get in the way of my career. He said I wasn't to turn into a punter down the pub that sits and says that he could have made it at the top level, but ended up on the drink and had too many nights out or had a dodgy game when a scout came to watch. Don't be that guy who failed to make it and does nothing but slag off footballers by saying that he was better than this guy and the next guy. Great advice. I listened from the early days at Fir Park and it helped take me all the way to making a contribution to my country beating a team of the quality of France.

I was disappointed when McLeish resigned as Scotland manager. George Burley was appointed as his successor. I thought about quitting the national team after McLeish left but I decided to stay on. That was a mistake.

14

THE PEP TALK THAT SAVED
MY IBROX CAREER

I FELT I started to struggle to find the necessary form for Rangers in late 2007 and into 2008. There was nothing obvious to people on the outside, but I knew things just weren't right. I had a few wee niggly injuries but that shouldn't have led to my dip in performances. When I got back to fitness I continued to fail to reach the required standard. I couldn't win high balls. I couldn't score goals. I had no assists. I didn't influence any part of a game. I struggled to pass from A to B. My confidence was shattered. I didn't feel like a capable professional footballer. My only contribution was helping Saša Papac in his role at left-back. It killed me. The weeks off-form became months and I couldn't find a way back. The fans picked up on it and they started to turn on me. Yet, the club was heading towards a UEFA Cup Final and going all the way with Celtic for the SPL title. Still, I'd never experienced such a loss of form in my whole career. I just couldn't do anything of note on a match day. I was the same in training. I couldn't even lift my legs at Murray Park. Yet, I still played in almost every game. I couldn't believe Walter Smith still picked me. He must have felt I was just one goal or one good assist away from breaking through that horrendous period.

When I was at Wigan I was a fighter but I felt there was nothing in me to come out battling at Rangers. I went into a shell. I didn't recognise the character I had become. Where was the

Lee McCulloch of old? Where was the Lee McCulloch that came through the system at Motherwell to get a move to England? Where was the Lee McCulloch that helped Wigan climb the divisions into the Premiership? And what happened to the Lee McCulloch that fought his way to get his dream move to Ibrox?

Walter had paid all that money for me and I felt I was letting him down. I watched several foreigners come in, and they would still be laughing and joking after a defeat. It looked as though their attitude was that they were going to get paid their weekly wages regardless of the result. They were able to switch off without a problem. I wasn't like that. I took defeats personally, particularly at Rangers. I took bad results home with me. Amanda and the boys knew to keep out of my road.

I remember many games at Ibrox where I'd be coming in at half-time extremely unhappy with myself. I was constantly concerned about what the Rangers fans were thinking about me. I was out on the left wing and was just an honest pro honoured to wear the jersey, give 100 per cent and make sure I gave my opponent as tough a ninety minutes as he could have expected. But my fear was that the Rangers fans wanted a tricky winger out there, someone who would beat three or four players and whip a ball in for the strikers. I'm sure that's what Kris Boyd wanted too. But I've never beaten a player in my life. That was never my game. I wasn't any good to the team wide left of a four. I've never had pace and been able to take on a defender and whip a ball in. I felt isolated and not in control of my own destiny as a Rangers player. I couldn't see what I was doing at home games to merit my place in the team. Away games were different, because a battle took place, but the onus was on us to attack and entertain at Ibrox.

Two games in my mind really stick out. Lyon at home was tough. Yet, I scored against Lyon away from home. I also felt I had a stinker after we played Hibs at Ibrox in March 2008. We won

2–1 yet that day I sat in the car park with my Rangers suit on and gave myself a right talking-to. I told myself to get my finger out or I was going to ruin things at Rangers. I struggled to cope. I was in tears driving home. I didn't want to let my dad down, didn't want to be seen as a Rangers failure. Some fans were giving my dad a bit of stick in the pub when he was out and about. My brothers were getting it at their work. Fans were on the phone-ins giving me verbal abuse. Going out for dinner with Amanda wasn't a pleasant experience. People said things to me. I was aware my kids were going to be starting school and I didn't want them to be on the receiving end of any verbal abuse. My wee nephew Dylan was going to high school and he also got it in the neck.

People would be shouting, 'You're pish, McCulloch,' stuff like that. It got to me. 100 per cent. But I always knew it would never totally defeat me and grind me into the ground. My biggest concern and fear was what it might do to my family. I didn't want any of them subjected to taunts or being dragged into any unnecessary situations. That would have destroyed me. I knew I'd handle it in my own way, but could they? It was horrible. I didn't mind the flak – I could handle it, but it made me ill at ease when my family were being picked on. I wanted to take the whole burden on. That drove me on more than anything. I knew I had to get my head right and move onwards and upwards. But it wasn't a good time. I felt helpless. Maybe I was trying too hard, I just don't know. What I do know is that the world of football can be a horrible environment and an unforgiving place.

I was in tears on at least three occasions in my car on the way home from games. I suppose every footballer has lows but I took it to heart because it was the club I wanted to play for and do well for. There was so much riding on being a success. It reached the stage where I didn't want to leave the house. I would have been happy to become a recluse. The Scottish mentality may also be that people like giving you a wee kick when you're down. They rarely congratulate you when you're doing well, but they're not slow to let you know if they feel you're not performing to a high standard.

I felt awful. Walter took me out of the team and I was named as a sub for a few games. I was then dropped from the bench and sat in the stands. It was going to go one of two ways for me – I either cut my losses and asked to get away to start afresh elsewhere or I got my head sorted out and made sure I battled through it. I decided on the latter option.

I also considered turning to a psychologist. I moved into rented accommodation in Lanarkshire when I rejoined Rangers. I was getting into my car one morning and a neighbour approached me, introduced himself and said he was a sports psychologist. He told me if I ever needed any help from him then to feel free to ask. I was sure one day I'd take him up on his offer. I never got round to doing it. I don't think there is any harm in sitting down with these guys but I was intent on getting through it on my own.

We lost the SPL title on the last day of the season. We lost to Aberdeen and Celtic beat Dundee United. I wasn't even on the bench for that game up there. In many ways, the end of the season came as a relief. I decided to go away, have a good break and sort my head out. My consolation was that if I could play in the Premiership then I had to be able to handle the SPL. I also had been through this scenario before. I was poor at the start when I first joined Wigan. I cost them more than £700,000 and couldn't handle it. I was going down there, perceived as a minimum twenty-goal-a-season man. I'm never that, but that played on me. I then found different positions away from being a centre-forward. I was scared I might be put up for sale by the club in the summer, that Walter wouldn't want me and no longer regarded me as an asset.

The football in the Premiership is different from the SPL.

Down south there is more time to play and more time on the ball. We had a rigid formation at Wigan and we liked to counter-attack. At Rangers the onus was on us to take the game to the opposition and make things happen. If we managed to sneak a draw here and there at Wigan in the Premiership then we would be lauded. At Rangers, if we dropped two points in any game we had an axe hanging over our heads and the media and supporters would claim we simply weren't good enough. There was very rarely any middle ground when it came to the opinion of people outside of the dressing room and manager's office. But the standard of sides in the SPL was good and it was disrespectful not to praise the opposition, especially if we got a draw at Fir Park or Tannadice or Tynecastle. The opposition were always pumped up to play us and they would have had a good win bonus to beat us, and there may also have been the added edge for some of them if they were Celtic fans and really wanted to put us down.

It was important to make sure I was back to full fitness after breaking my foot in an Old Firm game. I wanted to have a right good bang at it. People said Walter was being too loyal to me and I wasn't repaying him. But he showed confidence in me. I appreciated that. Sir David Murray pulled me aside in July 2008 and told me he had rejected a £1.5 million bid from Stoke City. He told me at Murray Park and he assured me I was to be a big part of the future at Rangers.

I spoke to Emile Heskey after I left Wigan and he asked me how I was getting on back up in Scotland. I told him it was great to be at Rangers but I was struggling to cope. For example, I went out for something to eat in Glasgow with Amanda and had a burger and chips in front of me, and within two minutes a guy came over, pulled up a chair and started eating my chips whilst telling me how good or bad a player I was. Emile has played for some massive clubs, such as Liverpool and for England, but even he had never encountered anything like that. There is no hiding place in the West of Scotland. When you play for Rangers your life is not your own. I think Tommy Burns once said that being an Old Firm player can be the best job in the world but can also be the most difficult to cope with as one half of Glasgow hates you and the other half think they own you. Funny but in some ways true.

The new season got off to a shocking start for the whole club. We lost to Kuanas in the Champions League qualifier. I had to get my finger out. We all did. A few games into the season I felt I was still not getting it right. I was depressed and had been for a number of months. I took my work home with me. During some of my really low moments, I had to find a release and I went on a few benders. My world was caving in – and I don't use that terminology lightly. I tried my best to stay strong and keep the people I trusted close to me. To help me cope and blank it out, I found myself going out for a few sessions on the drink. I thought it would help me come through the other side. Eventually. I knew I should have looked at other ways to cope with being down, but this was the simplest way of dealing with it. Nothing was going right on the park. I wasn't out every day but I would engineer a fall-out with Amanda so that I could escape and get to the pub. It's amazing how the self-doubt disappears after a few bottles of beer and a few vodkas, but I knew that going on benders would not sort it out long-term.

So I asked the manager if I could have a meeting with him. I spent the best part of half an hour with him, really opened up to him. I told him I felt my first season was a failure and that I was desperate to be a success at Rangers. I asked him to stick with me and to be patient. I assured him I would come good. He said, 'Jig, I know you will. I trust you. I brought you here for the long haul. I've seen players struggle to find their feet in the past but it works out in the end. You'll be the same. Relax and you will be a big player in this club's future.' He showed so much faith in me and he made me feel a million dollars. My confidence was high again. I felt a weight lifted from my shoulders, it was great. I came out of his office reborn and I never looked back. Great man-management. Without doubt, that little chat saved my Rangers career.

Part of our discussion was that he would play me as a sitting midfielder and at centre-half. He told me I was the one player in the dressing room that knew the game inside out. It was going to be a challenge because I'd played 95 per cent of my career in offensive positions. I was on the pitch to try and hurt the opposition. Now I was going to try and nullify them. He was true to his word and played me in both positions a few times. I enjoyed them. That was a turning point.

When I came out the office I phoned my brother Wullie. He knew I was buzzing, and was delighted for me after everything I'd been through. I was privileged to play for Walter – and of course for Ally, Kenny and Durranty – and he helped bring so much success to my working life. A European final and three league titles. My Scotland career also took off under him. I owe him so much. Even in the hospitality lounges at Ibrox he would always take time to speak to my parents and my brothers. And when my Rangers career got back on track I knew I couldn't do anything to jeopardise that. I had momentum in my game and I was relaxed. I felt good for the first time in long while. So, to avoid any chance of slipping back into a loss of form and any risk of depression, I decided to quit playing for Scotland.

15

WHY I WAS NEVER UP FOR THE CAP WITH BURLEY

MY EARLY impressions of George Burley were not good. I often thought he had a lack of belief in himself. Maybe that was because it was international management and not club management at which he'd been successful at Ipswich and Hearts. It started to go downhill very quickly under his leadership. It was quite alarming, actually. The discipline pretty much went out the window. Things started to happen that would never have been tolerated by Walter Smith or Alex McLeish. You know how it is when people, none more so than footballers, try to nick a mile if they think they've been given an inch. It was as if there wasn't the need to be at meetings on time. I'm not quite sure how to describe it, really put my finger on it, but it just wasn't right.

He seemed very nervous when addressing the players during team meetings at the hotel. He would get players' names mixed up. He sort of stuttered and was never convincing. He had a saying and we used to try and guess how many times he would say it before we went into the meeting. It was too easy to be unprofessional during Burley's time. Of course, he can't be blamed totally for that, as players need to be responsible for their own actions.

He brought in Terry Butcher as his assistant and Steven Pressley as a coach. I had massive respect for big Terry. Pressley was just thirty-three at the time and playing for Celtic. I didn't have a problem with Pressley but a few of the players did. It wasn't Pressley's fault. I'm not having a go at him. He was there to do a job and he tried to do it, but he should never have been put in that position.

Players sense when a manager has a weakness in his make-up. Some will pounce on it and others will make allowances. Too many players attempted to take advantage of Burley and they would be answering back during team meetings. They often disagreed with things Burley and Pressley would say. The atmosphere could often be cut with a knife.

We had a few beers one night at Cameron House during a squad get-together. We were a close squad and it was really a catch-up. Myself, Faddy, big Davie and one or two others were there. Pressley came in and asked us all to drink up and get to bed. We basically told him that we weren't leaving the bar as many of us hadn't seen each other in ages and we fancied a catch-up and that we were going to sit on and relax over a beer. He more or less pleaded with us and I felt sorry for him at that point. It wasn't fair on him, but we never moved. On reflection, and I can only speak for myself, I was wrong that night. I should have gone to bed, but that was the way it was under Burley and his assistants – there wasn't enough authority from them and too many players didn't respect them enough.

Pressley left the bar defeated. Nobody was nasty to him, but nobody was for following his instructions either. Big Terry then came in and asked us to drink up. Faddy played under him at Motherwell and they had a good working relationship. The next thing I knew, after a wee bit of coaxing from Faddy, Terry sat down with us for a few beers. Nobody was drunk and nobody was loud. But we had another couple of pints with him. It was a good laugh. Terry is someone I respect and look up to.

Pressley was very hands-on with the squad. He would take us for the warm-ups. I think a few of the boys resented that and a few really started to dislike him. I know a few of the boys were thinking, 'Who the fuck do you think you are, ordering us about?' which either way could be perceived as wrong, but maybe some boys just weren't having him. Pressley is a nice guy. He had a good career and I was okay with him when we played together. He looks as though he is going to have a very good career in management.

It was pretty much at that point I decided it was time to go. I could only see troubled times ahead. To be perfectly honest, I thought it was a bit of a shambles and I didn't want to be a part of it.

I rarely, if ever, spoke to Burley so I can't judge him as a person. I can only judge him as a manager. There wasn't a working relationship between us. He made my mind up for me that I should quit. He never made me feel welcome. He'd speak to a few of the lads but always ignored me, I don't know why, but it made me feel uncomfortable. If he didn't fancy me then he should have told me. Yet, he still picked me for his squads. It was quite strange, really. I just had a feeling we were never going to progress under him. Sure, Smith and McLeish were hard acts to follow, but Burley never got to grips with the job. I thought he was a bit of a bluffer. I wanted out, away from his set-up. It lacked professionalism and I was convinced we'd never reach the heights of the previous couple of years when we beat France home and away. It was also important for me to concentrate on getting things right at Rangers and that had to come before anything else. I decided to get out. I never played one game for Burley.

In the past, some players had had a quiet word with Walter and Alex, just to say to them they didn't want to be picked, but they'd be happy to help out in an emergency.

My immediate point of contact to make my feelings known was SFA employee Richard Simpson. He was the middleman between the players and coaching staff. It was a telephone conversation in the build-up to the opening games of the 2010 World Cup qualifying campaign. Scotland had a double-header, away to Macedonia and Iceland in early September 2008. I wasn't in the squad as I was injured.

I told him to pass on the message to George about my standing down from the international scene, but for whatever reason the message never got to Burley. I'd followed the protocol but, with the benefit of hindsight, I should just have phoned George myself.

At the time I thought things had all been taken care of, but they hadn't. I'd just thought that Burley had got the message and had chosen not to phone me to discuss it. When things then blew up, I felt like I'd been really let down. I wasn't pleased with Richard about what happened but we've had a chat about it since and we're now absolutely fine with one another. And, on reflection, the whole situation was my fault and I have to accept full responsibility for what followed. Really, I should just have missed out Richard and telephoned the manager directly.

The next thing I knew the press had got a hold of the story and all hell broke loose because Burley knew nothing about it. I then became a villain. I was accused of walking out on my country and not wanting to play for Burley. It was totally misconstrued. I got pelters. It got so bad I had to send Amanda away on holiday with the kids and her family. I felt it was better for everyone to be out of the way so I could deal with it myself.

It was a tricky one for me. There was so much I wanted to come out and say but then I also felt that it would be best if I kept quiet in the hope that it would all be forgotten about.

I spoke to Walter about it and asked for his advice. I told him all I told the SFA was that I didn't want to be considered for future squads. However, if they were ever stuck then I'd be happy to come back and help out in an emergency situation, similar to what plenty of players had done in the past. I decided to do an interview with Rangers TV in a bid to put the record straight. We agreed on the questions beforehand and I knew the answers I was going to give so I could try and get my points across very clearly.

One of the answers I gave to a question was, 'I feel like the whole country hates me because of my decision.' In my opinion I wasn't doing anything wrong. I felt the national team was going downhill and I didn't want to be part of it, but I never said that I was retiring from international football or would never again play for Burley. If circumstances arose in the future that meant I would have been required, then I would have reported for duty. Absolutely. However, I also felt the time was right to concentrate fully on Rangers and try to kick on at Ibrox. I was just not on form at Rangers and I had to be doing much better.

Of course, the newspapers picked up on my interview with Rangers TV and printed it all. Simpson got back in touch and claimed that I did not tell him I wanted to finish with the national team. We had a big fall-out and it all got a bit heated. Plenty was said but, ultimately, I should have made sure myself that the manager had got the message.

The whole situation has now blown over and we are okay again with each other. During my time with Scotland, Richard was always professional and good at his job.

Burley then phoned me and I explained everything to him. He told me I was going to be a part of his plans and he wanted me back. But I had made my decision and I wasn't for going back on it.

I was lambasted all over the country. Radio phone-ins, newspapers, television, they all had a go. I felt I was hung out to dry. There was no protection. I had to take it on the chin and I found it difficult.

My wee nephew got bullied at school. He'd not long started high school. A few of his pals were asking him, 'Who the hell does your uncle think he is?' That was tough on us all. I felt ever so sorry for him, but the whole sorry episode made me a stronger person. I had to really learn how to deal with things. It was the toughest spell of my international career, without a doubt.

On the park it started to go much more to plan. I felt I started to play really well for Rangers. I was relaxed and felt I had the right to wear that jersey.

Craig Levein took over from Burley in December 2009. Burley was sacked. The results he had as manager were very poor. I'd heard from one or two people that Levein was keen to get me back involved. Through a third party, contact was made and I made it 100 per cent clear I'd be delighted to go and play for him and Scotland if he wanted me. I knew I would get pelters from some people because they would not be moved on their opinion I had walked out on my country under Burley. I had a feeling some flak would come my way but I was willing to put up with it. My conscience was clear.

I was included in Levein's first squad, a friendly game against the Czech Republic at Hampden Park. Unfortunately I couldn't play in the game but I reported for duty to be checked out by the SFA medical team. It was also a chance to meet Levein and his backroom staff. After being out of the international team for a while I was thrilled to be back involved and I enjoyed my three days with the squad.

It also marked the return of Allan McGregor and Kris Boyd. Boyd also quit when Burley was manager. McGregor was banned by the SFA for his part in Boozegate. I'm not blaming Allan or Barry Ferguson for what happened during that sorry episode. To be honest, I was out of the international team by then, but I do know they felt they were hung out to dry as a few others were involved in that booze session at Cameron House after a 3–0 defeat to Holland in Amsterdam in March 2009. The team flew home right after the game and quite a few of them went straight to the bar for an almighty session. Some were just more cute than others.

That episode told me that the discipline had gone completely. Fact. I accept players have a responsibility to be professional, but there was clearly a lack of respect from too many players towards Burley, something I sensed from early on in his tenure and that's another reason why I felt it was best to get out when I did. I knew I was right at the time, and I stand by that.

Levein had a good track record in management and I felt this was going to be a new challenge for me. I was buzzing. I played in three Euro 2012 qualifiers for him – away to Lithuania in a 0–0 draw and a 2–1 home win against Liechtenstein. My last ever cap was in the 3–2 home defeat to World Champions Spain in October 2010. I should have played more times for Craig but I had to pull out of a few squads with injury. On one occasion – in the build-up to a friendly away to Sweden in August 2010 – I withdrew because I thought I'd had a heart attack.

I was suspended for the first two league games of the SPL season and this international game would have given me the chance to play a game. We were to report for duty on the Sunday afternoon. I was in the house on the previous evening and all of a sudden I felt pains in my chest, and I struggled for breath. Amanda phoned NHS 24 and when she told them the symptoms over the phone they told her they were sending an ambulance. We didn't want to alarm the kids so we decided it was best to take the car to Wishaw Hospital. They ran tests and kept me in. I was scared. The tests showed up that I had a viral infection from my time in Australia with Rangers during pre-season. It was in my system and it decided to strike that night. I don't know how I picked it up and I never will. I stayed in hospital for two or three days and I phoned Craig Levein to explain. He understood the severity of the situation.

Things improved under Levein but he and the players were

just not able to keep it going over a period and he lost his job in November 2012. I felt for him. Levein always phoned me to explain why I was being left out. That's why I totally respect him. He never ignored me. That's all a player can ask for. My time with Scotland has come and gone. I feel proud and privileged to have represented my country on eighteen occasions. I enjoyed almost every minute of it.

Gordon Strachan is the new manager and I wish him well. It's time for a new breed of players to come through and I hope they can achieve what everyone in our country desperately wants and that is qualifying for the 2016 European Championship Finals in France.

16

WALTER'S WINNERS

AFTER THE disappointment of losing the title to Celtic in 2008, there was a determination not to let it happen again, to the point where, for me, it became an obsession. That particular mindset started on the bus journey home from Pittodrie the night we lost to Aberdeen 2–0 and Gordon Strachan's men won the SPL after defeating Dundee United. Few words were spoken as we made our way back through the roads of Dundee, Perth and Stirling before we arrived at Ibrox Stadium at around 2am. I felt the resolve develop in my own mind and could see it in others, from Davie Weir to Allan McGregor, to Barry Ferguson and Kris Boyd. We weren't going to lose again. It was time for us to put a marker down. It dominated my thoughts during the summer.

The manager was given funds to spend in the transfer market and added Kenny Miller, Pedro Mendes, Kyle Lafferty and Andrius Velička. Steve Davis also made his loan move from Fulham permanent. We were sorry to lose Carlos Cuellar to Aston Villa for around £7 million as he was a brilliant player for us. But we replaced him with the charismatic and highly-capable Madjid Bougherra.

Before I go any further, I must tell a funny tale about Madjid. He got a good spell for Rangers. He was a confident player and the fans took to him. So did the players. But after a couple of years it appeared he wanted a move to try something different. He thought the 2010 World Cup in South Africa would be the perfect platform for him to show off his talents. Algeria's opening game of the tournament was against England. He was to man-mark Wayne Rooney. A solid performance could have clubs lining up for him, but he was a little conscious about his weight so before the game I heard he wrapped his tummy and chest in cling film to make it look as though his physique was better than what it actually was!

On a more serious note . . . We were dealt a crushing blow in the Champions League qualifier when we lost to FBK Kaunas 2–1 on aggregate. We drew 0–0 in the first leg at Ibrox but we were still confident of completing the job in Lithuania a week later, on 5 August. We took the lead through Kevin Thomson in the first half but they levelled just before the interval and scored the winner in the 87th minute. It was a disaster for the club's credibility and finances as we were all well aware at that stage the club was in a fragile financial state and Sir David Murray was willing to sell to the right buyer, a person capable of taking the club forward.

Walter Smith gave the players both barrels at full-time that night. I doubt the away dressing room at the rickety Darius and Girėnas Stadium had ever seen such scenes before. As a manager, Walter had the fear factor in him, to the point you knew at any time he could go off his head. On a few occasions when I thought he was going to go off on one, I was ready to duck for cover, picking my spot in the dressing room that would have seen me out of harm's way. That evening in Kaunas was the angriest I've ever witnessed him. It was our first tie in Europe after getting to the UEFA Cup Final and there's a point of view that we were still physically tired from the sixty-eight games the previous season and also mentally gubbed after losing out on the SPL title. None of that mattered a jot to the manager and was all an excuse anyway.

After the game he was going off his head. His face was like a tomato, veins popping out of his neck. There was a teapot within his reach and a few plates of sandwiches. He picked up the teapot and, like in a discus-style technique, he threw it against a wall behind him. It just missed our kit man Jimmy Bell's head by a matter of inches. Our masseur, big Davie Lavery, dived out the way, as if it was a hand-grenade ready to explode. It was strange to see a teapot bounce off a wall – not something that tends to happen every day in your kitchen! Walter went on to absolutely nail Kevin Thomson for his performance. He then gave a serious tongue-lashing to most players, one by one, and as he was getting closer and closer to me, I could feel my head drooping further and further, to the point it was buried into my knees. I had my eyes closed. I was scared. I got the verbals too.

On the flight home few words were spoken. I had to do the media after that game and I made it clear that the result wasn't acceptable for a club the size of Rangers and we had to realise that very quickly. Second best is never good enough. I had to get my finger out. We all did.

We had to focus entirely on the domestic campaign and that wasn't such a bad thing. After all, we had to win the title. It couldn't be any other way. We had taken seven points from our opening three SPL games, which was acceptable, but we know we are judged on Old Firm games and we faced Celtic at Parkhead in game four on 31 August. We won 4–2. We battered Celtic that day. Daniel Cousin was brilliant and scored the opening goal. He terrorised the Celtic defence. Kenny Miller came back to haunt his old club and grabbed a double. Pedro Mendes scored our other goal with one of the finest Old Firm goals ever seen, a raker from twenty-five yards. At full-time that afternoon the message was loud and clear: we were taking the title back.

Cousin was sold that night – transfer deadline day – to Hull City for around £3 million. It was a wonderful farewell present from him. What a player he was, but he was also a complex character and an unpredictable professional. Some days at training he was brilliant, other days he didn't give a toss. He was very frustrating to play with and, I'm sure, to manage. We just had to put up with it. He didn't have a great work ethic but when he was in the mood, when he was angry, he was a top striker. His first touch, strength, pace and heading ability were outstanding. He was as good as any striker I've played with.

The title race with Celtic was neck and neck, and it was vital to beat them in Old Firm games. They came to our place on 27 December and we expected to win. We lost 1–0 to a Scott McDonald goal. That put us seven points behind Celtic. It wasn't a good position to be in. It was important to win our next game and we went to Inverness and defeated them 3–0. By the time we next played Celtic we got a 0–0 draw at Parkhead and they were only two points clear. They were in our sights. We racked up six wins in a row in the league during April and early May to leave us just a point behind them. They were starting to crumble; we could sense it. We knew it and we had to take advantage.

We beat them 1–0 on 9 May. Steve Davis got our goal. We were now two points ahead with three games to go. In our next game we drew 1–1 at Hibs and Nacho Novo scored, but we'd lost our place at the top of the table on goal difference as Celtic had won twenty-four hours earlier against Dundee United. But when you get down to the nitty-gritty you need to have the mental strength to cope and we beat Aberdeen 2–1 at Ibrox on the penultimate weekend of the season. Celtic drew 0–0 at Hibs. We were back on top, two points in front.

The final game was at Dundee United and we knew a win would see us crowned champions for the first time since 2007. We were nervous but confident. Kyle Lafferty gave us an early lead. Mendes put us 2–0 ahead by half-time. Boydy wrapped it up with a third. We were the Champions, and deservedly so. I came on as a sub that day, as did Barry Ferguson, and it felt great to be a part of it all. When I was fit, Walter always made sure I was involved in all the big games, and that meant a lot to me. Considering what I had been through the previous season, with my crash in confidence and form, I felt great being a part of a title winning side. I felt a weight had been lifted from my shoulders. Needless to say, we partied for a few days to celebrate our title success.

We then won the Scottish Cup to make it a Double. It was brilliant. Another Cup success at Hampden. We didn't play particularly well against Falkirk but we got the win we needed, thanks to a Nacho Novo goal. It was a brilliant strike from twenty-five yards just after half-time. That success also sticks out for Kris Boyd. The season before he hogged the headlines for his goals and his moustache and it was the same this time, but for different reasons.

Boydy got whipped off at half-time. It was almost 100 degrees on the pitch that afternoon and, as far as Boydy was concerned, far too hot to play football. He sat in the dressing room at the interval and the sweat was lashing off him. His face was beetroot. We were shocking in the first half. Walter stormed in, and without a second of hesitation, pointed at Boydy and said, 'Right, you're off.' Boydy walked straight into the shower and stuck his head on a bag of ice to cool down. We were all pissing ourselves laughing. We managed to win the Cup and I was delighted. After the game, back at Ibrox for the party, we all had a laugh about what happened at half-time. Walter took a bit of stick and so did Boydy. The banter was flying. I told Boydy he only wanted to come off because he was hungry!

Personally, it felt good to end the season that way. I was much happier with myself than I was a year earlier. I felt I made a good contribution and was playing the way I should have been playing. To get my first Championship medal with Rangers made it all worthwhile. The full coaching staff were amazing.

We had some really good players at Rangers that year and we had to withstand stiff opposition from Celtic, but we were a better team than them and we deserved the title.

I really enjoyed playing with Pedro Mendes. Pedro was the type of player that would let me have the ball in a deep position and he would find a dangerous area to operate in in the opposition half. He liked to link with the strikers and also thread an eye-of-the-needle pass in the final third. He'd allow me to break up the opposition play and then play a forward pass, whether it was to a wide player or through the middle to him. He had exceptional ability. The downside to Pedro's game was that he hardly ever put in a tackle. He wouldn't go in where it hurt, that was for sure. If I played alongside Barry Ferguson or Kevin Thomson in the central midfield area then they wanted to drop really deep and it meant the partnership wasn't as effective although they were two quality players.

I also enjoyed playing with DaMarcus Beasley, who always stayed out wide and offered himself to receive a pass. And Steve Davis made things happen. He is a top, top player. He has the lot in his locker. Stevie Naismith was brilliant too. He arrived for £2 million from Kilmarnock and it took him a while to settle. Trying to find him a position in the team that suited him most was the biggest problem. He was also very unlucky with injury. He wasn't the tallest but he was fantastic in the air. He has a lovely spring and could out-jump players five or six inches taller than him.

Boydy was also brilliant for us. For all the stick he received, he scored when it mattered and bagged thirty-four goals for us in 2008-09 to finish top scorer. Sure, Boydy was a complete enigma. I'd do twice the running I'd usually do because he was in the team, but I didn't mind because I knew if the ball dropped in the box then he would score. Boydy had been targeted by a few clubs during that season, Alex McLeish's Birmingham City being the leading contenders, and they were willing to pay £3 million for him. Rangers found that to be an acceptable fee. Boydy, however, couldn't agree personal terms.

The club were keen to cash in on him. Rangers needed to bring in funds. The players were aware that was the case but it became clear during the 2009-10 season when we were defending our title. The manager was firefighting against the bank. The bank wanted the debt reduced and that meant there was pressure to reduce the wage bill and get players out the door. As the months wore on, the financial situation was well documented, albeit I never felt worried in any way when Sir David Murray was owner that the club would fold or go into administration.

Lloyds Bank had a huge say in the running of the club and it was clear to all that they wanted to reduce the club debt by millions of pounds to make it a more attractive proposition to any potential buyer. But, most of the time, everything seemed calm and normal. Walter was involved in a lot of it and it must have been hard for him to try and deal with all the stuff behind the scenes. But he hid it well from the players and protected us from all the off-field financial matters.

During the summer of 2009 a number of players were sold and moved on to help reduce the debt. We lost the likes of Barry Ferguson, Brahim Hemdani and Charlie Adam. The manager only had the funds to bring in one player, Jerome Rothen on loan from Paris Saint Germain. It wasn't ideal but we never felt sorry for ourselves. Towards the end of August, Sir David Murray stepped down as chairman and was replaced by the highly respected businessman Alastair Johnston. He made it clear his priority was to find a buyer for Murray's shares. But the club struggled with its finances and in November a debt of around £31 million was announced. It was a matter of concern for Lloyds Bank and they had the books under close scrutiny. During that period it led Walter to go public on the financial situation we were embroiled in and say that the bank was 'effectively running the club'.

The club at least had the knowledge it was going to bank a minimum of £10 million from the Champions League campaign. We were drawn against Seville, Stuttgart and Unirea Urziceni. We had a shocking campaign, though, and finished bottom of our section with just two points from the six matches. That particular campaign and losing to Kaunas in 2008 are real low points from my career. I wish I could erase them from my mind completely. Unfortunately, the lows seem to have stayed and haunted me. But the priority every year is to win the League Championship and we wanted to retain the title. Across the city, our rivals Celtic replaced Gordon Strachan with Tony Mowbray.

Our first league game was at home to Falkirk and we celebrated the unfurling of the flag with a 4–1 win. I scored our opening goal. The following week we went to Hearts and won 2–1. I scored our equaliser and Boydy got the winner from the penalty spot. We beat Hamilton the next weekend and followed that up with three consecutive 0–0 draws. It was then Old Firm time and we beat Celtic 2–1 at Ibrox. Kenny Miller got a double. We were in control at the top of the table and Celtic weren't proving to be serious challengers. Under Mowbray they talked a good game but they failed to produce when it mattered. We knew we were more than capable of brushing them aside.

On 30 December we beat Dundee United 7–1 at Ibrox. Boydy scored five goals that day. It was a brilliant achievement. The win also set us up nicely for going to Parkhead on 3 January. We were seven points ahead of them in the table and we knew that as long as we avoided defeat we'd be fine. Celtic dominated possession, without hurting us, but they took the lead through Scott McDonald in the 79th minute. I then equalised two minutes later with a header from a Steve Davis corner. I felt brilliant. It was a really important goal and I was delighted. Job done. When

I felt I had played well, I used to like to go home and give myself a wee treat of a glass of red wine and a Cadbury's Caramel! I used to say to big Davie Weir that I couldn't wait to get home to get wired in. He'd just laugh and ask if I dunked the chocolate in my vino!

We were on our way to the title and wrapped it up with three league games to spare on 25 April with a 1–0 at Hibs. Kyle Lafferty scored our goal. I played at centre-half that afternoon and it was new to me but I enjoyed the experience and it was nice to keep a clean sheet.

We kept up our proud record of two trophies per season by winning the League Cup again. We faced St Mirren at Hampden in the final. I was always excited about Cup finals. It was similar to an Old Firm game in terms of the level of expectation. As soon as I woke up, that was me, bang at it, and kick-off couldn't come quickly enough. But there was also that extra pressure that came with a showpiece game at Hampden. We knew we were expected to win and if we did there wouldn't be too many plaudits handed out. In contrast, we had it all to lose and there was no doubt we'd get it in the neck from all angles if we lost the game. I knew St Mirren were going into the match with nothing to lose. They would be legends if they won and it would only be a quick pat on the back for us if we won.

We didn't play well in the first half. We were well off it. Even the St Mirren lads appeared off the boil. Referee Craig Thomson sent off Kevin Thomson in the first half to leave us down to ten men.

Walter wasn't happy with our performance. As had become the norm at the national stadium, Walter was ready to give us both barrels at half-time. Walter didn't mess about. He ripped into us. In two stages. He told us we were a disgrace and questioned our desire to win the trophy. He then said, or more like screamed at us, 'Listen, I'm not sure how many medals I've won with Rangers, it might be nineteen, but don't dare come back in this fucking door unless another one is added to the total.' He then disappeared and came back in two minutes later. He started again and a few players were left in no doubt what he thought of them. He then said, 'I've got eighteen medals with Rangers and I want it to be nineteen. Now, the lot of you, fuck off. Get out there and win the Cup.' He must have left the dressing room to count his winners' total or get someone to verify it for him! Either way, brilliant.

Due to us being a man down, Walter pulled me aside and told me we were going to a back three and I was to drop back in there and play in defence.

It went from bad to worse out on the pitch. Danny Wilson then got sent off. We were down to nine men. In a Cup final. It was a case of defending for our lives and trying to buy time. We'd have been happy with penalties, under the circumstances. With a two-man advantage the expectation levels were now with St Mirren. It was a role-reversal. St Mirren had it in their grasp to win the Cup. They had to come and break us down though, and they didn't manage it. They didn't play as well as they could have and should have. I think they froze and didn't have the necessary togetherness and belief on the pitch to take advantage. Perhaps that scenario highlights the point I have made about the mentality required to cope with the demands of being a Rangers player. You have to deliver. Failure isn't an option.

So, it flashed through my mind that we were going to have to face one angry manager at full-time. I thought having to beat a team in a Cup final when we only had nine men was probably going to be too much for us, although I hadn't thrown in the towel. As long as it stayed 0–0 and we didn't take any chances at the back. And then we scored. Davie Weir passed to Stevie Naismith. His cross was met by Kenny Miller and he headed past Paul Gallacher. We didn't really celebrate. We wanted to save our energy to keep a clean sheet.

Saints had Michael Higdon and Billy Mehmet up front and both were powerful players. They loved a battle and loved attacking a high ball. It was left to me and big Davie Weir to try and stop them. It wasn't an easy shift. St Mirren had the bulk of possession but couldn't break us down. They ended up launching the ball but we held out and won the game over ninety minutes. It was an incredible feeling to win against the odds. Outwith beating Celtic and lifting an SPL title, that Cup win was as satisfied as I've ever felt as a Rangers player.

To win another Double was impressive and to do it with a tight squad made it all the better. We had to do without Pedro Mendes in the second half of the season as he was sold to Sporting Lisbon during the January transfer window. We had many heroes that season but special mention to the strike partnership of Boyd and Miller. They notched forty-four between them the previous season and followed it up with forty-seven in the 2009-10 campaign. Boydy was top scorer yet again with twenty-six.

Season 2010-11 was an almighty campaign for so many reasons. It was Walter's last season in charge and we wanted to do three-in-a-row for him. Celtic would come at us with fresh belief and vigour after they replaced Mowbray with Neil Lennon, but we were ready, knowing Neil would have the players up for it.

We lost a few players during the summer. Boydy left on a Bosman to head down to Middlesbrough. On a professional and personal level, I was sorry to see him go. We also sold Kevin Thomson to Middlesbrough for £2 million and Danny Wilson moved to Liverpool for a similar fee. It gave the manager some funds to play with and he freshened up the squad by signing Nikica Jelavič and James Beattie. Vladimir Weiss joined us on loan from Manchester City.

We were probably short on numbers in the squad but we had plenty quality. We won our first eight SPL games, as did Celtic, and it meant something had to give in the first Old Firm game of the 2010-11 season. We won 3–1. A Kenny Miller double and a Glenn Loovens own goal cancelled out Gary Hooper's opener. We lost the next two Old Firm games and drew the final encounter between us 0–0 at Ibrox. Allan McGregor saved a penalty from Georgios Samaras. It was a crucial save from the reliable keeper. Celtic were in the driving seat but we never gave up and our determination and quality got us into a position of being one point ahead of them with three games to go. We beat Hearts 3–0 and Dundee United 2–0 to take us into the last game at Kilmarnock. Again, a win made sure the title stayed at our place, regardless of what Celtic were able to do at home to Hearts.

It was a sweet, sweet day. We were three goals up inside eight minutes and won the game 5–1. I loved it. It was brilliant. For me, it was all about Walter Smith that day. He is Mr Rangers and he deserved to bow out with another title – the club's 54th – and also the League Cup in the bag after we defeated Celtic 2–1 at Hampden.

It was also important we gave a good account of ourselves in Walter's final European adventure with the club. We were in the Champions League and came out in Group C alongside Manchester United, Valencia and Bursaspor. It was an attractive section in many different ways and I was particularly excited about the Battle of Britain clash against Sir Alex Ferguson's men.

We opened our campaign at Old Trafford on 14 September 2010. A few days before that we were at Hamilton Accies on SPL duty and we won 2–1. I was a sub that day, as was Kenny Miller, as Walter told us he was resting us for the game at Old Trafford. We both came on at 1–1 and I set up Kenny to score a wonderful winner. It sent us down south in good spirits but we knew we faced an almighty challenge to avoid defeat in the Theatre of Dreams. I had played there before with Wigan and I was relishing the occasion. I wanted to make sure I enjoyed it. And I did.

We drew 0–0. We battled hard to keep them at bay and the whole team put in a terrific shift. It was one of our best ever results to come away from there with a draw. Our fans were brilliant that night and I'll never forget as we came back onto the pitch for our warm-down ten minutes after the final whistle and our fans were still inside the stadium. They chanted my name and I'll cherish that moment forever. They were jumping around, singing, dancing, and I honestly felt like joining in.

Our next game was at home to Bursaspor and we defeated them 1–0. Stevie Naismith scored our winner. It was a deserved victory and was all the sweeter because it was our first three points in the Champions League since we beat Lyon 3–0 in France in 2007. Back-to-back games against Valencia followed. They were a brilliant team at that time and had the likes of Juan Mata, Joaquín Sánchez and Roberto Soldado in their line-up. They were neck and neck with Barcelona in La Liga. Mo Edu gave us the lead at Ibrox but they equalised. We missed several chances and Walter said it was the most chances he can ever remember any Rangers side of his creating in a Champions League clash. We then went to Spain and the Mestalla Stadium. We were trounced 3–0. We just couldn't compete with them that night. We were a yard off it and we got punished.

Our final home game had Manchester United at our place. We had to win to have a chance of last 16 qualification. We had terrible injuries and I played in the middle of the park with Kyle Hutton. In my opinion, Hutton became a man that night. Steve Davis had to play at right-back. We battled hard and created a few chances but United won thanks to an 87th-minute penalty from Wayne Rooney. It was yet another great atmosphere at Ibrox. And they had the likes of Ryan Giggs, Dimi Berbatov and Rooney in their team so I suppose to not lose a goal in open play against them was good going. I was pleased with my display, and Sir Alex commented to me in person in the tunnel after the game that he felt I had played well. That meant the world to me. We may well have deserved to sneak a point but the consolation was that we were guaranteed third place in the section and a place in the Europa League.

Our last game was away to Bursaspor and we wanted to get something from it, both from a professional point of view and also to give the club extra funds from UEFA bonus money. Kenny Miller gave us a 19th-minute lead but they equalised through Sercan Yildirim. A draw was a satisfactory result, and the last 32 of the Europa League was next up.

We had to face Sporting Lisbon. A wee bit of added spice was that our former team-mate Pedro Mendes was playing for them. The first leg was at Ibrox and we went one up through Steven Whittaker. That would have been an excellent result to take to Portugal but they got a goal back in the last minute through Matías Fernández. I was injured and missed that game. We were underdogs in the return leg but we knew ourselves that we should never be written off. We knew how to get results away from home. El Hadji Diouf put us ahead after twenty minutes. But they went 2–1 up through Pedro Mendes and Yannick Djaló. We looked down and out but we kept at it and we were rewarded when David Healy's cross was met by Edu, and he scored yet another important European goal for us. We went through on away goals.

The European bandwagon rolled on and thoughts of another UEFA Final crossed my mind. But it wasn't to be, unfortunately. PSV Eindhoven knocked us out in the last 16. We drew 0–0 at their place but they defeated us 1–0 at Ibrox. But we emerged from that whole European campaign with great credit and it was important to do that for the club and for Walter after the previous season's disappointment.

The many European experiences I've had are something I'll never forget. I'm really proud to have been a part of them all under Walter.

Everyone has respect for Walter. He is a total gentleman, pleasant and down-to-earth. He is interested in you as a person and how your family is getting on. He is proper old school. He managed Rangers for a total of eleven years and had to adapt to new ways in the game. He spoke to me about how he had to change his style of management and embrace new methods.

One of the main things he found different was the introduction of sports science. It has pretty much taken over football. When I was young we played on a Saturday, off Sunday. In about it on Monday and Tuesday. Tuesday was a particularly hard day and it wasn't uncommon to get the legs run off you for forty-five minutes. That would be followed by a day off on the Wednesday. Thursday was a lot of crossing and finishing, shape and tactical preparation for the game on Saturday. Friday would have been short and sharp. A light session, some shooting practice and a few small-sided games.

Now you play Saturday, off Sunday. Monday is now known as a recovery day. Even pre-season has totally changed. The days of running up hills and sand dunes are gone. That's how it was when I was starting in the game, and Walter would have been used to that for forty years as a player, coach and manager. Now you don't run for longer than four minutes. We do four four-minute runs, with a three-minute recovery in between each run. So for someone from Walter's era, that must have been a big change to allow sports science guys to come in and be more hands-on from day to day. But we were in no doubt who was in charge. When we used to mess around at training, he would spot it. He wouldn't say a word, but every now and again you would glance in his direction and you would get 'the stare'. He didn't need to say anything. The fooling around stopped immediately.

He is a man I have a lot of respect for, and I'll always be indebted to him for signing me for Rangers and standing by me through my tough times. As much as I was pleased for Walter, the three-in-a-row campaign was a frustrating one for me personally. I felt down-and-out and depressed for long spells. I missed three months of the campaign after I had a cyst removed from my left knee. The recovery process took longer than anticipated and I was forced to sit out vital games during March, April and May, just as we took total control of the SPL. I did manage to play in the final few games of the season, but it couldn't make up for the lost time. Sure, the most important thing is to win the league title and to make it three-in-a-row, but I was desperate to play more games. There were times I thought I was getting there and just a week or two away, and then when I tried to push myself to the next level my knee just wouldn't take it. It was hard to lift myself out of the doldrums. At times, I was tormented with it. We were tight in numbers as it was and I was desperate to be available to Walter. Yet during one press conference Walter kindly said that I was his Player of the Year. That meant so much.

The lack of bodies threatened to take its toll on a few occasions but Walter's experience meant he was able to manage the situation to perfection. I won three SPL league titles with Rangers. Personally, my favourite season was 2009-10 when we made it two-in-a-row. As a person I had many challenges put in front of me and had to go through a huge range of emotions. It's a major achievement to lift any championship because it's not handed to you, but that season was a wee bit extra special. We also won at least one Cup every season to make it three consecutive Doubles.

I believe we were the dominant force in Scottish football at that time. Some people wanted to be critical of our style of football and thought we should have been more entertaining, but it's about winning football games and getting the end result. We knew how to do that. Three different Celtic managers – Strachan,

Mowbray and Lennon – all tried to get the better of Walter over the course of a league season and they were all found wanting. That says it all.

17

ADMINISTRATION

Craig Whyte bought Rangers in May 2011. We were just about to clinch three titles on the trot, in our win against Kilmarnock at Rugby Park. It was also Walter Smith's last game. Personally speaking, at the time I was delighted Whyte took control because he was supposed to have tens of millions of pounds at his disposal. I looked upon it as an end to the club's financial troubles and the beginning of a bright new era. It was a chance for everyone to move on and we all thought it would give the new manager, Ally McCoist, substantial funds to spend on new players to improve the squad.

Whyte never introduced himself to the squad at the end of that season. He first addressed us in the pre-season when we played our first Champions League qualifier in Malmö in Sweden. It was brief, nothing major. He didn't impress me. I remember thinking that his suit didn't fit him properly and he didn't wear a belt. He was very untidy. Call me old fashioned, but he did not dress the way the owner of Rangers Football Club should, like Sir David Murray and Charles Green, or 'Mr Green' as I call him.

It became clear pretty quickly that he did not want to deal with the players. We had a players' committee of Davie Weir, Allan McGregor, Stevie Davis and me. Ali Russell was our point of contact. I was not impressed with him either. We had to deal with him to get our Champions League bonus money sorted. In previous years we'd received a substantial amount of money for qualification and we looked for similar money from the new regime, but after two meetings we knew it wouldn't be forthcoming. We never agreed on a bonus. To be fair to all the boys, we never kicked up a fuss. We didn't go to the manager and didn't go to the media. We kept our counsel. Of course, it was academic, as we didn't qualify. However, that was not the point. Alarm bells set off in my head, although not loudly. I still felt things would be fine.

But the noise level was cranked up a notch around September-time. Most of the guys have breakfast at Murray Park every morning, whether it's a bowl of cereal or a slice of toast. It's a great facility. We read the papers and have a blether. We had every paper there, from the tabloids to the broadsheets. One morning they weren't there and word got around that the newsagent shop had withdrawn their service, as the club had not paid their bill. We couldn't believe this. I was gobsmacked. Initially I thought it must have been an oversight. We also used to have coffee machines around Murray Park and they quickly went out of use. The club had stopped stocking them up.

Now, of course, with the benefit of hindsight, he clearly didn't want to pay many people and the news later came out that he had told one of the employees in the finance department that he wasn't allowed to sign cheques for more than £100. It was incredible. Of course, the thing that brought the club down was not paying PAYE and NI contributions over the course of his time at the club and that amounted to almost £15 million. We never did get any bonuses sorted out. Nothing was ever agreed, but at least we were always paid our wages on time.

There had been a lot of talk and rumours about administration for a while but lots of people said there was no chance it would happen to a club of our size so we just worked on and treated it as another part of everyday life in the West of Scotland goldfish bowl. Don't misunderstand me, it wasn't all sunshine and smiles, and we were given one or two indications that things weren't always going to be sweet. For example, when Craig Whyte bought the club from Sir David Murray he inherited our bonus scheme for winning the SPL Championship in 2011. It was a deal agreed with the then chief executive Martin Bain and the senior players. It was a complicated deal we had in place and the amount of money the players received would depend on the level of debt the club had at that time. We felt, for example, we'd be in a good financial position as the club had sold Kenny Miller to Bursaspor for around £400,000 during that January transfer window and had also got rid of his wage. We also trusted Bain completely and thought we would be given access to the balance sheet if we wanted it.

On our return to pre-season we asked Ali Russell about the bonus money for winning the Championship. He kept fobbing us off with lame excuses. We tried and tried and tried, but he wasn't budging. We weren't allowed access to Whyte to speak to him about it. The players felt we were being treated with contempt. So who knows how Ally McCoist felt. It must have been such a testing time for him. In the previous two years we had always been paid the bonus money so we were shocked at Whyte's stance on this.

Reluctantly, we had to admit defeat and we gave up the fight after months of trying to get some form of bonus paid to us. It's hard to put an exact figure on it but I reckon I was due a minimum of £20,000. You multiply that by a squad of twenty players or so, and Whyte may well have saved at least £400,000 by not paying our 2011 title bonus. So, we were wary of him from very early on, but we still didn't see administration coming.

On Monday, 13 February 2012, Craig Whyte and Ali Russell came in for a meeting with the squad before training and told us that administration was very probably going to happen within ten days. Whyte told us that if HMRC didn't deal out of court in the big tax case, we'd get our full pay for the month then it would be up to the administrators.

This was a bombshell to us. Naturally, the players panicked.

My first thought was one of disbelief. Really, how can a club the size of Glasgow Rangers go into administration? How on earth has it come to this? And then anger set in. My thoughts turned to how it could affect my personal situation. I knew that if administration happened then the manager would have to pick players with not so much resale value to go. So I knew that at thirty-three I had virtually none, and my heart sank. It wasn't about money for me. It was more about Glasgow Rangers Football Club and what it meant to me to play for this great club. I was shocked and saddened that we appeared to be heading into the final days of the club as we knew it.

I knew my time at the club would have to come to an end sooner rather than later, but not in this way. It was very unfair. I was feeling cheated.

The following day when I got home from training I heard on the news in the afternoon that it had happened. 14 February 2012 will go down as one of the darkest days in the history of Glasgow Rangers Football Club. The players were texting each other and panic and worry spread so fast. Everyone feared the worst. I called the PFA and set up a meeting with Fraser Wishart. Allan McGregor and Steve Davis were involved in this with me. We set up a working committee from within the dressing room. At that stage, the players were happy enough for us to deal with it. We needed to know exactly where we stood legally. We arranged to meet at a pub in Milngavie, close to the training ground, as the media were everywhere because this had now turned into one of the biggest stories in the history of Scottish football. It made the headlines all over the UK and further afield.

The meeting was relaxed and we thought the best route was to round the boys up and discuss all angles and most importantly to stick together as a team like we had done for the past four years. We had to use the spirit that got us the trophies we'd won together.

The press were following our every move and we had to keep quiet on all fronts. Our first plan was the one we stuck to throughout – if anyone gets sacked then we will do all we can to let them know we are not happy, and we had a few tricks up our sleeve. We thought we'd be able to negotiate a wage deferral to help the administrators, as we felt we still had a chance of winning the league title and that would have kept us all focused.

My personal situation was that I was 100 per cent behind a wage deferral to help out the club. I had a great time at Rangers and they had been brilliant to me so I saw it as a chance to give something back. A couple of the players, understandably, said they couldn't afford to take a cut in wages. But if it meant saving jobs at Ibrox and Murray Park then I was totally in favour of the plan. People such as Laura Tarbet, Jimmy Bell, Davie Lavery and Tiny had been there for decades. They had put their heart and soul into the club and didn't deserve to lose their jobs. I wanted to help them in any way I could and so did the rest of the boys in the dressing room.

We were off the next day but I had to do something so I went to Murray Park for a light weights session to take my mind off things. The media were still at the main gates – television cameras, photographers and journalists all living out every second of this story, waiting for a big announcement or an insight from a player. I left later that day and got a text from Allan McGregor saying he and Steve Davis had just met with Ally McCoist to discuss the current situation. The gaffer wanted an insight into the thoughts of the players and what our plans might be.

My own thoughts were that, rightly or wrongly, I felt my days might be numbered at Rangers because of the new circumstances surrounding the club. I felt heartbroken at the thought of it. I called my mentor Davie Weir to speak to him about the situation and he was very honest. He agreed with my assessment. So, basically, I had prepared myself for the worst. And so the sleepless nights began.

Duff and Phelps were appointed as the administrators. The men put in charge of getting creditors their money and also trying to save Rangers were Paul Clark and David Whitehouse. I wasn't questioning their professionalism and their ability to do the job, but the players were a little concerned that they were given this task considering Craig Whyte's links to Duff and Phelps.

Clark and Whitehouse faced the players at Murray Park and we had several questions for them. During our first meeting with them I would have been more vocal, but, because I believed I was going to be one of the players sacrificed, I was quite reserved. They stood in front of us all and said that we would be paid for February but they could offer no guarantees after that. They then had to go and study the financial books to ascertain exactly what kind of mess the club was really in. It didn't make pretty reading for them. They told us that they were available to speak to us at any time and there would be constant dialogue between them and the manager.

My mind went into overdrive. Will I play on Saturday against Kilmarnock? Have I played my last ever game for Rangers? I was in meltdown. A number of the players were the same – many of us were Rangers fans. I felt sick.

The game came and I played up front against Kilmarnock. Ibrox was packed, every seat taken as our fans had responded to the pleas to do their bit to help Rangers get out of the desperate situation the club found itself in. 'Penny Arcade' belted out over the PA system and it felt like an Old Firm game. It was incredible. We lost the game 1–0, and we let our fans down. I was in tears as I walked off the pitch. I had the ball in the net but the referee disallowed it. Yet, television replays confirmed the goal should have stood. But when you're down on your luck . . .

It was an emotional day and as I turned up that afternoon I honestly felt it was going to be my last ever appearance in a Rangers jersey. The media was full of stories that ten or eleven of us were going to be sacked on the Monday morning as the administrators had looked at the books and had a plan to save the club. Ali Russell and Gordon Smith were told to leave in a cost-cutting exercise. Gordon had been brought in by Whyte as director of football. I liked Gordon. He was hung out to dry in it all. I felt sorry for him. He had the players' best interests at heart. Ali Russell was also brought in by Whyte, but I had no time for him. I felt it was only a matter of time before a number of players were going to be asked to go. On my way to that Kilmarnock game I parked in the school across from Ibrox, as I thought it was my last game and wanted to walk through the famous doors with my club tie and blazer on.

Monday came and the scheduled meeting between the players and administrators was delayed by forty-eight hours. The players decided to have another meeting with the PFA. A lawyer from the English PFA also attended the meeting. He had experience of such situations with clubs such as Portsmouth. The lads decided to send five players along to the meeting.

The lawyers were great with supplying the details we asked for. They got in touch with the administrators and were eventually given access to the books to see if there was a way we could come up with a plan to save money without any employees losing their jobs. It took time to get it all going and it was a frustrating and worrying period. It really was a waiting game.

During that period the atmosphere inside Murray Park was, to put it bluntly, horrible. Sure, I always felt privileged to play for Rangers and to be well paid for doing so, and we were treated like kings, but when that honour threatened to be taken away from me, it was something I couldn't stomach. It wasn't our fault but what we all knew was that it wasn't the fault of any single person on the books of Rangers at that moment and yet we were the ones going to suffer for years of mismanagement and recklessness.

A few days later, I received a phone call from someone with a good working knowledge of the club to say I was going to be one of the players to be sacked. I was told there was a list of players that were being told to go and my name was on it. I had no reason not to believe this guy and it confirmed my worst fears. He was adamant that my P45 was imminent.

I had to take action to save my own skin. I had one throw of the dice left and I wanted it to be a double six. I discussed my situation with Amanda and came to the conclusion that I should offer to play for NOTHING until the end of the season. I was willing not to take a single penny to help the club and its staff. The manager, Ally McCoist, was exactly the same. He obviously felt the club had been good to him, so it was a great gesture for him and once again showed he has the club at heart – not that that has ever been in doubt. I spoke to the PFA about this and got Fraser Wishart to put my offer in writing to the administrators. It was lodged with Duff and Phelps the following day.

The next meeting we had with the administrators was day fifteen of the process. As a team we couldn't believe how long this was taking and we found the lack of information from them to be absolutely staggering. In terms of cutting costs and being decisive, I'd never known an administration process to take so long. And we were receiving no information from anyone at Duff and Phelps.

That night, 29 February, at around 11.30pm, I received yet another phone call to tell me a national newspaper was running a story the following morning to say eleven players were getting sacked and I was one of them. Again, the guy who phoned was, in my book, reliable and well informed. I also knew where he was getting his information from. I appreciated his call, for giving me the heads-up.

I was also angry. I called the gaffer straight away and he said it was rubbish and we had a chat about a few things. He was meeting the administrators on a daily basis but insisted Clark and Whitehouse were telling him very little. The players were receiving next to no information, and the manager wasn't either.

The gaffer said he wanted to avoid, at all costs, being party to any list of players being drawn up that would be bulleted, and I understood why he would say that. I was coming towards the latter stages of my career and I was one of the higher-paid players, although nowhere near the level of salary three or four of the top earners were on. The only thing in my favour was that we did have a small squad and I was able to operate effectively in a number of positions.

The meetings between the players and PFA and the administrators became a daily event. Fraser brought in the PFA lawyers Bridge Litigation. Liam O'Donnell and Margaret Gribbon would assist us greatly over the coming days – they were excellent. Clark and Whitehouse said they were keen to sort out a package with the players and we were just as keen to settle on a figure and try to get on with playing football, but it was just so bizarre. There was so much going on that we weren't training until five at night.

In the administrators meetings we were all nervous but at the same time we were hitting Paul Clark with both barrels. Picture the scene – twenty-five angry players in training gear, sitting in a small room with Mr Clark standing in front of us fielding questions. Myself and Allan McGregor sat down with our bits of paper with questions and points all written down and we made sure they listened to every word we read out.

Looking back, McGregor was funny, he has a way about him that makes you laugh. He has a heart of gold and is a genuinely nice guy. He is very trustworthy and has been brought up in a similar style to me, although he comes from Edinburgh! He is very streetwise.

I would ask a question to put pressure on the administrators, but I would ask it in a pleasant manner and understanding tone of voice. McGregor asked questions in a sharp tone, as if he was ready to half the guy in two with a sword. He didn't hold back and I'm not too sure Clark and Whitehouse understood every word he said because of his accent. That said, it was very clear they didn't know how to take us during the meetings. Clark, on a few occasions, looked extremely uncomfortable when he was asked certain questions and I could see him shuffling backwards to hold himself up against a wall. We never intended to be cheeky or disrespectful, but we had to ask questions that mattered. We, more than anyone, wanted answers, so we were blunt with some of our questions. For example, we asked them if they had ever worked for Craig Whyte. We asked them if they were working for Whyte during this administration process. They answered 'no' to both questions. We then asked them if they had ever worked for a company owned by Craig Whyte and they stuttered a little but eventually said 'yes'. The room immediately filled with rage and anger. None of the players had any time for Whyte. We would eventually insist on (and get) our contracts being amended so that if Whyte ever got control of Rangers again ALL players could leave on a FREE. That shows how strongly we felt about what he'd done to this great club.

My opinion is that Duff and Phelps could have accepted the players' offer of taking wage deferrals. They initially said they would but then changed their minds because they said there would be tax implications. PFA lawyer Liam O'Donnell contacted the tax authorities and a tax specialist on behalf of the players and we found a way to take deferrals without there being any tax issues. Clark and Whitehouse refused to go ahead with it and we felt they had messed us about. Why agree to it and then make excuses? Excuses we'd shown to be wrong. It also heightened our suspicions of them having an agenda. Liam O'Donnell fired questions at them and they struggled to answer. They were extremely nervous. But we had to deal with Duff and Phelps.

The next morning Clark stepped back and Whitehouse took centre stage. He was very clear and wanted no more tricky questions. He told us that if a wage cut – not deferral – wasn't agreed today then he'd be terminating the contracts of up to fourteen players the following day. No further questions. Thank you. And then he and Clark walked out! The room was in shock – complete shock. We sat stunned. The gaffer was also stunned.

Fraser then took control. It had reached the nitty-gritty. The meetings were tense, and forthright views were aired by all. It was agreed we would all vote on the wage cut in a secret ballot conducted confidentially by the lawyers. The gaffer addressed us as a squad – we were all in it together. He was right. It all got surreal again as each player trooped through to the canteen to cast their vote. Liam and Margaret took the votes. Credit to all the guys – the massive cuts were accepted as long as no member of staff at the club got sacked. Fraser got that in writing from the administrators.

As it drew to a conclusion it was late in the day, and we were between meetings. Myself and Allan McGregor were stressed with it all so we decided to have a few beers. We went into our kit man Jimmy Bell's room and took a few cans of lager. We put them in an ice machine to chill. We then took great pleasure in drinking them all. It set us up nicely for the next meeting, the meeting where it all got sorted once and for all.

We decided that the highest paid players would take a 75 per cent wage cut, the middle group would face a 50 per cent deduction and the lowest earners would lose 25 per cent of their wages. Some guys, such as Gregg Wylde and Mervan Celik, decided to quit the club and go for nothing, as was their right. I took a 75 per cent cut and I didn't have a problem with that. I would have played for nothing, I really would have. During the three-month process it cost me around £200,000. Don't get me wrong, it was a sore one, but it was worth it. Glasgow Rangers Football Club and the fans had been good to me over the years and it was my way of giving them something back. I was more than happy to have sacrificed money to keep other people in a job and help keep both the club and my dream alive.

The players had no choice but to reluctantly agree to wage cuts of 75 per cent. Once we had agreed the principle of wage cuts as a group the PFA stepped back and allowed the individual players' agents to come in. Some of the boys then got clauses inserted into their contracts which allowed players such as Allan McGregor, Stevie Naismith, Steve Davis, Steven Whittaker, Maurice Edu and Kyle Lafferty to go for anything up to 75 per cent less than their market value. For example, Allan's value was around £4.5 million but he could go for £1.5 million.

In my opinion this was the worst mistake the administrators made. They should never have allowed those clauses. A wage deferral would have cost a new owner around £3 million and that made much more sense to me than losing around £12 million from the asset value on players. In a meeting with senior players it emerged Paul Clark had said to the PFA lawyers that the value of the squad wasn't worth £3 million. Allan was furious and he asked Liam to go into a private meeting with him and the administrators, to act as a witness. He was even more furious when he came out. But Paul Clark denied saying it in that context. I couldn't believe what I was hearing – it made no sense. These clauses were a disaster and would later put off potential buyers including Bill Millar, the wealthy American businessman. A huge asset had been written down. The PFA had repeatedly told Duff and Phelps this as they pushed for the sensible option, wage deferrals, as regularly happens in English football administrations. But they wouldn't listen.

The players were also willing to allow any new owner the chance to pay the outstanding wage deferrals over a two-year period. I had a problem getting to grips with the decision that was made not to accept that. This great club wasn't being treated properly. What was the agenda?

To be perfectly honest, I wasn't overly impressed with Clark and Whitehouse and I found it hard to have complete trust in them after the wage deferral issue and the lack of communication.

Companies were declaring an interest in buying Rangers and, rightly or wrongly, there was a widespread feeling that Craig Whyte may have been involved in some shape or form with one or two of the interested parties. There is no doubt he was slippery and it's hard to believe that he ever had Rangers' best interests at heart. The things he did during his time in charge and trail of destruction he left behind proves beyond all doubt what a disaster he was for Rangers. We made sure he could never return with our frees clause written into our contracts.

My stomach turned when stories of his time in charge of Rangers began to unravel. Even now, my gut still churns. It has left a horrible taste in my mouth to think he was able to come in and take the most successful club in the world and bring it to its knees. It was also disappointing that the SFA didn't heed warnings from the old Rangers board not to accept him as a 'fit and proper person'. There appeared to be a lack of due diligence on him from within Hampden.

What made it worse was that Whyte was from Motherwell, where I grew up. He attended the 1991 Scottish Cup Final at

Hampden Park between Motherwell and Dundee United. My cousin and brother were also on that bus, as was Whyte's sister, Adele. My brother dated her for a while. I was also at that Cup Final and it was a brilliant occasion. To see my hometown team beat Dundee United was memorable.

When he took control of the club, Whyte claimed he was a Rangers fan and had been all of his life. I'm not so sure that's the case. When he took over in May 2011, I don't think he would've known Nikica Jelavić or Saša Papac had they sat beside him in the Murray Park canteen. But he would have known Dougie Arnott!

We would have liked to have dealt with Whyte during the negotiation process but we never saw him again after he addressed the squad on 13 February. What a pity. We would have loved to have been able to get our hands on him, believe me.

He clearly had a plan from the start in terms of what he was going to do to Rangers. He gave huge wage rises to Allan McGregor, Steve Davis and Steven Whittaker during his first few weeks in charge. That should have started the alarm bells ringing. But we all trusted him at that point. However, for him not to pay his bills to small businesses was wrong. He sold the Arsenal shares that Rangers had in their possession for decades for more than £200,000. With the benefit of hindsight, we should have all listened more closely to John Greig, Alastair Johnston, Martin Bain, John McClelland and Paul Murray. They all knew the score and had clearly done their due diligence on Whyte, but, unfortunately, they didn't have the power to overrule Sir David Murray or the bank.

Sir David came in for some serious criticism in his final few years as owner. I happen to like him. When I joined the club he was very encouraging. He introduced me to Sir Sean Connery at the training ground and I got my photo taken with the best 007 there has ever been and ever will be. He came to the training ground quite a lot but was rarely in the dressing room on a match day. Sir David would phone me or text me after good results, but knew how to keep his distance. He was always impeccably dressed. He was Mr Rangers to me and from as far back as I can remember he was the main man at Ibrox. He made some great signings and was a master at hogging the headlines and maximising positive publicity. I spoke to him a few times on the phone before I signed for Rangers and he was great.

Plenty have blamed him for one reason or another when Rangers went through a bad stage, between the debt and the Big Tax Case. He had the finger of blame pointed at him for selling the club to Craig Whyte. It's unfortunate if he is remembered for that. Yes, it was a mistake, a monumental one, but he can't be held responsible for the decisions Whyte made. That is totally unfair. And, remember, there was pressure from Lloyds Bank to sell up to Whyte.

Sorting out the contractual issues off the park allowed us a bit of closure on that front, albeit for a short period. I certainly found it easier to concentrate on playing football after that. Of course, what was sort of missed in all of this was the fact we were deducted ten points by the SPL for going into administration. We had no chance of winning the league as soon as that happened. Before we went into administration Celtic were just four points ahead. Had we not been deducted the points I would have fancied our chances of winning the league. From a footballing point of view, that was the biggest crime of all. Mismanagement on so many different levels, for such a long time, cost us. We've won more league titles than any other club in the world and we could have had another one in 2012. Unfortunately, four-in-a-row had disappeared, but we had to keep going, try our best to get some victories and make sure we finished in second place.

Through the administration period I was moved up front and I started hitting form and scoring some crucial goals, like one away from home at Motherwell, to make sure Celtic had to wait at least one more week to win the SPL title. I rarely played well when I returned to Fir Park but I thoroughly enjoyed that one. I felt great relief to get the winner. I scored again the following week at home to St Mirren. The fans chanted my name that day and that meant everything to me, it really did. I was then voted the Fans' Player of the Month and that was a great honour and some satisfying news during such a trying time. Rangers fans are the best in the world, but they can be very demanding. That's what comes with playing with such a big, big club.

To hear them chanting my name gave so much confidence and it couldn't have arrived at a better time. We played Celtic in the final Ibrox Old Firm game of the season. In fact, some speculated it may be the last ever Old Firm game between the clubs on our park as there was all sorts of stories doing the rounds by that stage that we might close down. Listen, I never believed that for a minute but I suppose there always was a wee doubt hiding at the back of my mind as we were never totally sure the exact mess the club was in and what kind of trouble Craig Whyte had landed us in.

Celtic could have won the title at Ibrox and it was a game that would go down in history if it didn't go our way. We didn't want that happening on our watch. We also had to avoid defeat or else we'd have been the first team in the history of the club to lose four games on the trot at Ibrox.

Ibrox was bouncing that day, in a way I'd never seen before. Talk about our fans being up for it! Before the game the boys were obviously ready and well pumped up in the dressing room. Myself and McGregor kept shouting at each other to go and win the game. We stared at each other, eyeball to eyeball, and kept pushing each other like we were about to fight.

I told him to slap me to get me even more angry and he did so with his gloves on, then I just slapped him back right in the face. We didn't smile, we just kept on getting angrier and angrier. Steve Davis came over to see what was happening but he got pushed away. He looked at us with a stare as well. We were at fever pitch but we loved it. We were never going to lose that day.

We won 3–2. Amazing stuff. Sone Aluko, Andy Little and big Lee Wallace got our goals. Lee is another winner, my sort of guy. He is quiet and polite but mentally strong. He is one of the best left-backs in the UK. I think he is a definite Rangers captain of the future! Myself and Steve Davis went into Jimmy Bell's room after the game for a beer and we had a laugh as we recalled the pre-match antics!

I played up front and was absolutely delighted with my performance. I was named Man of the Match. I felt I made a significant contribution to our victory. The fans also spurred us on. They were absolutely first class and they deserved to enjoy that day more than anyone. The atmosphere inside Ibrox was incredible, I think the best I had ever heard and played in front of. It was the last time any of us had the chance to smile for a couple of months.

Over the piece, it was great for our fans to see us winning that game. They had been brilliant during the whole turbulent process and it was because of that the club retired the no.12 jersey in their honour. They set up the 'fighting fund' and have raised more than £500,000 that will be put to good use if and when it's required. Our fans are amazing.

RANGERS TIMELINE 2012

FEBRUARY

On the 13th of the month Rangers apply to the Court of Session in Edinburgh to enter administration proceedings. Owner Craig Whyte announces that the bill for the major tax case, concerning the improper use of Employee Benefits Trust under previous owner Sir David Murray, could amount to £75 million.

Just twenty-four hours later Rangers appoint administrators Duff and Phelps after a court battle with Her Majesty's Revenue and Customs. They effectively forfeit the title to Celtic after being docked ten points. Duff and Phelps reveal that HMRC lodged their petition to take Rangers into administration over the non-payment of about £9 million PAYE and VAT since Whyte's 2011 takeover.

Fears grow for the club's future but the Administrators insist that Rangers will continue to exist as a football club. Administrators announce that parties not connected directly with the club have expressed an interest in taking over from Whyte. Administrators also express concerns over Whyte's stewardship of the club. Whyte comes out to defend himself against a number of allegations and expresses confidence that investigations will prove 'every penny has been accounted for'.

The Scottish Football Association launch an independent inquiry into the activities of Rangers, specifically whether Whyte is 'fit and proper' to hold a position in the game. Rangers' attempts to sign Daniel Cousin are thwarted despite having announced his signature prior to entering administration. Manager Ally McCoist welcomes the SFA inquiry after his side's 1–0 defeat against Kilmarnock at Ibrox.

On the 21st it is revealed that Craig Whyte had made a deal with Ticketus to pay off Rangers' outstanding £18 million debt to Lloyds, something Whyte had earlier denied. Then forty-eight hours later Rangers Director of Football Gordon Smith and Chief Operating Officer Ali Russell agree to leave the club. A report on the club's financial dealings is received by Strathclyde Police. McCoist expresses pride at his players' focus on football following a 4–1 victory over Inverness.

Off the field, Rangers' woes worsen as they are fined £50,000 for failing to declare that Whyte had been disqualified as a director.

MARCH

On the 1st Ticketus call for a 'rapid and successful conclusion' to the administration process and say they are willing to hold talks with any potential new owners. The SFA confirm they will investigate claims made by former Rangers director Hugh Adam that payments made to players were not disclosed to the governing body. Duff and Phelps postpone a final decision on wage cuts and staff redundancies after refusing an offer from players to defer wages. Craig Whyte expresses 'enormous sympathy' over impending redundancies at the club. Administrators say redundancies are 'likely' as Rangers lose 2–1 at home to Hearts on the 3rd.

The Scottish Premier League have confirmed that their board have instigated an investigation into the alleged non-disclosure of payments made to players by Rangers. Rangers administrators consider a proposal from players overnight after failing to reach consensus over wage cuts.

On the 6th joint administrator David Whitehouse says they have been unable to reach an agreement on a wage-cut plan and that talks will continue on Wednesday. Mervan Celik and Gregg Wylde both offer to leave the club, and twenty-four hours later it's announced that liquidating the club is inevitable, a claim made by Rangers director Dave King. Administrators announce that the sale of the club has been accelerated after players fail to agree cost-cutting measures. Joint administrator Paul Clark rules out the prospect of European football for Rangers for three years.

Whyte is declared unfit to hold a position in football. The governing body say that Rangers face a charge of bringing the game into disrepute. Rangers administrators announce a package of wage cuts with players that have 'directly prevented substantial job losses among non-playing staff both at Ibrox and Murray Park'.

Former Rangers director Paul Murray confirms his Blue Knights consortium is finalising an offer to buy the Ibrox club with the surprise backing of Ticketus.

On the 15th Rangers are issued with notices of complaint over alleged breaches of five disciplinary rules. Whyte is alleged to have breached two rules. A hearing set up to determine whether Craig Whyte did indeed breach SFA rules is adjourned until 17 April.

APRIL

News breaks on the 4th from the administrators and they reveal they have received four bids for the club. Then seven days later Duff and Phelps admit they have had to delay the announcement of a preferred bidder for the club due to proposed changes to Scottish Premier League rules. Sale Sharks owner Brian Kennedy is told his revised verbal bid for the club is not 'capable of acceptance'.

On the 23rd all hell breaks loose when the club receives a twelve-month embargo on signing players and owner Craig Whyte is banned for life, whilst Whyte and the club are fined £200,000 and £160,000 respectively. The club intends to appeal the decision. Fans react with anger and disbelief at the SFA's decision, with many planning to boycott away matches. News also emerges that manager Ally McCoist has suspended striker Kyle Lafferty for two weeks – meaning he may have played his last game for the club – and admitted he'd be open to the club joining the SFL and entering the Third Division.

MAY

The move to find a buyer intensifies. American businessman Bill Miller is granted preferred bidder status ahead of the Blue Knights consortium. That was on the 3rd, and just five days later he withdraws his bid for Rangers. The Blue Knights follow suit and withdraw their interest in buying Rangers after their noon ultimatum to Duff and Phelps passes.

18

NEW ERA: THE GREEN SHOOTS OF RECOVERY

CHARLES GREEN and his consortium bought the club and he was announced as the preferred bidder on 13 May, the final SPL day of the season. We beat St Johnstone 4–0 that day at McDiarmid Park. I scored and Sone Aluko grabbed a hat-trick. Mr Green spoke to the players that day.

Then the club went into liquidation after HMRC rejected a CVA on 12 June. A newco was formed and we are now known as The Rangers Football Club. It's been comforting that the club still exists and we're still playing football, but it's not all been easy to take. But at least we have retained our 140-year history. It was sad in many ways. Nobody wanted it to end this way for Rangers but we had to try and keep a positive outlook. It's my view that we are still Glasgow Rangers and always will be. Nobody will ever take that away from us. What happened in terms of a newco doesn't change anything for me. Nobody can take away my memories and medals from the past few years. I'm sure if you asked the likes of John Greig and Richard Gough they'd say the same about their time at the club. The supporters will say the same. We all have to stick together to make sure this club can move forward.

With our registrations and contracts being transferred over to a newco, some players were then advised they could walk out for nothing. Quite a number of them chose to go down that road.

I wish Allan McGregor, Steve Davis, Stevie Naismith, Steven Whittaker, Sone Aluko, Kyle Lafferty, John Fleck, Rhys McCabe and Jamie Ness well. They all had had enough of the uncertainty surrounding the club. I don't blame some players for that. They had to keep playing at a high standard to save their international careers and their livelihoods. It should never be forgotten that many jobs were saved by their actions in the wage-cut vote.

On the first day of pre-season, 28 June, seven players had walked and we knew there would be more. When we were booted out of the SPL and voted into the SFL Third Division then that was the final straw. It was yet another low point in our history, perhaps the lowest of all. I felt a bit sick with it all and just wanted it to be over and get back to playing football again.

I made my mind up pretty quickly that I was going to stay with Rangers. I was not for going anywhere. Of course, I would have rather have been in the SPL or the First Division with Rangers. The SFL Division Three didn't hold too much appeal but I wouldn't turn my back on Rangers. It was a time to show support and loyalty. I wanted my conscience to be clear. It wasn't a time to quit the club. That would have been the easy thing to do. Since I was a kid growing up in MotherwellI all I wanted to do was play for the club. The last thing I would have done was walk away. Wearing the Rangers jersey is an important part of my life and I'd never have forgiven myself if I'd given that up. I see it as a personal mission to help get the club back up to where it belongs.

The senior players who did turn up for the first day of pre-season – myself, Kirk Broadfoot, Lee Wallace and Neil Alexander – expected to go through a rigorous examination. That is the norm. We thought we'd get blood taken and urine samples tested and plenty more. But it didn't happen. Again, it was an indication of how the lack of clarity off the park for Rangers was taking its toll with the football department. Everyone was all over the place and, quite rightly, the safety and well-being of the future of Rangers was paramount.

At this stage, Green was being slaughtered by many people in the media and by thousands of Rangers fans. The fans appeared not to trust him and lots of them didn't want to buy their season tickets. Walter Smith was part of a consortium that made a late bid but it was rejected. During that period, the players spoke a lot but we didn't know what was going to happen. We were in the dark. Completely. Mr Green saved the club and deserved to be given a chance.

The uncertainty made me feel vulnerable. At the start of July, I received a lucrative offer to go to the UAE and could have earned a net amount of more than £750,000 per year for two years but I turned it down. I felt that I couldn't just walk away. I was lucky enough to make my dream come true to play for Rangers and they had been so kind to me over the years with medals that I had to stay. I owed it to the club and the fans to stay.

But pre-season was a helluva time. Between administration, liquidation and transfer embargoes, the club didn't know if it was coming or going. I think I was in a bit of shock that the most successful club in the world could be brought to its knees. Many people and organisations played their part in it all.

The way we were treated by the SPL was the biggest disappointment to me. We had Motherwell in administration and other clubs flirting with danger, Hearts not being able to pay wages, that kind of thing. So why vote us out? They were going to lose money and the clubs had to be stronger and stand up to their fans.

I believe Celtic wanted us down in SFL Division Three. It made sense for them to think that way. It gives them a free run at the Champions League for the next few years. They would have known we'd have had to move our better players on, making us weaker. And they would get stronger. Unfortunately, that's what has happened in the past twelve months and the gap between the clubs on the park now is pretty big. We have some very good young players, and on our day we could give most teams a game. But, of course, we want to be beating Celtic and teams at that level on a regular basis and there's no doubt we'll need to strengthen the squad and add more experienced players as soon as we can. Having been up there until last year, it pains me to think of what has happened and how far we still have to climb to get back up to the top. That's the challenge we face, though, and we will rise to it in the coming years. I know we will be back. That's the challenge we have and we will rise to it in the coming five years.

I totally understood why the SFL voted the way they did. It was a no-brainer for them to put us into the Third Division and let us climb the leagues back to the SPL. They were right not to vote us into the First Division. Every SFL club owner / chairman / chief executive wanted a crack at us for financial reasons so they were right to 'use' us for a minimum of three years. It was a Lottery win for them, and good luck to them all. I'm also grateful they gave Rangers a platform to play football on and kept us in the professional game.

I'm also delighted that Mr Green and his financial backers came on board. It has worked out well. As I mentioned, the first time I met him was when we played our last game of the season, away to St Johnstone. He came into the dressing room to introduce himself. He stood in front of the players and told us that there would be changes for the better and that we had to trust him. He assured us he wasn't another Craig Whyte. We had just been turned upside down by Whyte and none of us knew the new owner. He didn't have a problem seeing managers off the premises down there and I'm sure that must have been of great concern to Ally McCoist. But Ally more than deserved his opportunity.

He then spoke to us again at pre-season and we got to ask him a few questions. I asked him if the gaffer would be getting money to spend on new players because we had just seen Allan McGregor, Steve Davis, Stevie Naismith and others walk out. In terms of experienced players, there was only myself, Lee Wallace, Neil Alexander and Kirk Broadfoot back at the club. He told me that money would be available.

From there, we have built up a good working relationship and I now trust him. He gave me a new contract in October. I took my lawyer Liam O'Donnell with me into the meetings with Mr Green and it all went well. He gave me a new two-year deal when he could easily have only offered a twelve-month deal. He told me that my deal would expire when I was thirty-seven and if I wasn't playing at that time there could be a place for me going all over the world representing the club in an ambassadorial role. But it was only mentioned in passing, it's not set in stone.

I think Mr Green appreciated the fact I did not walk out on the club in the summer. I was the first guy to state I was going to stay at Rangers and play for them regardless of the division we were in. I'd like to think that was a wee reward for my loyalty.

He also encouraged me to buy shares. He gave me a prospectus to look over and, after taking advice, I felt it was a sound thing to do. I bought £25,000 worth of Rangers' shares in December 2012. That's not an investment for me, I'm not interested in making money from the shares. That's something I did to do my bit for the club and also something that my two sons can inherit so that the family will always have an involvement long after my career at the club is over.

Charles Green definitely has substance to him and I think he is great for Rangers at this stage of our development. I've been very impressed with how he defends our club to the hilt. I think he is now immersed in Rangers.

MAY

On the 13th the administrators announce they have signed a binding contract to sell the club to a consortium led by former Sheffield United chief executive Charles Green. The Yorkshire businessman travels to the final game of the season, a win over St Johnstone at McDiarmid Park, and introduces himself to the players in the dressing room beforehand.

An SFA appeal tribunal rejects Rangers' appeal against a £160,000 fine and twelve-month transfer embargo. But on the 29th there is a dramatic twist and the SFA transfer ban is ruled unlawful in the Court of Session following a challenge from Rangers. Duff and Phelps publish Green's Company Voluntary Arrangement (CVA) proposal to creditors.

As one of the most dramatic months in the history of the club draws to a close, SPL clubs take on responsibility for deciding whether 'newco' clubs should be admitted to the competition but reject fixed penalties. Rangers' administrators provide files requested by SPL in their investigation into undisclosed payments.

JUNE

A crushing blow on the 12th when HMRC announce they will reject the CVA offer and force the club into liquidation. But Green tries to make sure it's business as normal and Rangers newco formally apply to acquire the SPL share of Rangers FC. The SPL agreed to consider the request to transfer the share. After a couple of weeks of deliberation, Rangers newco applied to transfer SFA membership, it being a requirement for a club to be an SFA member to be eligible to participate in the SFL or the Scottish Cup. The SFA confirmed that it had 'received an information pack from Sevco Scotland relevant to their membership application'.

JULY

The SPL vote by 10–1 to reject Rangers' application to play in the SPL. Kilmarnock abstained and only the old Rangers club voted in favour. Rangers then apply to join the Scottish Football League and this is accepted with twenty-five of the thirty clubs voting that the club should be placed in Division Three. Rangers are granted a licence by the SFA. On the 29th Rangers newco plays its first ever competitive game and defeats Brechin City 2–1 in the Ramsden's Cup.

Green warns Ibrox staff the club faces job cuts in a desperate bid to balance the books. The newco chief executive said there would be 'huge implications' of playing in the bottom tier of Scottish football and he admitted to employees: 'There will be job losses.'

FIFA announce Rangers won't get a penny for stars who quit Ibrox – but they could land an £800,000 windfall for Steven Davis. Green challenged the decisions of Davis, Steven Naismith, Jamie Ness, Kyle Lafferty and Allan McGregor. They all rejected the transfer of their contracts to a newco and negotiated deals elsewhere. Naismith joined Everton, Lafferty signed for Sion, Ness for Stoke City and Whittaker for Norwich. But FIFA have ruled Green is due nothing for any of them.

McCoist faces a hectic dash to rebuild his threadbare squad after Green accepted the SFA's twelve-month transfer embargo. The signing ban will start on 1 September, giving McCoist just forty-two days to acquire enough new players to take the club through to the January transfer window of 2014. It's one blow after another and the SPL continue their moves to strip the club of titles. Rangers chairman Malcolm Murray also sneers at SPL clubs alarmed by their finances and insists they'll be begging for us back within a year.

AUGUST

Sir David Murray denies any cheating took place during his stewardship after the SPL appoint an independent commission to investigate payments.

SEPTEMBER

Rangers refuse to co-operate with the SPL inquiry. The SPL-appointed commission sets a start date of 13 November for a hearing regarding alleged undisclosed payments during Sir David Murray's tenure.

NOVEMBER

The SPL hearing is postponed. Meanwhile, the tax tribunal allows Rangers' appeal in principle on a majority verdict and rules that HMRC's assessment should be 'substantially reduced'. Murray International Holdings 'MIH' welcome the findings, which they say, 'leaves minimal tax liability and overwhelmingly supports the views collectively and consistently held by our advisers, legal counsel and MIH itself'. A massive victory for Rangers and a huge weight is lifted.

Walter Smith returns to Ibrox as a director of Rangers. Smith will have a non-executive role.

DECEMBER

Rangers are drawn against Dundee United in the Scottish Cup and immediately a war breaks out between the clubs – Rangers announce they won't accept their allocation of tickets as they back fans' plan for a boycott. This is after United were seen as being one of the main clubs against Gers getting back into the SPL during the summer.

Meanwhile, Green reveals the Rangers share issue was a big success. Rangers fans buy around £5 million worth.

Around £22 million is raised due to an impressive response from institutional investors.

The year from hell ends with Rangers returning to Hampden, where a last-minute goal from Fraser Aird earns a 1–0 win over Queen's Park.

19

SIMPLY THE BEST DERBY
IN THE WORLD

I MISS playing against Celtic. The fact I've probably played in my last ever Old Firm game doesn't sit well with me. That's the main thing I've found from us being in the SFL. I loved the Old Firm baggage. For me, there is nothing better than getting my sleeves rolled up and getting wired in against our main rivals. Our supporters miss the games too. I always had respect for Celtic management and players because it's only when you have been in the heat of the battles – especially over a period of time – that you can understand and appreciate exactly what's involved. The Old Firm games brought the best out of me in some games but also made me lose it and the red mist came down on more than one occasion. The worst one was the 2009 League Cup Final when we lost 2–0 to Celtic after extra-time. Madjid Bougherra missed the game through injury so Kirk Broadfoot partnered Davie Weir in central defence. I was given the role of holding midfielder, to help and protect them as much as I could. I will go back to 16 April 2008 to explain the history of what led to the incidents in the League Cup Final.

April 2008 was an SPL game and we lost 2–1 at Parkhead. Shunsuke Nakamura scored for Celtic but we equalised through Nacho Novo. We were reduced to ten men after Carlos Cuellar was red carded for a deliberate handball. Allan McGregor saved the resultant penalty from Scott McDonald. But McGregor had a bad ankle injury and hobbled off. Neil Alexander replaced him. Jan Vennegoor of Hesselink scored the winner in the 93rd minute. These things happen.

But the referee that night was Kenny Clark and I thought he had a poor, poor game. Paul Hartley caught me very late in the 15th minute and was only yellow carded. For me, it was an awful challenge and he should have been given a straight red. He actually broke my foot with the tackle, that's how bad it was. I didn't realise it at the time and played on. Knowing fine well it was a bad one, I was surprised Hartley didn't apologise for it. It was out of character for him not to hold his hand up to a late one. There was no doubt Celtic – who were chasing us for the title and needed to win – used tactics that were to hammer it into us early doors, to put a few markers down. Some of their challenges were well over the top. They could have been stopped, but the referee didn't step in that day as we thought he should have.

We can now fast-forward to the League Cup Final in 2009 and Hartley was at it again with me. His challenges weren't nasty, they were just niggly, and in my opinion definitely late. Every time I released the ball to play a pass, his boot was left in. I knew what he was up to and this time he was sussed, but I didn't want to risk a red card. As it turned out, I just couldn't get the opportune moment.

Completely frustrated, I eventually snapped twice that afternoon. The first came at a corner and I was defending our box. He was in the vicinity and I remember shouting at him, 'Hartley, you're getting it from me. If I don't get you today then I'm coming to your house later.' I had totally gone. Stephen McManus tried to intercept and told me to calm down. I told him to 'fuck off' and repeated the threat to Hartley again. Hartley kept quiet. I knew he wasn't amused but I couldn't have cared less about how he felt. Yet I'd known him for years. We played football against each other in the Lanarkshire area when we were kids. We came up against each other in our early days in Scotland when he was with Hamilton and St Johnstone and I was at Motherwell.

We lost the game 2–0. At time-up, I sat on the grass extremely disappointed at losing the game and still raging with Hartley. The Celtic team celebrated to my left-hand side, no more than twenty yards away. Walter came over to me and asked if I was okay. I told him I was far from okay. He told me to calm down but I wasn't for listening to anyone or taking orders. I was my own man. I had unfinished business. I glanced over in their direction and could see them bouncing up and down and cuddling as they waited to climb the Hampden stairs to receive the trophy. Well, that set me off again. The red mist came down.

I got up and made my way over to them. Hartley was in my sights. He happened to be standing beside Gordon Strachan. I confronted him and challenged him to a fight. I said, 'Come on, right here and now. Let's get it on. Down the tunnel, wherever you like.' Strachan stared at me in disbelief. He had no idea what to think. Hartley was stunned. A few Celtic players spotted what I was up to and pushed me away, back to the Rangers end. I regret my decision but I was hurting badly.

Walter came back over and told me not to be so stupid and to calm down. But, deep down, I think he loved it to see that hurt and desire in me. At least, I hope he did. I suppose my anger also stemmed back to that league game when Hartley broke my foot.

Hartley and I are good friends and we laugh about it now. He was a really good player and I'm glad he had a terrific career as a player and looks to be going to do the same as a manager. We were doing our SFA coaching badges at the same time and travelled to Largs together every day for a week in the summer of 2012.

I struggled to sleep before Old Firm games. It was a mixture of nerves and excitement. I couldn't wait to get up out of bed and get on with it. Old Firm games were usually lunchtime kick-offs. So we'd have our pre-match meal around 9am. Some of the boys would still eat pasta or chicken at that time but I couldn't do that. I was two slices of toast with a poached egg. I always eat light, back to the days as a young boy at Motherwell. Stephen Craigan used to say that when you are out on the pitch you don't want too much food in the belly. He cited the example of a lion, in terms of when a lion is hungry it's on its paws and on the prowl, constantly on the move. Whereas, if it has eaten then it goes somewhere quiet, lies down and falls asleep. So, that thought has never left me. I'll have coffee, a slice of toast and a wee spoonful of scrambled egg. I only eat the bare minimum, just enough to keep me going. That's just one of my many superstitions.

I made my Old Firm debut in October 2007. It was at Ibrox in front of 49,000 fans. What I really remember was the wall of noise when I walked down the tunnel five minutes before kick-off. Honestly, it was like something had hit me, the roar was something I'd never heard before in football. It was as if it had the power to knock you off-balance. It was so, so loud. Just another aspect that's different about the greatest derby clash in the world. It feels totally different from any other game. It is different from any other game. It's as though it's a different football you're playing with and a different set of fans. The whole match-day experience is just incredible.

My first experience was brilliant. We won 3–0. Nacho Novo scored two and Barry Ferguson got our other goal. The only downside was that I had a perfectly good goal disallowed for offside, but I was onside. I slotted the ball past Artur Boruc. It jolted me not see that one count. It deflated me. I played on the right-hand side of midfield. I had Alan Hutton behind me and he was good to team up with. He had great pace and energy. I enjoyed beating Celtic, but I always tried to win with dignity and never, ever tried to rub their faces in it if they had lost to us.

During the many Old Firm games I played in I was deployed in several different positions – from wide right to wide left, centre-half, centre-forward and centre midfield. I did score in a 1–1 draw at Parkhead in January 2010. Celtic had the bulk of possession and we sat in, happy for the game to go that way. Celtic did score through Scott McDonald. My dad told me the television cameras showed Rod Stewart and his wife Penny Lancaster celebrating the goal. But it was short-lived. We had to come out a bit. We got a corner kick and Steve Davis swung it over. I peeled off Gary Caldwell, charged towards the front post, and headed it into the bottom corner. The goal was at the 'Rangers End' and it was special to do it in front of our own fans. I ran away towards them because I knew my brother Wullie and my nephews were in there and I tried to look for them. Next thing I knew Stevie Smith jumped on me, as did the rest of the lads, and I couldn't see a thing. It was an important goal. We had a nice gap and we knew avoiding defeat was going to see the title stay at our place. That was an experience!

During his previous time in charge of Rangers, in the nine-in-a-row era, Ally told us that Walter used to say, 'Let Celtic have the ball, they'll pass it around but they won't cause too much damage, then we can use Laudrup and Gascoigne and hit them on the counter, one, two, three passes and then bang – a goal.' Great tactics from Walter. Celtic may well have been more pleasant on the eye, but Rangers won the titles. Bottom line. Walter's team talks for Celtic games were perfect. He was never disrespectful towards Celtic, that was never his motivation. He used to focus on us and what a result would mean to the club. He'd spend time pinpointing any weaknesses in the Celtic team.

A key part of the build-up to Old Firm games was making sure that the foreign lads were angry and wanted to rip Celtic apart. We had to drum it into them that Celtic were the enemy and losing was just not an option. On one occasion, just an hour or so before kick-off, Daniel Cousin was on his phone playing games. We had to take it off him. I hated seeing a team-mate being laid back. I wanted him charged up, ready to give every ounce to win the game.

Some of the lads would go into a cubicle and be sick. I could hear them throwing up. I took that as a sign of nerves but I thought that was a positive. I'd rather have that than one of the lads filing their nails. That said, the foreign lads did wonder what the hell was going on when it came to our masseur, Davie Lavery. Davie was up at 5am on the day of every Old Firm game. He'd have a room at the hotel all decked out in photos of Rangers scoring winning goals in Old Firm games and there would be Union Jack towels on the treatment table. The treatment room at Ibrox would be the same.

Davie also liked to get involved in team talks before Old Firm games. Walter would emphasise the point not to get caught up in the atmosphere and let our hearts rule our heads. It was hard enough to win an Old Firm game with eleven men, never mind if you were a man down. As Walter came to the end of his talk, big Davie would appear from nowhere and just say his piece. I think he used to get so wound up that he lost the place a wee bit, but I guess it was just his way of dealing with the pressure. He would shout out, 'Right, lads, let's get into them and show we are scared of nobody. We must win this game today. Now, get fuckin' intaaaeee theeeemmmm . . .' And he would then disappear out of the dressing room.

Our kit man, Jimmy Bell, is Rangers daft. He also drives the team bus for Old Firm games and Cup finals. The rest of the time it will be the designated driver from the bus company. When we played at Hampden he'd be there at least seven hours before kick-off. He got there early to make sure we always got the home dressing room. He never failed. The only time he had no control over it was when we played Queen's Park at Hampden in SFL Three and they were not for being moved even though Jimmy tried his best.

For Old Firm games, he would have his own routine, and on the bus to Ibrox or Parkhead, he would put his own music on with three minutes to arrival. He would belt out 'Simply the Best' as we made our way to the front door of Ibrox or Parkhead. The lads all knew to switch their own sounds off and just soak it up. It was a ritual. We all loved it.

I firmly believe a certain type of mentality is required to survive in Old Firm games over a number of years. You need to be able to cope with the pressure on and off the park that comes with the fixture. You need to be able to look your direct opponent in the eye and believe you are going to beat him. Regardless of my opponent, I always felt I could do that and always knew at some point I would have to go in where it hurts to survive the ninety minutes and to help Rangers win the game. I didn't have a problem coping if things got a bit tasty. The positive is that if I played well then I'd have the chance of becoming a hero. But it's borderline and the negative, the exact opposite, is never far away, whether that is getting a red card or being short with a pass-back and it costs a goal. Defeat to Celtic is horrible and something you don't forget in a hurry.

Beating them brings unbelievable pride and joy. I thoroughly enjoyed our 2011 League Cup Final win over them. It was Walter's last Old Firm Cup Final and Neil Lennon's first as Celtic manager. I felt it was important Walter went out a winner on that front. After all, he is the Master. Steve Davis gave us the lead. Joe Ledley equalised for them. The game went into extra-time and Nikica Jelavić got our winner. Brilliant. A well deserved win for the Rangers. Job done for Walter.

We're expected to win every game and when we do beat Celtic or lift a piece of silverware, it's more of a relief knowing that we've succeeded and the job is done rather than it being about celebrating a success. The fear of losing drives me on every day in my working life and that will always be the case. I rarely dwelled on any success. I enjoyed the moment for a day or so and then I moved on. Walter and Ally drummed that into us.

I had a healthy respect for Stephen McManus. He loved a tackle and would get wired in, a bit like myself. But he always shook hands at time-up. No grudges were held and nothing was carried forward to become a problem off the park. I also got on well with Robbie Keane. I marked him in his final Old Firm game for Celtic. I had a day out with him and Alan Hutton down south a few years ago and we reminisced over a few beers. He enjoyed his time at Celtic and during our chat about Old Firm games he said he felt it was important to stay calm and not get involved. I suppose that's fine for a player to say that when he is on loan from down south but when you're Scottish and steeped in the tradition of it all, it's not quite so easy. For example, if we lost an Old Firm game, my dad was almost suicidal. He couldn't handle it and looked for a way to escape it. The flip side is that when we won he would go daft. When I scored that header at Parkhead he ran out the house and into the middle of the street to do a celebration dance. He was off his head.

One of his treasured possessions is a VHS tape of Rangers' victories in Old Firm games. It has three hours of highlights on it. His favourite game on it is when Rangers beat Celtic 5–1 at Ibrox, a game where Ray Wilkins scored a brilliant thirty-yarder. My dad knows the commentary by heart. He'd sit and watch it constantly. He'd have a cup of coffee and a packet of biscuits and sit back in his favourite armchair and still jump off his seat when the ball went in, even though he'd seen it a hundred times before. I loved watching it with him when I was a kid.

20

LEE-DING OUT MY TEAM

IT WAS Saturday, 1 September 2012, and I was in training at Murray Park, as normal. The transfer window had closed the night before. There was a bit of activity at our place, mainly players leaving. Carlos Bocanegra had been transferred to Racing Santander in Spain on a season-long loan deal. Carlos was our captain. It meant someone had to take over that important role. I wanted to be given the privilege of being captain of Rangers but I wasn't expecting to be asked. I didn't build up my hopes.

After training I went to speak to Kenny McDowall about a private matter. Kenny is an approachable guy and I've never had a problem asking him about anything, whether it's things that concern football or off-the-field matters. Kenny told me the gaffer wanted to see me. I finished my business with Kenny and went to the manager's office.

The gaffer told me to sit down. Kenny was there, as was Ian Durrant. The manager started off by asking how I was and then burst into a story about how Walter Smith pulled him aside in a hotel in Dundee and told him he was going to be captain of the club for the remainder of a season. He admitted it was a moment in his life that he'll never forget. He then asked me if I would like to accept the role of being captain of Glasgow Rangers for the season. Needless to say, I accepted with open arms and thanked him, Kenny and Durranty for picking me for this honour. To be perfectly honest, I was emotional and had to go to the toilet to get myself together. This was an honour I had dreamed about but never thought would happen!

On my return, we sat in his office and the manager explained to me what he wanted from the dressing room and other things about the team. I felt like saying to the three of them that I would run through brick walls with that armband on and if you want anything else done then consider it sorted. No need for questions to be asked. I really opened up to them, told them I was absolutely buzzing to be their captain and promised them I would not let them down.

After I left I had lunch with Durranty and he was his usual self, taking the piss out of me. He loves my mum and dad and was saying that my dad must attend our game the following day, at home to Elgin City. In his usual witty way, he said he expected to see my dad in the players' lounge with his suit on, football boots on and wearing a captain's armband, staring at everyone. He said Mum would have the Rangers jersey on with my name on the back of it. Oh, and she'd also wear an armband. We had a laugh about it – well, he did!

I was still in a state of shock. I couldn't help thinking about how my old man was going to feel the next day, watching me lead out the team from the Ibrox tunnel and onto the pitch in front of nearly 50,000 Rangers fans. I knew he was going to be so proud of me. To be honest, I was proud of myself. I knew Mum would be saying, 'Go on, son' with a smile as wide as the Clyde.

But I kept the good news to myself. I thought it was best that way. I didn't want it to dominate everything for the next twenty-four hours. I wanted to remain focused. I only told Amanda. Naturally, she was chuffed to bits and admitted it wasn't before time. But she was also able to quickly detach herself from the euphoria. So, as cool as you like, asked me, 'Well, Skipper, what do you want for your dinner?' I smiled. Amanda can be very laid back and that rubs off on me in a very good way.

In a way, being appointed captain was also a nice reward for Amanda and the kids. The problems that surrounded the club for the previous six months were not easy on them either. I made their lives very difficult because I brought my work home with me and couldn't switch off. I was snappy, moody and unfair on them. It put a tremendous strain on my relationship with Amanda. There were times she would have been well within her rights to tell me to pack my bags but she tried extremely hard to be understanding. I wasn't a good person to live with during most of that period. Callum and Jack never really understood what was going on. All they said to me was to tell the manager to pay the bills so their daddy could keep his job. My parents certainly felt it too. It took a lot out of Dad because he loves the club so much. Mum was on the phone every night, concerned for me and my family. They were both probably more shook up than me. Thankfully, it's all over now and we are where we are.

I barely got a wink of sleep the night before the Elgin game. I tossed and turned. I eventually admitted defeat and got out of bed around 6am. I couldn't get my club blazer and tie on quickly enough and arrived at the stadium around three hours before kick-off. I was so proud and on such a high. I had been captain on five previous occasions, all away from home. So, this was even more special. My first time at Ibrox, in front of the Bears.

Jimmy Bell moved my seat in the dressing room that I'd had from my first day at the club and I was now sitting in the official captain's seat, which is placed directly underneath a certain picture of an important and admired person. Again, I felt so proud.

I went into the game on ninety-nine career goals and was feeling really excited but a little nervous. I wanted to score. But, more importantly, I just wanted to win. The feeling I had as I walked down the tunnel was unreal. Absolutely took my breath away as the roar of the crowd hit me. The Rangers songs came on and it was also televised live on Sky Sports. It was ideal. I struggled to keep my composure but reminded myself it was important to act properly, in the manner of previous Rangers captains such as the successful John Greig, Davie Weir, Richard Gough, Terry Butcher and Barry Ferguson.

I had lived the dream of playing for my boyhood heroes but to captain the club was unreal. My dad watched the game at home with my mum and he had a beer and sang along with the fans, proud as ever. I did have a big thought for my old man as I got to the end of the tunnel and heard the roar from the Bears. In a quiet moment to myself, just before kick-off, I thanked the auld yin for everything and then focused on the game.

Being the captain was never going to be easy but it was a challenge I felt I was ready for and something that I would enjoy instead of being nervous about the responsibility. Barry Ferguson had always joked when he was captain that not many could handle the weight of the armband but I was more than ready for that weight on my arm and the challenges it would undoubtedly bring during the course of a campaign.

We won the game 5–1 and I scored two of our goals. It took me through the 100-goal barrier and also got my career as captain off to a winning start. When I got home after the game Callum and Jack ran towards me and said, 'Hey, Captain, heard you scored a goal each for us today.' That meant so much. For my boys to say that to me brought a tear to my eye. It made one of the best and proudest days of my life totally complete. Behind the births of Callum and Jack, that was the best day of my life.

But being at Rangers is all about trying to improve on the previous day. We are not allowed to dwell on good moments. That's the way it should be. I feel a huge sense of responsibility to help the club climb through the ranks again and get back to the top. As captain I have dozens of decisions to make every day and I often speak to Davie Weir for guidance and for his wisdom. He has always been full of encouragement. He was a great leader to me and the rest of the players when he was captain of Rangers and I'd love to be even half as good as he was on and off the park. When Davie was here the dressing room had plenty of experience in it and the boys could look after themselves, but the role does have different challenges nowadays.

I feel a huge responsibility to the young players at the football club. I stress to them the importance of working hard, being good listeners and being willing to learn the game. Several of the lads have coped with playing in front of almost 50,000 fans every other week and to do that when they are still teenagers will stand them in good stead. But as this club moves forward, they will need to show they are good enough to play in the SPL a couple of years down the line. I have rammed it home to them that they need to put every ounce of effort in and make sacrifices. Even though Andy Murray isn't a footballer I have told the young players they should look to him as a role model. I'd love to be able to get Andy into our place and let him talk us all through the graft he has put in to get to the very top in tennis.

I've got total admiration for successful Scottish sportsmen and women. A lot of Scottish people like to focus on negatives, but I prefer to concentrate on the positives. I have the utmost admiration for Andy. I was up out of my seat when he won the US Open and Gold at the 2012 Olympics. When he was breaking through I watched him at Wimbledon and he had all that incredible pressure on his shoulders because Tim Henman had retired and Andy was now the Great British hope. But he lacked stamina. He would crumble at Wimbledon in the fourth or fifth set. Now, when I look at him I see a total transformation and he has rid himself of that 'Glorious Failure' tag. His fitness levels are unbelievable, and the muscle tone on his body and strength he generates in his play is fantastic. From the outside looking in, I think the biggest thing he has added to his play is mental strength. Whether it's down to Ivan Lendl or not, he now looks a player that knows he can win and has the quality, fitness and temperament to get over the line, regardless of the opponent and the venue.

I played tennis and badminton when I was younger but golf and boxing are my other loves, apart from football. In the past year or two I've got involved at the Rob Roy ABC in Lanarkshire. The boxing training has been good for my fitness. It's fun putting on the gloves and battering a punch bag. I would have liked to have been a professional boxer. My all-time sporting hero is Muhammad Ali. He was rightly named 'The Greatest' and I have nothing but total respect for him. I have all of the DVDs of his fights, from the *Rumble in the Jungle* against George Foreman in *Zaire* to the *Fight of the Century* against Joe Frazier in New York. He is a man I'd love to meet. He'd be welcome at Ibrox any time.

I also have total respect for the World Champions we've had in Scotland in the past few years, guys such as Ricky Burns, Willie Limond and Scott Harrison. They are dedicated sportsmen and the work and effort that goes into each fight must be phenomenal. They push themselves to the limit every day and have been rewarded for the sacrifices they have made.

I want to make sure that when I do hang up my boots, or leave Rangers, which could be as early as the summer of 2015, I leave the dressing room in good health. By that I mean the youngsters have matured into good people, good professionals and are totally committed to getting Rangers back to the top. The young players have approached me about different things about being at Rangers and I'm happy to give them any guidance I can. Some of their requests have really taken me aback and one of the youngsters asked if I could help his mum find a job. I was really touched that he thought enough of me to speak to me about a matter such as that. Actually, it was quite overwhelming.

I only hope the young professionals don't follow in my footsteps when it comes to my superstitions and weird habits. I have a set routine for all games that must be adhered to. When the boot hamper is packed for games I take my boots out of it and spray them with Febreze because they stink. I then take my insoles out and give them to Jimmy Bell to take separately to the game. I then go into the sauna the day before the game and clean my boots. I also use an Italian oil to rub on them. Jimmy swears by this oil. Rino Gattuso got him it from Il Ciocco in Tuscany. It help keeps the leather on my boots lovely and soft.

I wouldn't go into the game in the right frame of mind if I wasn't satisfied with my routine. If we lose I will change the routine, but just tweak it here and there, nothing drastic. And it's not premeditated what I will change. It will be a spur-of-the-moment decision. It's not a personal thing, about whether I play well or score a goal. It's about the team winning, that is the be all and end all. If I scored a hat-trick and we lost 4–3 I wouldn't be happy and would examine my superstitions. It's about the team as a group winning games and Rangers getting the right result. It's weird to explain.

It's all rather strange but that's the way I am. I used to be worse. I went through a phase of cleaning the alloy wheels on my car every Friday night before a Saturday game. Sometimes I'd be relaxing in the house and I'd remember I hadn't cleaned them. So I'd go out and get stuck in, sometimes in the pelting rain. There I'd be with my waterproofs on, on the deck of my driveway cleaning my wheels. It's crazy, I know. Believe me, standing there with my bucket of water and sponge I'd question my own sanity!

I also think I may have OCD. I don't have it whereby I have to make sure all the tins and cereal boxes are all neat and tidy in the kitchen cupboards. No, it's more about having a routine and making sure my clothes are always hung up properly in the wardrobe and my shoes are all organised in a particular way.

It must also stem from my dad's background in the Navy. He is very neat and tidy – 'a place for everything and everything in its place'. Dad loved talking about his Navy days and sometimes we would take the mickey because of it, but I know I'm going to be exactly the same as him and ten, twenty, thirty years from now I will be telling my kids, and anyone else who'll listen, about me being captain of Glasgow Rangers FC.

Another area I would talk about to anyone who will listen is the issue of depression that seems more common in the footballing world today. I've heard too many horror stories in recent years about former players getting seriously depressed about being out of the game. I can totally understand why that would happen. It's something that terrifies me. Depression is very real and it's out there. Football must tackle this very serious issue and help provide answers.

Many footballers and, indeed, sportsmen, have spoken about it. Robert Enke, the German international keeper, suffered from it and took his own life at the age of just thirty-two. He had been suffering from depression for six years and had been seeing a psychiatrist. He committed suicide by standing in front of an express train in 2009. It was tragic.

Off the top of my head footballers who've played in Scotland, such as Paul Gascoigne, Neil Lennon and Dean Windass have opened up on it. It gets to people in different ways. It sounds horrific and I can totally understand where they are coming from and why they have ended up having to deal with such a problem. However, it does still seem to be a bit of a taboo subject. Perhaps people in sport need to raise awareness of it more. Everyone knows what to do if they have problems with alcohol or drugs, but it's not the same tackling depression.

The Sporting Chance Clinic in London – founded by Tony Adams – does excellent work on that front but I believe we need prevention, need to get to the root of the problem before it sets in. Footballers are used to an environment of being with twenty other footballers day in and day out, having a laugh and then being idolised by thousands of football fans on a match day. But it doesn't last forever. The moment arrives when it comes to an end and you have to find something else. Trouble is, there is no substitute for being involved in the game. Nothing can touch it. Many footballers retire from the game never having to worry about working another day ever again. But the money isn't what it's about. It's about being busy, having a purpose in life.

For me, it's also about your upbringing. I come from a working-class family and it's in me to work every day. People work until they're sixty, sixty-five or seventy. I feel I should be the same. Yes, I'd like a nice, long holiday when I hang up my boots, but nothing more than that. I don't want to play golf for the rest of my life. That's just not me. I will have to have a purpose, something that drives me on, stimulates me. Hopefully, it will be being involved in football in some capacity, but I know I can't take that for granted. And I know I would struggle without it.

21

SFL WINNERS

NATURALLY, I was delighted when we clinched the SFL Third Division title, for the good of the club. It was our goal for the season and we got there with a fair bit to spare, as was expected of us and what we expected from ourselves. Of course, it was strange having to play in the bottom tier of Scottish football, but Rangers Football Club had no choice. The SFA and SPL played games with our club and let everyone down. So much happened to the club between the start of June and the start of August that it's hard to know where to begin. On reflection, it was a ludicrous period. Scottish football's hierarchy made a total mess of the situation. Even more despicable than that, many people in a position of authority revelled in our misfortune to create a civil war within our game. Sporting integrity? Do me a favour.

It started when it was found out Craig Whyte didn't pay PAYE and NI contributions to the tune of around £15 million. That led us into administration and on the road to ruin. HMRC were still in pursuit of £49 million from the club, dating back to Sir David Murray's tenure, as they believed the club had avoided paying tax on an EBT (Employee Benefit Trust) scheme. Towards the end of 2012 the taxman lost the case when an FTT (First Tier Tribunal) decided the undeclared payments were loans and not earnings and were therefore not subject to income tax. However, this wrangle and investigation ran on for more than three years. Had a decision been reached earlier then we may have avoided the scenario that unfolded after Whyte had been found out.

As it was, HMRC rejected the offer of a CVA (Company Voluntary Arrangement) from Duff and Phelps on 12 June, which condemned Glasgow Rangers Football Club to liquidation. It also meant that Charles Green's newco had to apply to play in the SPL in season 2012-13. That was rejected and we were thrown out. We were left without a home. Us ending up in Division Three was relished by many in the SPL. Inevitably we had to move on some of our better players, which obviously weakened our team. We have some very good young players, but at the moment we're not ready for Celtic. It pains me to say it. Our old rivals at the moment are the gold standard of the SPL and are pretty much guaranteed European football for the next few years. That's the challenge we have and we will rise to it and through it in the coming five years.

We'll need a year or two to get back into the SPL and then we'll need a period of time to adjust and build a squad to challenge Celtic. A long, long road is ahead of Rangers but we have people at the club ready for the challenge. They will take it head on and make sure the club comes out the other side, bigger, better and stronger. Like Ally McCoist said when we went into administration, 'We don't do walking away,' and I know he means that. I agree 100 per cent.

Other things happened to the club during that dark period in the summer of 2012. We were handed a transfer embargo by the SFA judicial panel, which meant we weren't allowed to sign players during the January and summer transfer windows in 2013. We were also banned from playing in European football for three years.

We were then hounded by an SPL investigation to decide if we should be stripped of five SPL titles for alleged dual contracts for some players between 2000 and 2011. The SFA wanted Charles Green to voluntarily relinquish titles as part of an agreement to get us into the SFL First Division. Everybody wanted a boot at us. A few got in on the act and those who were on the outside wanted their pound of flesh. The conduct of some people within Scottish football was appalling. Some people wanted us found guilty without a hearing.

Too many chairmen and owners cut off their nose to spite their face and it has backfired for many. They allowed their fans to make the decision for them. What a cop-out. In return, the fans guaranteed they would make up the financial shortfall of not having Rangers in the top flight by boosting the average attendance figures and turning out in force. It didn't happen. A few clubs have been let down by their fans. As a result, the manager will have his budget cut and it will mean the product on the pitch is unlikely to be as good. What an almighty mess. Some other clubs didn't look at the bigger picture and it has backfired spectacularly.

Our club got treated abysmally and yet there was nothing we could do. We were powerless. Our only thought was to exist, and we had to take anything that was going. The SFA held back our Club Licence until the last moments before we played our opening game of the season away to Brechin City. It meant our pre-season was shambolic, an absolute joke. Just six players turned up for our first day back at training. We had to cancel our pre-season trip to Germany and we were only allowed to play games behind closed doors. It was totally unfair on Ally McCoist, his backroom staff and the remaining members of the top-team squad.

I didn't know if I'd ever kick a ball again for the club. In fact, there was a period of about two weeks during July when I had a constant worry the club would shut down and cease to exist. And I mean that. I was scared that was going to happen because I just couldn't see any way out for us as a football club. I remember thinking Rangers were too big to go into administration. Bang. It happened. Rangers are too big to go into liquidation. Bang. It happened. So, I thought our club may well have been forced to shut its doors and never be allowed to re-open. I had the feeling we were getting our medicine, taking our punishments, but it still wasn't enough for some people. They wanted more and more; they wanted to twist the knife. There appeared to be deep-rooted hatred of Rangers and jealousy which took precedence over the well-being of Scottish football.

I also had a situation to deal with during the summer with SFA chief executive Stewart Regan. It came to my attention in June 2012 that there was an offensive tweet on his Twitter account. It was a tweet about wanting me hung. I was livid, but I let it go. I was prepared to let developments unfold without forcing anything. The following day, Darryl Broadfoot, the SFA Head of Communications, phoned to say Stewart had made a mistake and had not intended to send the message. The offensive tweet had been sent to him and he had intended to save it as evidence, as he was to report all bigoted and sectarian tweets. But, instead, he accidentally sent it. I told Darryl that I understood mistakes happen but I'd prefer to hear it from Stewart. Late that night Regan phoned me. He said that he would say sorry for what had happened but, in his opinion, there was nothing to say sorry for. But he wanted to make it clear that the offensive tweet had been sent in error and there was no ill will on his part. I told him I wasn't happy, as I didn't want to be linked with being hung. It only puts ideas in the heads of the morons. But I believed him when he said it was accidental and by the end of the phone call we agreed to put it to bed and move on.

As a football club we found some open arms and comfort from the SFL. They had a vote on whether they wanted us or not and twenty-five out of their thirty member clubs voted us into their

Third Division. Game on. In a way I've felt it's made the club a more family club as everyone knows where they are and we're all pulling in the one direction.

I had always said I would never walk out on Rangers and that after going through so much to get to the club, I wasn't going to quit. But I did have a wee wobble just before the competitive season got underway.

A big part of me also missed some of the experienced lads that had left the club, in particular Allan McGregor. He left the club and I was surprised at his decision but totally understood where he was coming from. However, I got the feeling he didn't really want to go because he is Rangers through and through. Not long after he made that decision he phoned me to say he felt he had made a mistake and wanted back. I informed the manager, but, of course, it was impossible for that move to happen. I tried my best for Allan. Not only is he my mate, he is a leader on and off the pitch. He's invaluable.

I got my head together and had to concentrate on getting myself ready for a massive season in the club's history. I didn't want to let anyone down. Anything other than winning the league would have been an absolute disaster and embarrassment.

Our first game was away to Brechin City in the Ramsdens Cup. After a disastrous pre-season, we cobbled a team together. Due to the lack of games, few of us were anywhere near the level of match-fitness we'd been used to in the past. We won 2–1 after extra-time. Andy Little scored our opening goal and I got the winner.

Our first competitive game at Ibrox was against East Stirling and kick-off had to be delayed due to the size of the crowd. The stadium was bursting at the seams. Nobody envisaged that every seat would be taken. We won 5–1 and I scored two goals.

In terms of league games, the season was fairly smooth for us. We had to dig in in many games and grind out results.

That was fine. We lost away to Stirling Albion and at home to Annan Athletic. Both were real low points. I don't want to sound arrogant but we beat ourselves in those games. That's the way it was, for whatever reason, but we were always going to have one or two hiccups along the way. When the going gets tough and things aren't going to plan, when there is internal and external pressure, then that's when you really find out what people are made of, how they react in the face of adversity. Some go away and hide. Some blame others to deflect any deficiencies away from their own doorstep. Expectation levels at Rangers are very high and more than a few employees have been found out over the years. I keep telling the young boys to work hard and never take anything for granted.

After the Stirling defeat, we played at home to Queens Park in a Glasgow derby. There was pressure on us going into that game and we knew we needed to show a reaction from the previous week's embarrassment. We were drawing at half-time and our fans booed us off the pitch. I was far from satisfied with our performance. I played centre-forward and didn't have a good first half either, but I felt, as captain, I had to say something. In the dressing room I had a right go at Ian Black. I told Black his level of performance wasn't acceptable and the team needed more from him. He wasn't happy and had a go back at me. I was standing up, drinking a bottle of water, and I threw the bottle of water in his direction. It bounced off the wall, just above his head. I then went for him and both of us had to be held back. Calm was restored before we went out onto the pitch. We went out and won the game. I picked out Blackie because I knew he could handle the fight. I knew he could take it and react in the right way.

I felt Black played well in the second half and what I said to him had the desired impact. I didn't want to have a go at him but something needed to be done. He was in the engine room of the team and is one of our more experienced players. It needed to be said. Kenny McDowall came to me at full-time to say I was quite right to have a go. I apologised to Blackie at full-time for throwing the water bottle in his direction.

Big Davie Weir attended that day. His dad had sadly passed away earlier that week. I attended the funeral. Davie stayed on for a couple of days and was in the directors' box. I wore a black armband as a mark of respect for Mr Weir. When I scored the first goal that day I ran away, pointed to the armband and waved up to Davie. He was chuffed. Davie told me his dad would have loved that.

Davie wasn't one for saying much in the dressing room before games or at half-time, but I remember he exploded one afternoon when we were in the SPL and away to Aberdeen. Kyle Lafferty was having a shocker and Davie absolutely ripped him to shreds. Davie's veins popped out of his neck and he had a horrible look in his eye as he gave both barrels to Lafferty. Walter Smith was the manager then. He stood back and let his skipper get on with it.

During my time at Rangers I served under four captains. Barry Ferguson led the club to the treble in 2003 when he was just twenty-five years old. Barry wasn't one for talking to the rest of lads in the dressing room before games or at half-time to gee the boys up, but on the pitch he never stopped. He talked non-stop, most of the time it was moaning and sometimes he would go over the top with it, but there was method in it. Barry was always thinking of the bigger picture. I know some of the new signings found it very difficult to cope with and they weren't particularly fond of Barry because of it. But, after a while, they had total respect for him. The players would be out of their shell after six months and able to cope with most things that came their way. Barry felt it was better he shouted at them rather than nearly 50,000 getting onto them from the stands. Every player gets a honeymoon period from the supporters and that was when Barry would give it tight to the new lads.

That's the kind of thing I've taken from Barry and into my captaincy. Every young player at the club will say I'm a moaner – sometimes to the point of being a nasty piece of work on the park – but I'm doing it for their own good. I'm on at them constantly to win their tackles and their headers, and if they do something good I will tell them to make sure they follow it up with another positive. I've not allowed them to rest on their laurels. I've been there with fans on my back. It was a horrible, horrible place to be in and there was no hiding from it. For the young players to be ready for the SPL in one or two years' time they need to be able to cope with stick, and if they give the ball away, they need to look for possession right away. I speak to the young players all the time, make sure they've been motivated and that everything is good in their world. I've enjoyed seeing them thrive and it has humbled me. They put up with a lot of listening to me moaning and shouting and also advising them to keep away from the bevvy and not to go out most weekends. I'm only doing it to get the best out of them and that's what matters to me most. A few came to me over the months for advice and, sometimes, a sort of shoulder to cry on. I've been comfortable with that, as, in many ways, that's what I'm there for.

Robbie Crawford is inquisitive. He has a good head on young shoulders. He has an excellent attitude. He always asks questions, he's very thorough. I can tell Robbie lives and breathes the game. I like that. He reminds me of myself when I was a young player at Motherwell, always asking questions and gathering information and knowledge from the senior professionals. I'll be very surprised if he doesn't go a long way in the game. He works away quietly in the background but he is going to be a very effective player for Rangers for many years to come.

The captaincy has brought many mixed feelings and emotions.

As captain you have to put yourself second and the team first so any personal glory for me is no gain and it's all about team glory – but I've always been this way through my career anyway. The young players have helped keep me fresh and enthusiastic, although I've always found it easy to be motivated. I don't want to sound like a saddo, but I have been up for every game this season. Listen, I might not have played well in all of them but I give my all. That's the way I've always been and I'll never change – whether it's a pre-season friendly or a training game, I'm all in, all the time. I'm not ashamed to say that and I'm not doing it to deliver a cliché.

Yet there were some things the Third Division was unable to deliver, obviously – the main one being playing against Celtic. I miss the Old Firm games. I loved playing in them. I'm sure Neil Lennon and Ally McCoist will be glad of a rest away from the pressures and strains of the Old Firm, but I'm not of that mind. As I've said before, I may well have played in my last ever Old Firm game and that is a painful thought for me. I was envious when I watched Cetic play in the Champions League and beat Barcelona. I've missed the SPL. I can't hide from that. I can't tell any lies. However, I think there had to be a fresh start. We had to get away from some of the clubs and some of the people in the top division. Let them see how they would handle life without us in the top division. It's been refreshing to play at other grounds too because it does get monotonous going to the same grounds every season, week in, week out.

The standard in our own play has dipped in the past season, there is no doubt about that. But we lost so many top players that it was inevitable that was going to happen. It would be ludicrous to expect inexperienced teenagers to come in and fill the boots of someone such as Steve Davis, Steven Whittaker or Stevie Naismith. That was never going to happen. That's why I fully expected 2012-13 in the SFL Third Division to be so tough in many ways and I did expect more than a few disappointments over the course of the nine- or ten-month period.

In the early part of the season, the first round of fixtures, the opposition played as though it was a World Cup Final. Every side was organised and up for it. Every player was pumped up to the maximum, so much so that it's the only time in my career I can recall two players high-fiving each other when they blocked one of my shots from the edge of the box to send it out for a corner kick. They celebrated as if they had clinched the three points. It was the away game at Annan Athletic when we drew at their place. For me, that kind of sums up what we've been up against this season. But I'm not criticising the opposition for it, they've been perfectly entitled to be that way and I totally understood where they were coming from.

I thought SFL Division Three would have been easier than what it was. Some defenders have good experience and know how to handle themselves. The best thing has been the patter on the park. It's been brilliant. In the games we managed to go a couple of goals ahead, the opposition would sort of put the tools away and their focus was on who was to get my top at the end of the game. A couple of the Elgin City boys had a barney on the pitch about it. In front of more than 45,000 fans at Ibrox their players were going at it hammer and tongs. I gave my jersey away in the first few games but then Jimmy Bell got me into trouble. He told me to stop doing it. Any player that asked for my jersey was to go and see Jimmy. A few players from other teams would chap our dressing room door at full-time asking for Jimmy Bell. They'd tell him they wanted my jersey and he would tell them, in the nicest possible way of course, they weren't getting it. After the Elgin City game in March up at their place, their skipper asked me for my jersey and I told him to see Jimmy Bell. He told me I cracked that one with him in our previous meeting at Ibrox and this time he wasn't taking no for an answer. So, I took my jersey off on the pitch and gave it to him, seeing he was so keen to get it.

There are some players who will leave the boot in now and again and a few also like to tell you that they're Celtic fans and that they hate Rangers. I don't have a problem with things like that, it's all banter; we got that every week in the SPL too. What is also different from the top flight is that the playing surfaces are very close to the terracing and stands. You are so close to the fans, they are right on top of you and it can be very intimidating.

I found the away game at Elgin City on 16 March a nervy one. It came the week after we'd lost to Annan at Ibrox. It was 0–0 going into the last twenty minutes and we needed to win the game. Another one of Lee Wallace's rampaging runs down the left won us a penalty kick. It counted that afternoon in Elgin. It was a massive game. For me to get the chance to take that penalty and make everything right again was extremely important. I had to lead by example and take responsibility. I scored from it and it was a massive win for so many different reasons. A few people would have had plenty to say if we hadn't won it. It felt about as important a game as I'd ever played for Rangers.

Winning the league aside, another high I had was captaining the team the day Rangers celebrated its 140th anniversary. We were at home to Stirling Albion and we won 2–0. It was great to see so many Ibrox legends attend the game, including the Greatest Ever Ranger, John Greig. But it was sad another Gers great, Sandy Jardine, couldn't attend that day. Sandy had been diagnosed with cancer of the liver and throat and was recovering after a life-saving operation. Thankfully, he is well on the mend and was able to attend a home game against East Stirling on 2 March. He received a thunderous welcome that day from the Rangers supporters and that must have been very moving for him. The Rangers fans have been brilliant to Sandy and the way they have continued their applause in the second minute of every game for him has been fitting and derserved.

Personally, to break the 100-goal barrier as a professional footballer also gave me tremendous satisfaction. To score more than 100 goals as a professional footballer has given me a tremendous buzz. I take great pride and satisfaction from it considering I rarely ever played as a striker during my time at Motherwell, Wigan and Rangers. To score the 100th goal on the day I was captain of Rangers at Ibrox Stadium was a huge thrill. I just wish I had played more games this season, though. I picked up a bad ankle injury at the turn of the year and that kept me out for seven weeks. It was very frustrating.

The fans have given me and the team unbelievable backing in the past twelve months. Over the course of the season, they were absolutely incredible. Off the park they made sure the Share Issue was a huge success and it raised more than £20 million to help take the club forward. On a match day they have been our twelfth man, their passion and commitment there for all to see, travelling up and down the country. They have been an integral part of keeping the club alive and they set a new world record a few times over with highest attendance in the league. They have had it tough at times with some of our performances, but they never turned their backs. The Blue Order have been amazing. Sometimes Ibrox can be a little bit quiet but these guys are non-stop for ninety minutes and really give the players a lift. Long may that continue. Overall, for all of our fans, I doubt they'll ever have to go though anything as bad as the past eighteen months. I'm sure they won't.

For me, the final part of bringing an end to the misery came on 28 February 2013. After a year-long whispering campaign and people labelling our club 'cheats', an investigation by an SPL Independent Commission, chaired by Lord William Nimmo Smith, announced that Rangers were cleared of gaining any unfair sporting advantage by the use of EBTs and dual contracts. It took them more than six months to gather evidence and come to their findings, but it wasn't good enough for some. People wanted up to five titles taken from us and I was a part of three of them – in 2009, 2010 and 2011. It was a disgrace there was even an investigation in the first place. What a waste of time and it also cost more than £400,000 in legal fees. Nobody was ever going to take my championship-winning medals from me, that was for sure. And let me make it absolutely clear. I never had an EBT and I never had a dual contract. I won my medals fair and square. We all did.

The verdict from the commission was great news for the club. For that period of around a year, it was like a cancer that ate away at us, bit by bit, day by day. People wanted us dead and buried. Simple as that. I hope the worst of it is now over. Surely it must be. Really, can anything else negative happen to us? I think we'll kick on next season and we'll be much better. It's about getting back into the SPL as quickly as possible.

The past year was about winning games, that is the be all and end all in football. But we have to win and also play a certain brand of football. Our fans want to be entertained and they deserve to be entertained. We have to give them better football. And we will. I understand why people expected us to win 5–0 every week and play the part-time sides off the park in some kind of Barcelona-style, but, realistically, that was never going to happen.

For a period during the first couple of months of the season I reckon there was an air of depression in and around the club. Some people might not have been aware of it, but I felt it existed. I felt depressed sometimes, no doubt. Under the circumstances of everything that had gone on, that was inevitable. We had all been through so much, taken right to the very edge time after time – the manager more than most – and we had to battle hard to come through the other side.

Because of circumstances, the manager didn't have much to work with in the summer and was even limited in the amount of signings he could make in the SFL, but the players he brought in made an impact and made a significant contribution to us winning the League. The coaching staff made sure we all integrated and we had some real positives, such as Chris Hegarty and Andrew Mitchell becoming Northern Ireland Under-21 players and our other kids such as Fraser Aird, Kal Naismith, Robbie Crawford, Lewis Macleod and Barrie McKay played as though they've been in the first team for years. The boys all have great togetherness and it's a pleasure to work with them. Dean Shiels and David Templeton both made a good impact on the park and were very professional off the park.

Our more experienced players have also played a huge part in the dressing room and on the pitch. Lee Wallace and Neil Alexander have been class this year and a help to me in my captain's role. The manager, Kenny McDowall and Ian Durrant have stayed strong and got us one step closer to where we all want to be.

We have now secured title number 55 in the club's illustrious history. I'm very proud to have been a part of it as we are one of the most successful clubs in the world of football. This title has given me the most satisfaction because of everything the club has been through, and to be captain is extra special. Of course, we would all have preferred it to have been another SPL Championship success, but circumstances outwith the control of the manager and the players prevented that. We are where we are and we will continue our pursuit to getting back to the top of Scottish football. Considering the dire situation we were in during the spring and summer of 2012, we have made great strides since then. We are heading in the right direction but patience and togetherness will remain key to it all. With the help of our loyal fans we will get there.

22

LEE MCCULLOCH'S DREAM TEAM

I CONSIDER myself extremely fortunate to have played with and against some of Europe's and the world's greatest players. I spent countless hours on my line-ups, taking into consideration the merits of my team-mates and opponents. I'm pretty sure at one point my shortlist was about thirty-five for each side. So, it's fair to say, having to select a Dream Team and an Opponents' XI has presented me with the most agonising decisions I've had to make in writing this book. But it's also been lots of fun. I can't include every good player I shared a pitch with, and I hope I don't offend anyone.

I based my team on a mixture of abilities and also have some guys that I would want in the trenches beside me if I were playing in a game to save my career or life. I firmly believe team spirit and togetherness is every bit as important – if not more important – than ability.

I've also selected eleven of my toughest opponents. Having played as a centre-forward, central defender and central midfielder, it's been extremely beneficial in assessing the many different players I came up against. Some of them made my life as a footballer really difficult and that's why they have been chosen. I'm sure it would have been an interesting game between my dream team and toughest opponents!

But here is my Dream Team selection and, needless to say, you do not find me in the dream team. I'm not worthy of a slot in there, not to mention the fact I'd prefer to give the guys a chance of winning the game! As I've not selected myself I would happily be the bus driver or help wee Jimmy Bell with the kit. Or maybe I would just buy a season ticket to watch the lads perform!

DREAM TEAM (4-4-2)

Goalkeeper
GARRY GOW: Gowzer has been my close mate since we were both apprentice footballers at Motherwell. He is a strong character, very brave and also has a madcap streak in him, which is typical of goalkeepers. We went through a lot together on and off the pitch so he has to be my number one. He has ability and also has a big nose to help him fly through the air! He is one of the very few people who nickname me 'Cully'. Why? Well, when I first joined Motherwell everyone called me Lee. I never had a nickname. Football being football, every player must have a nickname and Alex McLeish called me 'Cully'. Not very original! The lads didn't even laugh at it and quickly ignored it. But Gowzer has stuck with it.

From our early days at Fir Park we clicked right away and became close pals. He'd come down to my mum's house for lunch between training sessions. But he was a lazy boy at doing his jobs for the senior players. He hated cleaning boots and setting out the training gear. So I'd do it for him. He used to laugh and call me 'brown tongue'.

He was a brilliant keeper and I remember getting him Keeper of the Tournament when we were in Spain. He got a beautiful watch for it and he's never shut up about it from that day. We lost to Real Madrid in the final. We all got skinheads for the final, which was amusing at the time. Willie McLean was the Youth Team manager back then and I think even he managed to raise a smile at us. Gowzer moved on to play for different clubs and I'm delighted we still remain in close contact.

Defence

GED BRANNAN: Ged played with me at Motherwell and Wigan and is a central midfield player but he was also extremely effective at right-back, and that's why I've chosen him in that position. He was solid in the tackle and was also good at taking and delivering set pieces. Every player he played against knew they were in a game.

He took me under his wing when he arrived at Motherwell. He really helped me coming into the first team at Motherwell, which I was grateful for, and gave me lots of confidence which I needed at that time! He is a top bloke, typical Scouser that loves a drink but has a great attitude. He was loud and confident, but in a nice way.

Ged came in at a time when John Boyle was spending money. He came up here with his wife Melanie and they stayed in Motherwell. He showed me the ropes, the do's and don'ts of a dressing room and general advice as to how to get on as a young professional. He loved a right good bevvy but used to tell me to be a better professional than he was, to pick and choose the right times to socialise.

LEIGHTON BAINES: Bainesy is different class. Simple as that. He was coming into the team at Wigan just as we started having success. I played on the left with him and he is undoubtedly developing into one of the best left-backs in world football at the moment. Without question, he is the best left-footed player I've ever played with. Along with his wand of a left foot he also has great pace and can be as hard as nails. I'm delighted to see him playing regularly for England as his dedication and willingness to learn is second to none.

I played when he made his debut for Wigan. After his fourth or fifth game Paul Jewell said in his team talk, 'Bainesy, just you keep doing what you've been doing. I've had Alex Ferguson on the phone and he's told me he wants first refusal on you.' How good was that? We all knew he was going to be a star. For a Scouser, he is quite a quiet guy but he does love a good laugh! He just likes to sit back and soak it all in. He's also honest and hardworking. We were very close at Wigan and still keep in touch.

DAVIE WEIR (Captain): My skipper has been there for me in the past as a shoulder to cry on and moan on and, basically, to annoy the hell out of him! He is now into his coaching career and I know he will be a leader of men as a manager at a big club. He has all the credentials and respect of his peers.

He skippered Rangers in the Champions League when he was forty and that sums the big guy up. On the pitch he could be a nasty bastard. Even when we were in training he loved to get a kick at you, let you know he was there.

I knew Davie from the Scotland squads. He was a senior player and I was in the Under-21s. But that mattered not a jot when I played for Wigan and lined up against him at Everton when he was centre-half. I tried to make a run inside the box to get on the end of a free-kick. I was stopped in my tracks as Davie elbowed me bang in the middle of my nose. He then stared at me, as if to say, 'Well, come on then. What you got to offer me?'

Off the park, he is a gent and has some of the best one-liners going! He also has great teeth (he'll be buzzing I said that!).

MATT JACKSON: Mr Wigan and our captain through the good times. A very good player. Matt had an amazing attitude and was a great example for young kids! Having him and Davie as my central defensive pairing must mean the combined age is touching ninety, but that wouldn't matter to them or to me. They know the game and that's what matters.

Matt helped me through my Wigan days by showing me different areas. He also found me a house there. We had different managers and different players coming and going all the time and that made it quite a challenging dressing room, sort of hard to get momentum going and togetherness built. But he kept working at it and made sure foundations were put down. He showed authority and leadership and helped cement the boys together. Yet, strangely enough, he wasn't the most confident of guys, he was quite shy. Was quite rightly a fans' favourite.

Midfield

JIMMY BULLARD: Where do I start? A wee guy, just skin and bones to him, really. Easily the worst hair in football but a lovely guy and the best banter in the game! A typical Cockney off the pitch. On the boys' nights out in pubs he would usually take his top off and get the full pub to count him to twenty topless press-ups, then pour a pint over his head and finish off with a song!

Jimmy was a brilliant player and had a fantastic level of fitness as he went from box to box for ninety minutes and never seemed to tire. He was the most confident player I've ever played with, sometimes it bordered on over-confidence but I didn't mind that in him.

In our debut season in the Premiership he was just unbelievable before games as the teams stood in the tunnel. We were little Wigan Athletic, newly promoted and expected to be the whipping boys. Jimmy would be standing there with the likes of Steven Gerrard, Frank Lampard and Paul Scholes opposite him for the top teams. Jimmy did not give a monkey. He used to shout at the top of his voice towards the opposition, 'Don't come in the Bullard dog house because you'll get bitten.'

After a few weeks he'd tell us he was going to scream it at the top of his voice and that we had to respond by barking back, 'Woof, woof'. So, he shouted it in the tunnel and the rest of the boys kept quiet. Not one of us gave the response he was looking for. So, he shouted it again and then answered himself with, 'Woof, woof.'

He took to the Premiership without a problem. Some of us were a little apprehensive and sort of dipped our toes in, but Jimmy just got in there with both feet and was inspirational in our debut season.

He was also a busy boy and loved to make an appearance on Soccer AM. He used to tell us Tim Lovejoy was desperate to get him on all the time but we later found out his agent was on the phone to them non-stop asking for Jimmy to get a gig.

BARRY FERGUSON: Like myself a Lanarkshire lad, and his dad, Archie, would sometimes take us to play in games together when we were kids. We played together for Rangers and Scotland and he was a leader on the park. Always played with his head up, looking to play a pass. Had very good vision, never hid and always demanded possession. On the park, maturity beyond his years from an early age. A total winner. And I believe a guy cut out to have a great future in management.

PAUL DALGLISH: Another close mate at Wigan. He played well wide right of a midfield four and was very direct, loved to run at the full-back. On his day was a really good player. I had sympathy for him – I think we all did, actually – having to run out with Dalglish on his back, as his dad was the best Scottish player ever. That must have been a huge weight to carry around. All things considered, Paul coped very well. He was lightning quick and had a great right foot. He maybe just didn't believe in himself enough.

Off the pitch he loved a laugh and had amazing one-liners. It wasn't pleasant to be on the receiving end of his tongue. Paul Jewell didn't really take to him as Paul Dalglish used to wind him up. One day he parked his Porsche in the gaffer's parking bay and when confronted by Jewell he gave him both barrels, turned the situation around on its head. Jewell was wearing a tight T-shirt and he told him he looked like a fat member of the band Boyzone – who were the in-band at that time.

Paul Dalglish never introduced me to Ronan Keating but he did take me out for lunch one day with the former glamour model Jordan, aka Katie Price. She was in Manchester for a Manchester United game. I think she might have been dating Dwight Yorke at that time. She was good company and she told Paul she liked me!

JAMES McFADDEN: He started off at Motherwell as my boot boy and I tried to help him as much as possible by giving him encouragement and guidance. I took to him straightaway. Yet, he used to slaughter me for only giving him a £40 bonus at Christmas. He casts that up every time we meet! When you looked at him he stood out immediately as he had a ponytail and would sometimes have red streaks through his hair. But his ability put all that in the shade. He was ultra-talented, blessed with a gift to play football. On countless occasions, I watched his spaghetti legs turn great defenders inside out!

His first game for the first team was during a pre-season and he played on the left wing. He was only seventeen and he went out there to prove a point as he felt he should have been given a top-team debut sooner. He quickly became a player that couldn't be left out of the side and he earned the respect of the senior professionals very, very quickly.

He came from a tough part of Glasgow and you could see he was willing to work and fight to make his way in the game.

A good boy and a right good laugh. Faddy developed into a Scotland hero and I'm delighted for him about that. A lovely lad with a fantastic family. We'll be friends for a long time to come, that's for sure.

Forwards
KRIS BOYD: I don't think Kris got enough praise or enough respect from too many people in the game. I felt for him a lot of the time because the negatives in his game received too much attention. He got far too much stick at Rangers, but you have to have a high level of ability to score the amount of goals that he did. He was a ridiculously talented finisher, could rattle them in from anywhere inside the box with either foot. One of the best I've ever seen. To be the highest ever goalscorer in the history of the SPL says it all. Also takes a bit of beating when it comes to sticking away his pre-match meal!

Sure, he didn't enjoy playing the lone striker role. He played up front on his own in a game at Celtic Park and he didn't get a sniff. It was backs-to-the-wall stuff for us. He came off the park at the end and said, 'That's the best ninety minutes I've ever had at playing hide and seek, because I can't remember touching the ball.'

During the many more productive games he had, when we had the ball he would position himself to get a goal. As his team-mate, it didn't bother me if he wasn't running about daft and going into channels all the time. Goodness, the amount of time I had to do his running for him was frightening! But I knew if we got a decent ball into the box he would score. That was his job, and if every player was as lethal at their jobs as Boydy was at his, then the game would be in a better place.

I have so much time for him as a person and we are close mates. He's a down-to-earth boy from Tarbolton in Ayrshire. He's had a solid upbringing and I can see similarities between his dad and mine in the way we've been reared about the game of football.

Loves life and loves a laugh. Grew a moustache for a dare for the Scottish Cup final against Falkirk – that's my kind of guy. Also spent nearly £10,000 on a new set of teeth, and if you can remember his old ones then it's the best cash he's ever spent. Has one ear higher than the other and that's why his wife Christine calls him Shrek! Right, that's enough of a pounding for him!

JOHN SPENCER: From the first day I met Spenny at Motherwell I took to him and looked up to him. Bubbly, funny, a great attitude and very kind. He made sure he took time out to speak to everyone at the club and was always pleasant to my mum and dad. When he arrived at Motherwell it was a great signing as he'd had a career down south at Everton and Chelsea. He knew the game and passed his knowledge on to me. He showed me the right runs to make and when to make them. That was massive in my development. He also helped me to relax in the footballing environment because it can be a very unforgiving place. I think he was a very good finisher and would be a great foil for Boydy. Spenny was a big influence on me as a footballer and as a person.

Substitutes

ALLAN McGREGOR: AKA Stiff Eddie or Chicken Legs! Up there with the best ever keepers this country has produced. An honest, hardworking pro and hates losing. Also fancies himself as a bit of a striker, so more back-up for the bench! I miss him and was sorry to see him quit Rangers. We're in constant contact and I know he misses the club. I think he will be back playing for Rangers in the not too distant future.

ANDY GORAM: One of my heroes. Played with Andy at Motherwell. A nice guy and very funny. Also a top goalkeeper and used to show it training and in games – when he could be bothered to turn up! I'll never forget his penalty kick save from Pierre van Hooijdonk in an Old Firm game at Parkhead.

ALLY McCOIST: Another hero of mine. Still loves to play in games and is still different class at putting chances away. In his heyday he won Golden Boot awards and his patter is also right up there with the best. Very witty. In training he liked us to call him the 'Gas Man' because when he came on as a sub he'd turn the heat up a few peeps!

STEVIE SMITH: Comes from Blantyre and he thinks that makes him as hard as nails. Aye, right! The wee man was unlucky at Rangers through injury when I was there but is a top player! Someone I got really close to and still am. Hard as nails in the challenge and a great crosser of the ball. Takes a bit of stick as he looks like Shaggy from *Scooby Doo*! Takes pride in his appearance, which also translates into Poser!

JOHN FLECK: Wee Square-heid, as we used to call him at Rangers, is a fantastic footballer. I was disappointed he didn't fulfil his potential at Rangers but he's still young and talented enough to play at the very highest level in the UK.

A lovely kid but not the brightest! I remember at our pre-match meal on the day we were playing Kilmarnock at Rugby Park to clinch three-in-a-row and Flecky was with me and Davie Weir. Considering what was at stake that afternoon, we were all a little nervous and started to talk about things other than football, to take our minds off the game. The chat turned to Fleck's family and big Davie asked the wee man what his mum's name was before she got married. Flecky was deadly serious and replied, 'Christine. Why you want to know that?' Me and Davie just buckled. We couldn't stop laughing. I had to leave the room to calm myself down. But Flecky still didn't get it. He then started to lose the rag and then said, 'What are you two laughing at, ya couple of pricks?' That just set the pair of us off again. Flecky was an unconscious comedian. His patter that day took our minds away from the big game, but in a good way. We went on, of course, to beat Kilmarnock and clinch another SPL title.

He had another cracker one day when in conversation he stated that I used to play for Wigan. I said, 'Yes, that's right.' Flecky then asked me whereabouts in London Wigan is!

Flecky was my roommate and is a class guy. He isn't daft but just doesn't think before he opens his mouth! Obviously, he won't have a clue what I've written about him – not unless the book is also out on audio!

WULLIE McCULLOCH: I was going to put myself on the bench but it's best for the team if the place goes to my big brother, Wullie. When he was younger he was an amazing talent and had much, much more potential than me. He was a centre-forward and would regularly score fifty goals a season. Chose to go away from the game when he was at secondary school but that doesn't take away his talent. Go on, Wullie son! He also made it onto the bench in Davie Weir's Dream Team.

DAVID LAVERY: Big Disco Dave is my close mate. He has been my psychologist and my shoulder to cry on. Officially, he is the Rangers masseur and a very popular person. Would run through brick walls for any player at the club. And for Rangers. During the administration period he offered to also take a 75 per cent pay cut in a bid to help the club stay alive. For me, it sums the guy up. Incredible vision with his Homer Simpson-style eyes! Capable of opening up any defence with either one of his two left feet – if only someone would pass to him! That's why he will get a run out!

Manager

WALTER SMITH: The only guy I can think of who'd have the respect of the dressing room in order to keep that lot in check! An out-and-out football man, with the knowledge and CV to sit in any company. Was great for my career and also never really had to lose the plot with us. He had an icy stare, a knack of just looking at you in a certain way if he wasn't happy with you. It was as though you'd taken a few slaps off of him without him having to lift his hand!

Assistant Manager

PAUL JEWELL: Would be a great no.2 for Walter. Was brilliant for us at Wigan and I'll always be grateful for that. An old-school manager and he didn't take any shite from any players. Fancied himself as a bit of a player and also liked a laugh at the right times.

Kit Man

JIMMY 'THE KAISER' BELL: He is Mr Rangers and loves the club more than life itself. Seriously. But is also a grumpy wee man. He is very close to Davie Lavery and they are seldom apart. The boys have often wondered if there is something going on between them! His son, Martin, is following in his footsteps, learning the trade as club kit man. Martin is a cracking guy and also loves the Bears.

OPPOSITION XI (4-4-2)

Goalkeeper

DAVID JAMES: I played against David a few times and always thought he was a top quality keeper. He had a huge presence and appeared to be a great communicator and organiser on the pitch. I scored against him twice – both times when he played for Portsmouth. One of the goals was a volley from the edge of the eighteen-yard box and it flew past him. Harry Redknapp pulled me at the end of the game at Fratton Park and told me I had scored with a special strike. We then played them at home and I scored the winner against him again and that gave me a real boost of confidence against England's no.1.

Defence

SOL CAMPBELL: I played against him a few times and I rarely got a kick. He was such a strong and powerful guy, muscles popping out of areas of the body I didn't even know existed. I would try to shield the ball, hold it in and lay it off as it came up to me, but he'd more or less just brush me aside and take possession. He was just massive and had a brilliant turn of pace.

ANDY MILLEN: I was a young boy, still trying to properly establish myself as a regular pick for Motherwell and a respected and capable SPL player. Andy had a solid career at Kilmarnock and Hibs. In one game at Fir Park – I think Andy was at Hibs – under the floodlights, Andy tried to demolish me physically.

At the time Hearts were linked in the papers with paying around £1 million for me, a move that never came off. Andy constantly kicked and elbowed me. He'd nip my skin at corner kicks, every old trick in the book. He also shouted in my ear, 'A million pound for you, you're not worth anything near that because you're pish.' Now, I don't know Andy and I'm told he is a very nice guy. He was also a very good defender who maximised his ability to have a career in the game at a high level to play beyond forty. For that, I have total respect for him.

ARTHUR NUMAN: A Rangers legend. Great pace, great left foot and a wonderful person. I played for Motherwell on the right-hand side one afternoon, directly against Arthur, and he just kept bombing forward. He constantly had me on the back foot when the roles should have been reversed. I don't think I got out of my own half at Fir Park that day. He was also a gentleman and spoke to me throughout the game, tried to encourage me, which I totally appreciated. A great career in the game and I'm surprised he is not involved in coaching at a high level because he has all the attributes.

RINO GATTUSO: Played for Scotland a few times against him when he was an integral part of that successful Italy team that won the World Cup in 2006. He also helped AC Milan to numerous successes over the years. Kept things simple but was so effective. Also loved to talk away to opposition players and his patter wasn't too bad!

Came to Rangers as a kid and retained such a strong affection for the club. His career blossomed after Dick Advocaat sold him to Salernitana. A player who never gave up on the pitch and would be like a little terrier dog, snapping away at your ankles and never letting go. Had a magnificent career and worked hard to achieve all he did.

I've chosen quite an attack-minded team so Gattuso would be crucial in this line-up, to give the defenders some cover in front of them as the rest got on with their business of attacking the opposition.

Midfield
CRISTIANO RONALDO: Played against him for Wigan at home and away when he was at Manchester United and felt extremely privileged to have done so. He was lightning quick and had mind-boggling skill. A genuine world-class talent and I'd have loved the opportunity to play in the same team as him.

One lunchtime we were meeting at a hotel for a game and

Manchester United happened to be using the same place. The bold Ronaldo got out of his car and waved over to me. I was delighted and thought, 'Bloody hell, he must know who I am.' Of course I had a Wigan tracksuit on and I'm guessing he was just showing professional courtesy to another footballer. He wouldn't know me from Adam, although I told the boys he shouted, 'Alright, Jig!'

LIONEL MESSI: The world's best player came to Ibrox with Barcelona to play against us in a Champions League game. To be honest, by his own standards, he didn't really do too much that night. Maybe I had him in my back pocket! The game finished 0–0. At the Nou Camp, I played on the left-hand side against him. I was meant to help out left-back Saša Papac. I ended up side by side with Saša, I just couldn't get up the pitch as Messi was always in possession and going at us.

I often hear people say that defenders should just put him up in the air to thwart his threat, but it's not as easy as that. I just couldn't get close to him. Back then, in 2008, he wasn't as big a name as he is now. He was still really emerging and developing into the world brand he now is on and off the park. But for such a wee guy, he really tore the game up. A wicked change of direction, wonderful quick feet, and you just can't get near the ball when he's in possession. He is like a PlayStation footballer. I tried a few slide tackles on him but ended up ramming into the advertising boards! There is no equal to him in the modern-day game and I'm truly honoured and humbled to have shared a football pitch with him.

PAUL GASCOIGNE: He is my hero and I was lucky enough to meet him at Ibrox and play against him. He elbowed me right on the nose at Ibrox during a game and I was delighted he touched me! My eyes were watering and my nose was bleeding but

I just got on with it. I actually would have thanked him for it. An amazing player, and what a laugh off the pitch! Genius. When I tried to play against him, he'd do things I never expected. He'd show me the ball, leave himself wide open and I'd think I was going to go in and nick it from him. Then. Bang. The ball was gone and so was he. He'd be rampaging towards goal and I had tackled thin air. Total arrogance. But he had the ability to back it up.

Walter Smith often talked about him and how he used to float in and out of games. His concentration would wander and you'd maybe see him whistling or looking up to the sky. Walter, or someone else under instruction from the manager, would then have to have a word, cajole him, and ask him to get involved. Those few words would spring him into life and he'd invariably go on to become the match-winner. When he clicked few could match him.

I remember Barry Ferguson and David Graham nicked a pair of his boots when they were apprentices to give to me. I was very proud to have worn a pair of Adidas Predators with Gazza on them.

HENRIK LARSSON: Simply brilliant. One of the best strikers I've ever played against. I remember I played against Celtic one night for Motherwell in 1999 and they battered us 6–0. I think Henrik scored four. He was just ridiculous that night. It was the best performance I've ever seen a striker come up with when I've been on the same field. Our keeper that night, Stevie Woods, took some stick in the dressing room after the game. Some of the lads accused him of diving out of the way of Henrik's efforts on goal!

His movement was different class. When I was a young striker I was told to try and learn from Larsson, study his movement and try to get anywhere near that standard he set. Different managers and team-mates told me to do it. It was all part of my education as a young professional. He had great all-round ability and very good pace.

Forwards

DUNCAN FERGUSON: A player I respected for what he could do on the park. And a player, quite frankly, I was scared of. He could kill teams off with his ability in the air and his presence. But having played against him a couple of times down south I also knew that if you got on his wrong side then he wouldn't think twice about hooking you.

He played for Rangers and it didn't really work out for him at Ibrox for different reasons after bursting onto the scene as a kid at Dundee United. He blossomed at Everton and also had a good spell at Newcastle United. He returned to Everton and I think he regarded Goodison Park as 'home'. He seemed comfortable there and had an excellent rapport with the fans.

I know from talking to his former Everton team-mates such as Davie Weir, James McFadden and Gary Naysmith that they rated him ever so highly as a footballer but held him in higher regard as a person. That says a lot. I was lucky enough to meet him on an SFA coaching course in the summer of 2012 and he was a gentleman. He offered me advice about what to do when I stop playing and I valued his wisdom. He is a ferocious worker and I feel he will have a very good career in coaching and management.

THIERRY HENRY: I played against him in the last ever competitive game Arsenal played at Highbury. It was a great occasion and I felt privileged to be there with Wigan, providing the opposition on such a momentous afternoon. It was a lovely day and the pitch was like a bowling green. Cut into the grass was 'Highbury' and the date of the game. The atmosphere was unbelievable, like a carnival day.

We went 2–1 up when David Thompson scored with a free-kick. And then Henry started trying and took over. He was on a hat-trick with a few minutes to go and Arsenal had a free-kick from a wide area, about thirty yards out. I was marking Henry inside the box and I remember he said to me that I would never beat him in the air and that he was going to score again. Well, he didn't score from that set play but did get his third from the penalty spot. He had a sense of humour on the pitch and I found him to be a lovely guy. It was a great experience to play against him in his prime.

Wonderfully gifted and one of the best players from the past twenty years in world football.

Manager
JOSÉ MOURINHO: I played against Chelsea a few times when he was the manager there. One game, at Stamford Bridge, sticks out in my mind. We lost 1–0. John Terry scored the goal. I was meant to be picking him up at the corner kick from which he scored. Later in the game, a Chelsea player poked me in the eye and I went to ground just in front of the dugouts. Paul Jewell and Mourinho had an argument about it. In the post-match press conference Mourinho accused me of cheating and it became headlines the next day. On one hand I wasn't happy with him for labelling me a cheat, but on the hard hand I was buzzing he knew who I was.

A top, top manager and I've hardly ever heard a player that has played for him say anything negative about him. A real players' manager. I like that.

23

WHY I'LL GIVE SOMETHING BACK TO THE GAME I LOVE

AS I'M coming to the end of my career I'm conscious my body is not the same as it used to be, although in the 2012 pre-season – the twentieth of my career – I was once again in the top group for fitness and running. I take real pride in it and I'm really strict with my diet nowadays. Gone are the days of a Big Mac meal and a bottle of Irn-Bru and a packet of sweets on a Friday before match day. Although I have to confess, I do find it difficult to resist having a right few biscuits with a cup of tea.

I've even taken a leaf out of David Weir's book by only adding slimline tonic to a vodka on the odd occasion I have a drink. It still hits the spot quite nicely and I've seen me in a few states after a few large, but it's all about the calories now and keeping the fat off. I certainly have matured on that front from the days when John Spencer joined Motherwell at the latter stages of his career and tried to get me off the lager and into wine. I followed his words of wisdom and got myself a pint of wine! Scary!

In the past two or three years I have taken it all seriously. To try and prolong my career as long as possible, I've been doing gyrotonic as well, which is stretching your full body with machines and also a little bit of Pilates involved. Young ballet dancers do it to make themselves more supple, and I feel that everything I do helps. I find running to be very therapeutic and if I'm stressed or down, I'll go for a forty-minute run to clear my mind. I'm still doing the boxing training and enjoy doing that with my friends, James and Martin Lyon, both from a lovely family.

No matter what I try to do to help prolong my career, I know I can't go on forever. I will start to put plans in place for when I hang up my boots but I've already started to do a few things for when that day finally arrives. I'm going through my UEFA Pro Licence just now and it's something I see myself wanting to do in the future. Coaching and management definitely appeals. I have enjoyed the different aspects to the SFA coaching badges. It's an excellent course. Obviously it involves lots to do with football but there are other aspects to it, such as making a lengthy presentation to the rest of the aspiring coaches and qualified coaches.

Now, I'm still very shy. I'd love to be more outgoing but it's just not in me. My parents and brothers aren't like that. They are outgoing. Amanda and the kids are also very sociable and easy to talk to. I guess I must be a bit of a strange dude. I hate the way I am when it comes to that.

Yet, if I ever become a coach or a manager, I know I will be able to stand up in front of twenty footballers and handle it no problem. I'll put on a training session or give a team talk with my eyes shut. I'm relaxed when it comes to football, although not cocky, but ask me to do something formal in front of people I don't really know and I become supremely shy. It's so annoying. It's something I've tried to work on. It will be an ongoing thing.

At this stage of my life, I feel as if my career has just about gone full circle and I find myself being the way I was as a young YTS lad at Motherwell. I used to pester the senior players to teach me the game and now I'm pestering the coaches to teach me that side of it. I've got involved with the Youth set-up at Rangers and enjoy doing my bit at Murray Park with what I hope will be the next generation of players at our club. I've been closely observing training sessions and trying to get in on the conversations about their philosophies on this side of the game. The Rangers coaching staff at youth level – Jimmy Sinclair, Tommy Wilson, Billy Kirkwood and Craig Mulholland – must be sick of the sight of me and tired of me grilling them for information and any wee nuggets I can glean from them.

My view is that coaching is an art, a thing of beauty, and tremendous satisfaction can be gained from putting on a training session that the squad of players enjoy and don't want to end. Training sessions have to be full of quality and to achieve that there must be plenty of preparation.

I would love the chance to be a manager in the future if I'm lucky enough, having been with a few great ones in my time, such as Billy Davies, Alex McLeish, Paul Jewell, Ally McCoist and Walter Smith. I will absolutely take a little bit of each of their styles with me. Although the game doesn't change significantly, they have all been different in many ways.

To give me as good a chance as possible, I'm learning French. A tutor comes to the house once a week to give me lessons. My sons are also involved as it will be good for them to have another language in their locker as they progress in life. We'll do this every week for the next two years. I will do the SFA Media Course off my own back to have another string to my bow. Every bit helps, I feel.

I've been working quite a bit with the Rangers Under-15 side and the coaches have been most helpful, patient and understanding with me. They can't do enough for me. I'm thoroughly enjoying it all.

Over the years, the youth system at Rangers has been on the receiving end of some stick from time to time but I suppose that's just being at a big club. Perfection is demanded at every level but it's impossible to produce that all the time. Still, the fruits of Murray Park are there for all to see. It's a wonderful facility. It's been there for more than a decade and has helped to produce some excellent players such as Alan Hutton, Charlie Adam and Allan McGregor, to name but a few. They were all top players for Rangers and have reached the top of their profession. We now have to hope the likes of Lewis McLeod, Robbie Crawford and Barrie McKay continue to show their excellent early promise and maintain their development into what I'm sure will be first-class players for Rangers. But I've told them time and time again not to take anything for granted and that this is just the start. I have reminded them of a startling statistic which is that only one per cent of footballers that join a club as a fifteen- or sixteen-year-old on a full-time basis actually still play full-time at thirty-five. I've told them the story Alex McLeish used to tell me and that they should not be sitting five years from now full of excuses and hard luck stories. 'Be the guy on the telly, not the guy shouting at the telly.' Be dedicated and always be ready to make sacrifices.

The game has changed from the days when I was a lad at Motherwell. Youngsters are allowed to solely concentrate on football now. The days of cleaning boots, washing the manager's car and painting the toilets are long gone. I actually think there was no harm in that kind of thing and I would still have the young players doing certain duties, but they are treated like diamonds from the start and that means some adopt the attitude they are sparkling footballers before they've even played a handful of first-team games.

They are given the best opportunity to make the grade. They want for nothing, really. Sports science is a huge factor in all of football and that has resulted in some massive changes in the game in the past decade. I'm not having a pop at any of the sports science guys employed by a football club but when I was younger we used to run for forty or fifty minutes at a time, at a good pace, and have loads of sprints to do. Players sometimes dropped like flies and most would be sick at the side of the running track.

But I believe that kind of thing was good. It helped to bring a togetherness in the squad and a mental toughness to individuals.

There was a story that a high profile manager on his first day in charge told all the players to run on the track until he told them to stop. He sat on a seat at the sideline and watched. Watched until they dropped, one by one. He took a note of the names until he was down to his last six players still running. He ended up building his team around those six players as he thought they were mentally the toughest in his squad.

There is a major emphasis on weight training and that involves a gym session every other day. Afternoons are spent in the gym rather than on the training field. I think somewhere along the way we have lost sight of the priorities of a footballer and what it takes to win football games. I remember Tony Fitzpatrick came away with a great saying a few years ago: 'Hard work only beats talent when talent doesn't work hard.'

Because of the emphasis on weights and flexibility tests, lung tests, saliva tests, jump tests and blood tests, I wonder if the standard of the game has dropped from a while ago. It seems to be about fitness and physique first and then talent and ability next. If it continues down this road, players are going to need a motorbike on the pitch to keep up with the demands. Maybe I'm just saying that because I'm getting on a bit!

I'm also wary of these enhancing products on the market now, the tablets and muscle builders that are thrown into players' faces. I'm not so sure it's wise to take stuff like that. I refuse to take the sachets and gels on offer at half-time during games. It's a personal choice but I don't want to pump my body full of stuff that will make my heart race faster. No thanks. We've seen enough sports people with heart trouble in recent years. The plus for me is that the sports science guys have brought in diet awareness across the board in football!

Adam Owen is the Rangers sports scientist. He has played the game and also has his coaching badges. He is very good at his job, knows how to keep a happy medium to his philosophies. He is definitely up there with the best in his profession and is a sound guy.

I like to try and stay fit and can't see myself becoming a fat ex-footballer. But maybe I will turn into a retired guy with a massive belly and pat it every now and again and say, 'Well, it's all bought and paid for.' That's what my dad does. I would love to be a coach and love a go as a manager when I feel I'm ready but once I retire from football I will have a break and spend some time with the family. I feel I owe them a bit of uninterrupted quality time.

Being a footballer has allowed me to go to some fantastic destinations but we rarely get to explore the cities. We land in the airport, get taken to the hotel, then to the stadium and back to the airport. When I retire from playing I'd like to take a couple of months off and go travelling. Doing a round-the-world cruise really appeals. I also want to visit a few places in America and South Africa. I love golf and if I get a few games under my belt, find a bit of form, I can play off 10. I've been fortunate enough to play on some lovely courses such as Royal Lytham, The Belfry and Celtic Manor. I want to play the Old Course at St Andrews – that's an ambition, and so is getting a hole in one. I've hit the pin a few times, though. I grew up with golf and Gregor was the pro at Wishaw Golf Club. My heroes were Seve Ballesteros and Ian Woosnam. I'd also love to go to America to sample a Ryder Cup. The last weekend in September, every second year, is the best viewing on television. I will get to it one day, for sure. I want to go to the Bernabéu to watch a Real Madrid v Barcelona game. El Classico. Can't beat it. I was lucky enough to play at the Nou Camp but never Madrid's ground. I always wanted to draw them in the Champions League.

I want to switch off completely. Eat and drink as much as I

want. Not do a single bit of exercise for a few months and be quite happy if I come back four stone heavier. Live the way I've wanted to live all my life. From the day my dad set out circuit training exercises for me in the house until I became a full-time player and had to always watch what I ate and what I drank because I was paranoid about my weight. I can go away on holiday and not worry about superstitions to prepare for my game. In many ways, I can't wait until I retire. I know I will miss playing and the banter in the dressing room when I hang up my boots, but I'm equally looking forward to letting myself off the leash and not being restricted by anything.

When I finish with football what I won't do is be extravagant. I won't blow fortunes on things but I will look at one or two investments. My favourite holiday destination is Portugal. I went there as a kid with my parents and brothers and go back there most years with Amanda and the kids. We love Vilamoura and I'd like to eventually buy a house out there, all being well. I've been to Dubai and it's a lovely place with quality hotels, but I'm not the type to go somewhere and spend the equivalent of £9 on a beer when I can get it for less than half that price in Portugal. It's just not me. The Motherwell boy in me tells me to get a grip of reality.

I know football has given me and my family a very comfortable lifestyle but I will look after the pennies. That may be construed by some as being stingy and they can have that opinion if they want, but I'm just not a 'Flash Harry' and never will be. Even when it comes to fashion, I see some of the lads buying training shoes at £250 and paying £3,000 for a suit. I can't understand that. I shop now the way I shopped when I was a teenager earning a very modest living. For example, I refuse to pay £175 for a designer label shirt when I can buy one out of Zara for £30. I love to buy nice clothes but I will not pay over the odds. Maybe I am tight but I think I'm just sensible.

I did lose the plot a bit when I signed for Wigan and spent a right few quid on cars. I was being silly. That's almost the extent of my extravagance. I bought a nice Rolex watch for myself and one for Amanda a few years ago but John Spencer helped to get them for me at cost price. I wouldn't have paid the mark up for them in the shops. There was an eight-year waiting list for them and they are lovely. I've also bought them as an investment for the kids.

Another long-term investment has been our beautiful house in Bothwell. Every time I drive through our gates I feel so happy. We bought two acres of land and knocked the house down. Started from scratch. The back garden was a jungle and we put that right. We designed it all and it took more than two years to build and get it the way we wanted. I spoiled myself and designed the basement, built a cinema room, a bar, a sauna and steam room. I hope we're there for the rest of our days and pass it on to the kids.

I still have kept in touch with most of the pals I grew up with. I was lucky to play with Motherwell, Wigan, Rangers and Scotland, so many of my dreams came true and when I take a moment to think about some things that have happened to me it can all feel quite surreal. It's also given me so much pleasure to see my dad being so proud of me and it gives me enormous satisfaction that I've helped fulfil some of his dreams. For him to watch me playing for my country and leading Rangers out as captain in front of 50,000 fans has made it all worthwhile for me. I know if I sit in the stand at Ibrox twenty years from now and watch Callum or Jack play for Rangers then it will reduce me to tears. Floods of them.

I look back on my career and I have so many people I owe a debt of gratitude to. Alex McLeish has probably been my favourite manager, in terms of the way he moulded me from a young age and instilled good habits. He made my parents feel

I'd always be well looked after and that was also important. We were putty in his hands from the day we met him. Walter Smith gave me my dream move to Rangers. I'll be eternally grateful for that. Billy Davies is the best tactician I've played under. He was scared of no team and gave us great self-belief. We used to keep three players up front when the opposition had a corner kick. He tested other managers. He was thorough in his preparation and left absolutely nothing to chance.

Paul Jewell was good for me and made Wigan Athletic such an enjoyable experience. He used to scare the living daylights out of me though. He was a fiery character, a true Scouser. He could cut you in half in two seconds. I've been lucky to have some solid team-mates, guys I now regard as friends and always will. From Garry Gow and John Spencer at Motherwell, to Gary Teale, Matt Jackson, Leighton Baines and Jimmy Bullard at Wigan, and Davie Weir and Kris Boyd at Rangers. Matt Jackson knows the game and was great at giving little pointers to me. Davie was the same at Rangers. The experience both had was invaluable. Davie was the best at speaking to the young players and making the new signings feel part of the club. He has a lovely manner. I've been trying to emulate big Davie since I was given the armband.

I played with some extremely talented footballers too. At a young age, Barry Ferguson was class, everything about him was elegant, and although his passing and first touch were both great, he had excellent pace and was good in the air, qualities that may well have been overlooked about him. Emile Heskey had the lot – pace, power, first touch, lethal finisher and a threat in the air. He came in for a bit of stick now and again, but on his day there were few better. In terms of opponents who made my life a misery, the one guy who immediately comes to mind is Cristiano Ronaldo. He was my toughest opponent. I played against him for Wigan a few times and he was simply unstoppable. Incredible strength and pace, clever movement, wonderful spring that enabled him to win so many great headers and, of course, the step-overs. He really did put fear in me every time he had possession.

I'm lucky enough to have played in some huge games for club and country. Memories I will cherish and that can never be taken away from me. Scotland beating France home and away was so special. Scoring for Rangers in the Champions League in the 3–0 away win at Lyon was incredible. Drawing 0–0 against Barcelona was a brilliant performance, a result against all the odds. Beating Reading in 2005 and Sheffield United in 2007 for Wigan brought so much joy for different reasons. I scored against Reading. Big Jason Roberts cut down the right-hand side, squared it and I arrived from the back post to slam it home from eight yards. We had to win to make sure we gained promotion to the Premiership. A few family members and friends travelled down and they were on the pitch at the end. The goals on my debut for Motherwell are right up there. The headed equaliser for Rangers against Celtic at Parkhead in 2010 is the best I've ever felt after finding the back of the net.

Parkhead is one of the best grounds for atmosphere. I loved playing at Old Trafford, Anfield, the San Siro and the Nou Camp, for the history of such great clubs. Ibrox is a special stadium and is my favourite, but the other one I'm most fond of is White Hart Lane, home of Tottenham Hotspur. Everything about it is class – great atmosphere, great dressing rooms and first-class hospitality lounges. Wigan always played well there. I don't know if I will ever get back to such great arenas in a working capacity in the next ten or twenty years. It's when I say that out loud that reality bites about what the future holds for me. Fingers crossed I remain active in football, in some shape or form, whether that's helping kids to progress and develop in the game or something along those lines.

I believe a coach has to put in the hours on the training ground and that's something I would do. That kind of role demands knowledge, time and patience. It has to be about wanting to improve the players you have in your group and that means working tirelessly with them, especially young professionals. I know I would relish that kind of challenge.

Who knows what the future will hold and as I'm getting older I think about it a lot. I get nervous and anxious about what it will bring, that's for sure. What does concern me is what will happen if I don't find anything to do and I end up sitting about twiddling my thumbs. That would drive me crazy. Yes, I may well have financial security but I will need to be active, have a purpose in life to get me out of bed in the morning.

All I can hope for is that the next fifteen years are half as rewarding and as satisfying as the last fifteen years. If they are, I will have no complaints.